PRAISE FOR *MONEY M*

"As a nonprofit board member and treasurer, I find this book invaluable. It teaches important financial concepts and gives detailed examples of what should be reported and how. Melisa makes it easier for anyone to be comfortable giving direction to bookkeepers, speak intelligently to their board and donors, and understand tax accountants."

—JOANNA BECK, Founder and CEO, Beck Insights; Treasurer, National Association of Women Business Owners–Charlotte

"This book is a much-needed straightforward and intelligent resource full of engaging examples and illustrations that provide insights into the financial reporting of nonprofits. A masterful teacher and expert on nonprofit accounting, Melisa writes with clarity and technical confidence in an engaging and very readable manner."

—ROBERT DURAK, CPA, CGMA, Director, Audit & Accounting Technical Services—Public Accounting, AICPA

"Melisa explains complex financial concepts with easy-to-understand language that even those new to the nonprofit world can understand. I highly recommend nonprofit board members, executive directors, or anyone that works with nonprofit finances read this book to better equip themselves to deliver on their missions."

—HEATHER BLAKE, CFO, Girls on the Run International

"*Money Matters for Nonprofits* is a must-have resource for any nonprofit board member who seeks to assess and comprehend their nonprofit's financial statements. Melisa's detailed examples make the learnings straightforward, relatable, and easy to apply."

—ANGELA HOSKING, MBA, MSN, RN, NE-BC, CEO and Dean Northeastern University Charlotte, nonprofit board member

"Melisa captures the key elements facing nonprofit board members and explains them in a way that is understandable while still comprehensive. This book would serve well as required reading before joining a board."

–FRAN BROWN, CPA, Managing Partner, CapinCrouse

"*Money Matters for Nonprofits* empowers board members to achieve their mission by removing the mysteries of accounting and auditing. Melisa gives you a clear understanding of the numbers that drive nonprofits. Harness the power!"

–CHARLES B. HALL, CPA, CFE, MAcc,
Partner, McNair, McLemore, Middlebrooks & Co.

"Melisa Galasso combines an impressive career in professional accounting and adult learning to offer a fresh, practical, and effective guide to nonprofit financial oversight. This is a must-read for nonprofit boards and professional staff alike!"

–MARK MCSWEENEY, CAE, VP, Association
Strategies, Raybourn Group International

"As a former nonprofit auditor and current CFO of a nonprofit, I have seen firsthand the need in nonprofit boards for knowledge and clarity about financials. Melisa's clear language and examples help bridge that "GAAP" for board members. Whether you've been on boards for 50 years or are completely new to the scene, this book will give you great insight."

–CHRIS BROWN, CPA, VP & CFO,
Arkansas Colleges of Health Education

"There is a real need for those involved in governance of nonprofit organizations to understand their fiduciary responsibilities. Melisa explains these responsibilities in easy-to-understand terms that everyone involved in these organizations can put into practice."

–MICHAEL BRAND, CPA, CGMA,
Member, BMSS Advisors & CPAs

"After reading this book, regardless of their prior accounting knowledge, board members will understand their role in the financial reporting process and appreciate how their role serves their organizations."

–BRIAN TODD, CPA, Shareholder,
Clark Schaefer Hackett CPAs & Advisors

"Melisa's ability to teach in a highly informative, entertaining manner is truly amazing. Her book helps members of nonprofit boards interpret financial statements, enabling them to lead their boards with true strategic insight."

–SHARON H. BRYSON, MEd, CEO,
North Carolina Association of CPAs

"This book should be a companion for any board member, grantor, or other user of a tax-exempt entity's financial statements. If you want context for well-informed decision making, read this book and learn from one of the best accounting instructors out there!"

–KATIE DAVIS, CPA,
Higher Education Practice Leader, James Moore

"Joining a nonprofit board comes with fiduciary responsibilities that many board members are unprepared for. Galasso skillfully puts complex accounting and financial principles into simple, everyday language that can help every nonprofit board member."

—**JAMES MATZDORFF**, **CPA, Director, CohnReznick**

"A must-read primer for all nonprofit board members! Melisa provides a well-defined road map that is understandable, insightful, and full of valuable information."

—**KATHRYN FLETCHER**, **CPA, MBA, Partner, Draffin Tucker**

"A great resource for all (especially nonfinancial) nonprofit board members. The concepts in the book are supported by fun, easy-to-understand examples."

—**THERESA BATLINER**, **CPA, Assurance Partner, Not-For-Profit Services Team Leader, MCM CPA & Advisors**

"I'm recommending that all my clients share this book with their boards. There is no better way to advocate for your organization's mission than by equipping yourself with the acumen to evaluate financial situations and ask management the right questions."

—**TINA M. DZIK**, **CPA, Partner, Cohen & Company**

"Melisa Galasso has made a topic that often intimidates most nonprofit board members approachable, understandable, and readable. A decisive contribution to nonprofit board governance, this book will help nonprofit board members committed to the serious work of moving forward the organizations they serve."

—**ANDREA WRIGHT**, **Partner, Johnson Lambert**

"This book contains valuable information on the basic fiscal operations of nonprofit organizations. I have been involved in auditing and consulting with nonprofit organizations for over 45 years and I would highly recommend this book to new nonprofit board members with limited knowledge of nonprofit financials and reporting."

—**TIMOTHY NOVOTNY**, **Maloney + Novotny LLC**

"I have the utmost admiration for Melisa's knowledge and her ability to take complex topics and present them in ways that are completely understandable."

—**DAN KLOHA**, **Partner, 415 Group**

"Melisa Galasso shares her expertise in an easy-to-understand guide for nonprofits. It's a must-read for nonprofit board members."

—**MELODI BUNTING**, **CPA, CMA, CGMA,**
Senior Manager, Advisory Services

MONEY MATTERS FOR NONPROFITS

How Board Members Can Harness
the Power of Financial Statements by
Understanding Basic Accounting

MELISA F. GALASSO, CPA

Published by River Grove Books
Austin, TX
www.rivergrovebooks.com

Distributed by River Grove Books

Design and composition by Greenleaf Book Group and Mimi Bark
Cover design by Greenleaf Book Group and Mimi Bark
Cover image used under license from ©Shutterstock.com/rawf8

Publisher's Cataloging-in-Publication data is available.

Print ISBN: 978-1-63299-591-9

eBook ISBN: 978-1-63299-592-6

First Edition

This book is dedicated to all the nonprofits and nonprofit board members making our world a better place in appreciation for all of your hard work and for the impact you make.

CONTENTS

PREFACE

While I can't imagine being in any other profession, I didn't go to college to become an accountant. I excelled academically in high school, but I wasn't exposed to a wide variety of potential professions I was interested in. I only knew I wasn't going to be a doctor (to this day, the sight of blood makes me queasy), and I could never make it as a politician (I tend to say what's on my mind, and I have absolutely no poker face), but I hadn't quite landed on what my path to a successful career might be.

I was the oldest of three girls and the first of my generation to go to a four-year school, and my mother's only advice was to major in something that would allow me to support myself one day, so when I applied to Georgetown University, I applied to the business school. Despite growing up in New York, I was not a Wall Street expert of any kind, but I felt it was a pretty safe bet that business graduates found their way to successful jobs. My very first class on my very first day as a college student was Intro to Financial Accounting. I didn't really know what an accountant did, but I had pretty much written that class off as a tedious prerequisite on my way to finding my purpose. I certainly didn't expect it to change my perspective forever. My professor,

Dr. Srinivasan Sankaraguruswamy, introduced me to a new language of business. The concepts of debits and credits instantly made sense to me. When my trial balance actually balanced, I was hooked.

In the spring semester of my freshman year, I enrolled in Intro to Managerial Accounting, which focuses on cost accounting for manufacturing. Let's just say making widgets was not my thing, and a career in accounting suddenly seemed a lot less likely. But as all great professors do, Srini spotted my potential and encouraged me to take Intermediate Accounting my sophomore year. Intermediate was a two-session course similar to the intro course. Both courses focused on financial accounting, which is my wheelhouse. I still loathe managerial accounting to this day!

I found Intermediate Accounting fascinating. I loved bonds and leases and things most of my peers hated. It came easily for me. My professor for Intermediate Accounting, Dr. Kirsten Anderson, would become my faculty adviser. I would babysit for her later in my college career, and even further down the road, her daughter would babysit my daughter so I could attend my college reunion.

During my upperclassman years, my passion for accounting helped me earn a position as a teaching assistant and then as a research assistant. I cherished my time in the accounting department. Outside of my minor in French, most of my electives were in accounting.

I graduated from school and accepted an offer from one of the Big Four accounting firms. I took all four parts of the CPA exam over a two-day period with two thousand of my closest friends at the Dulles Expo Center in November during the prime of cold and flu season. It was not a pleasant experience, and I wouldn't find out I'd passed all four parts for months. At the time, passing all four parts in one sitting was pretty rare. I had found my passion.

I would continue my work in the profession, moving from public accounting (performing financial statement audits for large public companies) to industry (working in accounting departments for various companies) and then to internal audit (evaluating internal controls for private companies). During this time, the CPA exam review provider I had studied with reached out about a part-time position teaching CPA review. In college, I had been happiest helping make accounting approachable to students who found it difficult, so I took the position.

Just a couple of years later, while I was pregnant with my daughter, I learned that a part-time adjunct faculty position had opened up at Georgetown. I was teaching CPA review in the evenings and on weekends around my day job in internal audit. I applied for the spring semester position, which was, ironically enough, Managerial Accounting. The dean hired me for the spring position, and I left the corporate world.

I spent a few years in academia, teaching freshman accounting. I noticed some very interesting things about my students. For the record, all of them were pretty brilliant. For the most part, they were accepted into Georgetown because of their academics. They were hard workers and they cared about their grades, sometimes more than I would have liked. But even some of my hardest-working students just didn't do well on exams. I found grading very binary—there were students who really grasped the material, and students who just couldn't grasp it no matter how much effort they put in. They studied hard and came to my office for extra credit, but it just wouldn't click for them. Because it had come easily to me in college, I hadn't realized how difficult accounting was for so many.

Those students who loved accounting and excelled in the course have gone on to be VPs at banks or partners at accounting firms, but I'm just as proud of the students who just never clicked with accounting and went on to start their own companies, become major marketing gurus, and achieve other successes. These people are just as important to a business and to society as those accounting naturals.

After a few years, my husband and I moved to Charlotte, North Carolina, where I found a public accounting position in a national office of a CPA firm. This position utilized 100 percent of my talents. Part of it was technical, and part of it was learning and development for the staff and partners at the firm. I had the opportunity to do a significant amount of training, and I obtained my Master Trainer designation from the Association for Talent Development, a nonprofit association that supports talent development in the workplace. I was also exposed to the inner workings of the American Institute of Certified Public Accountants (AICPA), the institution that certifies CPAs and writes the auditing and attestation standards. In 2014, I was accepted into the AICPA's Leadership Academy: a four-day leadership program for young accounting professionals, which I credit with getting me where I am today. At the conclusion of Leadership Academy, students are asked to write a letter to themselves, which the academy sends a year later. My letter said that if the frustrations I was currently facing at work hadn't changed, it would be time to consider some new options. When I received the letter, I knew I wanted to build a training business. I wanted to make accounting and auditing more achievable and approachable. I took baby steps to get there, going part time at the firm while I created Galasso Learning Solutions.

Pace of change is a real issue for accountants, and I had the luxury of not carrying a client load so I could track the standards and absorb them, to then disseminate them to others in a more manageable way. As part of my Leadership Academy graduation, they asked us where we wanted to volunteer at the AICPA. I applied to be part of the Technical Issues Committee (TIC). TIC is responsible for reading exposure drafts of proposed changes and providing feedback on behalf of smaller entities, including nonprofits. TIC worked collaboratively with the standard setters to improve accounting and auditing. My three-and-a-half-year term was incredibly rewarding and led me to serving on the

Financial Accounting Standards Board's (FASB) Not-for-Profit Advisory Committee (NAC). The NAC is an advisory body to the FASB that provides timely feedback on the development of standards that impact the nonprofit community. I'm humbled to be part of an amazing group that is able to influence nonprofit accounting. I also have the honor of meeting and networking with some of the best and brightest CPAs in the nonprofit industry. I continued to focus on my technical training while studying adult-learning theory and best practices in training. I passed the Certified Professional in Talent Development exam, which tested my abilities in training delivery and instructional design. While working part time at Galasso Learning Solutions, I began incorporating best practices in adult learning into my courses to make them more impactful and have better return on investment for participants.

In 2020, I left public accounting for good to work full time as the CEO of Galasso Learning Solutions, which at that point had grown significantly and offered a variety of learning opportunities for firms. With my background in nonprofit and government accounting and my training in adult-learning theory, I've since built up a client base of amazing CPA firms committed to quality and making a difference for their clients. I have the privilege of keeping them up to date so they can serve small businesses and nonprofits around the country. I recognize the importance of their work and am proud to serve as a guide as they serve the organizations that make our world a better place.

INTRODUCTION

While the people serving on nonprofit boards are nearly always enthusiastic supporters of the mission who truly want to improve the organization, they are often ill-equipped to understand the financials. I hear daily from my CPA-firm clients about how their clients' boards aren't interested in the audit update because it doesn't mean much to them. These boards are full of fabulous people who want to help the nonprofit succeed, but they lack the financial education to make informed decisions and truly have a two-way conversation with the CPA firm.

Having served on nonprofit boards, I've seen passionate board members from all walks of life—the schoolteacher who wants to make a difference, the marketing expert who wants to help get the nonprofit exposure, the manager whose company is a big sponsor of the organization. While many of them understand some corporate finance, very few understand the nuances of the nonprofit financials. They are great people who do great things, but they do not have enough nonprofit accounting experience to hold management accountable and meet their fiduciary responsibilities. As with my college students, even those for whom accounting doesn't come easily serve a vital role on the board.

They just need a small primer in accounting to understand the financials so they can evaluate the organization and management.

I often teach courses on nonprofit fraud. Lack of proper governance and poor internal controls are nearly always the reasons the fraud is able to go on for so long, devastating the organization. A board is doing its nonprofit a disservice if it doesn't proactively protect the organization and ensure funds are being used appropriately. There are MBA programs for nonprofit finance, and I've even taught classes for a certificate program. I have to say these are very expensive and time consuming and most board members don't have the time or resources to invest in them.

My clients often ask if there's a book I could recommend. Sadly, all the books I've read in this area focus too deeply on the debits and credits that most board members don't need to know, or focus solely on corporate governance with a chapter devoted to accounting at a very high level. Board members don't need to be able to book the entries; they just need to understand the financials enough to evaluate the organization and hold management accountable.

After years of being asked about this nonexistent book, I decided to write it. I've spent most of my career trying to make accounting less scary and more digestible. I've volunteered with the best and the brightest in the nonprofit arena. I've experienced firsthand the importance of the board and its relationship with the CPA firm. I know the value these board members bring with their experiences and backgrounds and what they really need to know to make a difference. This book is the result of my desire to fill the void in nonprofit board education.

We start with a review of what the responsibilities of the board actually are, then introduce the basic financial statements for nonprofits. We then cover the details of each financial statement and provide diverse examples from real nonprofits. You'll find methods for evaluating your nonprofit, including using the concepts of ratio analysis, benchmarking, and trends, as well as nonfinancial considerations.

Finally, we conclude with an overview of the role of the independent accountant and the various services that nonprofits can use to obtain assurance about the accuracy of financial statements. You'll also find a set of questions to get the CPA discussion started.

You won't find any in-depth discussion of debits or credits in this book. In fact, you'll find nothing here but what you, as a board member, really *need* to know. You *need* to be able to read financial statements, identify errors, and question items you are concerned about. This book will provide you with a language to have the conversations that demonstrate true two-way communication and board governance. I hope it makes a difference for you and your organization!

KEY TERMS

Accounting terms are sometimes rather wordy, but they don't have to be intimidating. To help you get familiar with these terms before seeing them in practice, we've provided the following list of acronyms and definitions—these are plain English definitions instead of the formal definitions you would find in standards or regulations to make them easier to understand and apply.

ACRONYMS

AICPA (American Institute of Certified Public Accountants or Association of International Certified Professional Accountants): This is the organization that writes the auditing standards for the Generally Accepted Auditing Standards. It also has a nonprofit section membership to provide nonprofits with excellent tools and education.

ASC (Accounting Standards Codification): This is the reference used to cite Generally Accepted Accounting Principles using topic numbers from the Codification. Topic 958 is the section for nonprofits.

ASU (Accounting Standards Update): To update the Accounting Standards Codification, the Financial Accounting Standards Board issues an update to denote the changes and then provides the line items that need to be updated. Each ASU is numbered with a year and number for referencing. For example, ASU 2020-07 addresses nonprofit gifts in kind.

CPA (Certified Public Accountant): This person has passed the CPA exam and is required to follow an ethical code of conduct and take continuing education in order to protect the public interest.

FASB (Financial Accounting Standards Board): This is the organization that writes the Generally Accepted Accounting Principles. It is made up of seven board members who vote on changes to accounting standards. The FASB is part of a nonprofit organization, the Financial Accounting Foundation.

GAAP (Generally Accepted Accounting Principles): These are the rules of accrual accounting as written by the Financial Accounting Standards Board.

GAAS (Generally Accepted Auditing Standards): These are the rules the auditor must follow when performing an audit of financial statements. These standards are written by the Auditing Standards Board of the American Institute of Certified Public Accountants.

GAGAS (Generally Accepted Government Auditing Standards): Written by the Government Accountability Office, these standards apply to audits of nonprofits and governments, who often receive state or federal funding. GAGAS layers on top of the Generally Accepted Auditing Standards.

DEFINITIONS

Accrual basis: GAAP is a type of accrual accounting where revenues and expenses are booked when the transaction happens and not necessarily when cash exchanges hands.

Agent/intermediary: In an agency transaction, this is the recipient organization who receives funds from a donor who is then required to provide the funds to the ultimate beneficiary.

Aggregation/disaggregation: Aggregation is to lump things together that have common traits. Disaggregation is to break things down into smaller buckets.

Assets: These are the things a nonprofit owns that it could sell or use for its own benefit. Examples of assets include accounts receivable, inventory, and buildings.

Assurance: There are different levels of assurance a CPA can provide. The highest level is reasonable assurance, which is not a guarantee but requires the most work to ensure the financial statements are accurate. Limited assurance is a step down. The CPA does less work (inquiries and analytics) to look for errors in the financials. As with a compilation service, the auditor can give *no assurance*. They do not check the accuracy of the financial statements.

Attest/attestation: An attest engagement is where a CPA provides a report. Reviews and audits are examples of attestation engagements.

Audit: This is a service provided by a CPA to provide reasonable assurance that the financial statements accurately portray the financial position of the nonprofit. This is the highest level of service a CPA can provide on financial statements.

Capital campaign: This is when a nonprofit is creating a fundraiser to pay for a capital asset like a building or for funding other major initiatives.

Capitalization: This is when something is recorded on the statement of financial position as an asset. For example, a nonprofit capitalizes a building. Instead of recognizing an expense for the building, it records it on the statement of financial position and then records an expense over its useful life (depreciation).

Cash basis: This is referred to as an "other comprehensive basis of accounting" or "special purpose framework." These labels indicate that it is not GAAP. *Cash basis* accounts for a transaction when cash exchanges hands.

Cash flow (inflow/outflow): Cash inflows are when cash comes into the nonprofit, such as when they sell a good or service or receive a donation. Cash outflows are when a nonprofit uses cash, such as when they pay their bills.

Conflict of interest: This is a situation when an individual's personal interests are in contrast with the organization and could compromise their judgment. It could be due to a family relation, friendship, or financial reason.

Depreciation: This is a type of expense that shows how the allocation of a long-term asset can be spread over its useful life. This helps the nonprofit see how the asset is used up over time.

Disclosures: These are the narrative explanations for the financial statements. They are an integral part of the financial statements and are found at the back of the financial statements. They provide information for additional analysis.

Dual-entry bookkeeping/accounting: In accounting, a journal entry always has two parts: a debit and a credit. The journal entry balances when the debits equal the credits. An entry can never not have an equivalent in the opposite direction.

Endowment: This is an investment fund set up by a nonprofit. Donors set aside these funds for very long-term purposes to ensure the longevity of the nonprofit.

Exchange transaction/exchange revenue: This is when one party receives approximately the same value as they pay for a good or service. Exchange transactions generate exchange revenues.

Fair value: This is an exit price, which is the amount you would get to sell something you already have.

Fiduciary responsibility: This is a duty to act in the best interest of the nonprofit. A board member acts as a fiduciary to the nonprofit.

Fiscal period: This is the annual period for the nonprofit. Many nonprofits have a fiscal period that runs from July 1 to June 30. They could also have a period that runs from January 1 to December 31. The organization gets to pick what period it wants to use.

Fixed assets: This is another term for property, plant, and equipment (PP&E). These are the long-term assets of the organization.

Form 990: This is an information return required by the IRS for nonprofits (except for churches and other houses of worship) that provides detailed information about the organization, its activities, and its financial status.

General expenditure: These are the expenditures that cover the day-to-day operations of the nonprofit. While there is no formal definition, nonprofits should determine what they interpret a general expenditure to be for disclosure purposes.

Gifts in kind (contributed nonfinancial asset): These are when a donor contributes supplies or other items for use in the organization instead of a cash donation.

Intangible assets: These are assets that lack physical form but have value to the organization, such as intellectual property.

Internal controls: These are actions taken by a nonprofit to reduce the possibility of error in the financials. They can be preventative and stop an error from happening (e.g., the general ledger not allowing an unbalanced entry) or detective, where they identify and correct the error as part of a process (e.g., the review of a bank reconciliation to ensure all book-to-bank-statement differences were identified and appropriately corrected).

Investing activities: These are a type of cash flow that relate to buying or selling long-term assets.

Liabilities: These are the debts of the organization. They can be formal (notes payable) or informal (accounts payable).

Liquidity/liquid asset: Liquidity is the ability to pay your bills. Liquid assets are assets that can easily be converted to cash to pay bills.

Material/materiality: An item is material if it would influence the judgment of a reasonable user. Financial statements are not exact to the penny. If the revenue of an organization is over $1 million, an error of $50 is not material to the organization, as the error wouldn't impact the user's decision-making. An error of $500,000 would clearly impact the user's judgments and is therefore material. CPAs calculate materiality to determine at what point an error is material and no longer acceptable.

Net assets: This is what is left over after all liabilities are subtracted from the assets. Nonprofits do not have owner's equity like for-profit entities.

Net realizable value: This is the value of an asset that can be realized upon its sale, less a reasonable estimation of the costs involved in selling it.

Operating cash flows: These are cash inflows or outflows that don't belong in any other category of cash flows. They often relate to the mission of the organization (e.g., employee salaries or receipts of cash for selling goods or services).

Payable: This is an amount a nonprofit owes a creditor. An example of a payable is accounts payable, which are the amounts owed to others that are short term in nature for purchasing goods and services. Wages payable is the amount the nonprofit owes its employees.

Presentation: This is how an item appears in the financial statements. It can be presented in the financial statements themselves (e.g., a line item on the financials) or in the notes as a disclosure.

Receivable: This is an amount owed to the nonprofit by a customer or donor. Accounts receivables are all the amounts owed to the nonprofit by all their customers.

Recognize/recognition: An amount is recognized in the financial statements when it is booked by the accountant and entered into the system. There are GAAP requirements for when an amount may be entered. These items are unrecognized until they meet the requirements.

Release from restrictions: When the nonprofit meets the purpose or time restriction, the amount is moved out of net assets with donor restrictions and into net assets without donor restrictions.

Restricted/restrictions: Unlike with providing funds to a for-profit organization, when a donor provides funds to a nonprofit, they can tell the organization how they want the funds to be used. They can specify what types of items they would like them to spend money on (purpose restrictions), or they can tell the nonprofit that they have to hold the money for a period of time before they can spend it (time restrictions).

Reverse (a transaction): This is when an element previously recognized from the financial statements is removed, and something else is recognized instead. In double-entry bookkeeping, one thing has to come off so something else can be recognized.

Single Audit: This is a type of audit required when a nonprofit receives more than $750,000 in federal funding. A Single Audit is performed by a CPA in compliance with the Uniform Guidance.

Statement of activities: This depicts the revenues, expenses, and changes in net position of a nonprofit during a particular period, typically one year.

Statement of cash flows: This displays the different ways a nonprofit generates and spends cash. It is broken into three categories: *operating cash flows*, *investing cash flows*, and *financing cash flows*.

Statement of financial position: Sometimes referred to as a *balance sheet*, this depicts the assets, liabilities, and net assets of a nonprofit.

Statement of functional expenses: This explains how expenses can be categorized by function (purpose) and nature (general ledger account). It is an optional statement; the information can instead be presented as a note disclosure.

Trial balance: This is a list of all the accounts used by a nonprofit along with the ending balances in the account at a given point in time. A trial balance should tie to zero when all the account totals are added together.

CHAPTER 1

GOVERNANCE

You likely wouldn't consider joining a nonprofit board (or reading this book) if you weren't passionate about your organization's mission. However, beyond advocating for a worthy mission, nonprofit boards assume many legal, fiduciary, and oversight responsibilities that can be difficult to understand. It is important to ask yourself a number of questions to ensure a good fit and to ensure a full understanding of the commitment. One question recommended by BoardSource, an organization that focuses on providing support to nonprofit organizations, is: "Do you understand the roles and responsibilities of being a board member?"[1]

FIDUCIARY RESPONSIBILITIES

Most of the legal responsibilities of board members come from common law (as opposed to statutory law). The Model Nonprofit Corporation Act is drafted and updated by the American Bar Association's Nonprofit Organizations Committee of the Business Law Section. The model is used by states and either adopted fully or used as the base for state law. The act grants each attorney general and secretary of state certain oversight functions for nonprofits. Chapter 8, paragraph 801, "Requirement for and Functions of Board of Directors," states, "A nonprofit corporation must have a board of directors." In addition, "(1) all corporate powers must be exercised by or under the authority of the board of directors of the nonprofit corporation; and (2) the activities and affairs of the corporation must be managed by or under the direction, and subject to the oversight, of its board of directors."[2]

Board members act as fiduciaries of the nonprofit, which means they're responsible for the mission and resources of the organization. States set requirements for board conduct. Boards are legally responsible for duty of care, duty of loyalty, and duty of obedience.

- **Duty of care** requires staying informed about the organization, participating in meetings, and ensuring the mission is properly carried out in compliance with laws, regulations, and statutes. This includes making informed decisions when voting, reviewing, and updating policies, and reviewing financial information.

- **Duty of loyalty** ensures that members of the board always put the interests of the nonprofit before their own. Conflict-of-interest policies can help ensure that board members do not find themselves in a position where personal interests and professional duties or responsibilities clash by requiring them to disclose any potential conflicts to the board for approval.

- **Duty of obedience** requires board members to follow relevant state, federal, and local laws and regulations and ensure the mission is carried out. This includes ensuring appropriate returns are filed and deciding what is within the organization's mission. Boards should have policies that cover topics like board recruitment, composition, attendance, and quorums. Board evaluations help ensure members are meeting their fiduciary responsibilities.

BOARD RESPONSIBILITIES

BoardSource has identified ten basic responsibilities for board members, falling under three broad roles—establishing organizational identity, ensuring resources, and providing oversight.[3]

Establishing organizational identity includes

- ensuring effective planning
- determining the mission and purposes, and advocating for them

Ensuring resources includes

- selecting the chief executive
- ensuring adequate financial resources
- building a competent board
- enhancing the organization's public standing

Providing oversight includes

- supporting and evaluating the chief executive
- monitoring and strengthening programs and services
- protecting assets and providing financial oversight
- ensuring legal and ethical integrity

OVERSIGHT RESPONSIBILITIES

Oversight is one of the main responsibilities of a nonprofit board. Independent Sector, a membership organization that focuses on nonprofits and provides policy leadership best practices, has identified thirty-three principles that help nonprofits evaluate their oversight.[4] The principles fall into four main areas—legal compliance and public disclosure, effective governance, strong financial oversight, and responsible fundraising.

Legal compliance focuses on understanding laws and regulations impacting nonprofits. In the United States, the IRS makes determinations about tax-exempt status. Nonprofits (with the exception of churches and other houses of worship) are required to file annual informational returns to the IRS. Noncompliance can lead to a nonprofit losing its tax-exempt status. The board of a nonprofit is responsible for ensuring that the proper returns are accurate and submitted in a timely manner. Nonprofits are also subject to state laws that can bring liability to board members if not followed.

TERMINOLOGY

Note: A quick point on terms. The term *nonprofit* is a legal concept. *Tax exempt* is a tax concept, and *not-for-profit* is an accounting term.

While this book is focused on nonprofit organizations, the term *nonprofit* is sometimes used interchangeably with *tax exempt*. However, not all nonprofits are tax-exempt organizations, and not all nonprofits are charitable organizations. The National Football League for a long time was a tax-exempt organization! Charitable organizations, entities whose purpose is to achieve a benevolent mission and where profit stays within the organization, are typically 501c3s per the Internal Revenue Code. Other nonprofit organizations can be membership organizations (like golf clubs or alumni associations), and they fall under 501c7 in the tax code.

There are differences between accounting standards for nonprofits (ASC 958) and tax requirements. For accounting purposes, the Financial

Accounting Standards Board (FASB) uses the term *not-for-profit*, which is defined as "an entity that possesses the following characteristics, in varying degrees, that distinguish it from a business entity:

a. contributions of significant amounts of resources from resource providers who do not expect commensurate or proportionate pecuniary return;
b. operating purposes other than to provide goods or services at a profit; and
c. absence of ownership interests like those of business entities."[5]

Entities that meet these criteria are the types of organizations that can apply the accounting concepts addressed in this book. Tax status is not a consideration for determining appropriate financial reporting.

For ease of use, this book will use the term *nonprofit* to describe the organization.

The legal compliance principles also focus on best practices in policies. Nonprofits should have well-documented policies that the board approves. Policies around whistleblowing, conflicts of interest, data retention, social media, and ethics are important and drive the tone at the top of the organization. The board should regularly review and update policies and stay alert for new policies that may be needed. COVID-19 provided opportunities for nonprofits to consider policies related to remote work and telecommuting, cybersecurity, and staff leave.

Donor expectations can also have a big impact on the priorities and policy setting of the board. As societal trends evolve, issues like diversity, equity, and inclusion along with environmental, social, and governance disclosures can impact the policies of a board. Pressures to ensure representation of women and minorities encourage nonprofits to review their selection criteria and outreach to ensure diversity of thought. Sustainability and the environment have become more pressing issues. Donors are looking for disclosures about these topics even though they are not currently mandated by any sources. Ninety percent of S&P 500 companies published Sustainability Reports in 2019 compared to just 20 percent in 2011.[6] While the S&P 500 is composed of large publicly traded companies, nonprofits are trending in this direction as well. A study by Ott, Wang, and Bortree found that "few nonprofits in the sample provided sustainability content; however, nearly all universities . . . had a designated sustainability landing page on their websites."[7] As societal focuses change, boards will need to ensure they don't lose donors for appearing tone deaf or being late to the game.

One of Independent Sector's principles explains the importance of having a board: "A charitable organization must have a governing body that is responsible for reviewing and approving the organization's mission and strategic direction, annual budget and key financial transactions, compensation practices and policies, and fiscal and governance policies."[8] Serving on a board means being responsible for setting the mission, vision, and strategic direction for the organization. These are big tasks. Staying relevant, executing on the mission, and ensuring the nonprofit achieves its mission are all the responsibility of the board.

Staying relevant means ensuring the mission is kept up to date for changes in society while preserving the core goals of the organization. A nonprofit with a mission to cure a particular disease or serve veterans of a particular war may find their mission no longer relevant when the cure is found or many years after the war is over. The nonprofit may need to expand or potentially even change its mission. An example of a nonprofit that changed its mission is the March of Dimes. The March of Dimes' original mission was to find a cure for polio. However, as polio was eradicated, they shifted to focusing on the biggest health risks to moms and babies.[9] Changes need to be formally approved by the board and communicated to donors and even the IRS.

The oversight function ensures that all resources are used to achieve the mission. Setting policies and procedures allows management of the organization to know the limits and helps the organization stay on task.

The board is also responsible for hiring the executive director (or CEO, etc.). That person is responsible for hiring and oversight of all other employees. The board needs to ensure they hold management accountable but also not meddle in day-to-day functions. By providing clear directives, setting key performance indicators,[10] and providing a budget, the board ensures that management has the information they need to steer the nonprofit in the right direction. Evaluating and compensating the chief executive also falls to the board.

The third area of board focus is financial oversight, which, among other responsibilities, includes ensuring the financial statements are accurate and complete. Boards can hire independent accounting firms to perform various engagements regarding the accuracy and completeness of the financials. However, the oversight and presentation of the financials cannot be delegated to the independent accountant. The board is responsible for financial oversight. One of the key objectives of this book is to provide the content you need to exercise this principle.

Finally, nonprofits often require charitable contributions or grants to operate. Fundraising is a priority for these organizations, and often the board leads the fundraising process. Again, strong policies—such as gift acceptance policies, donor privacy policies, and processes around acknowledging contributions—are important. Boards should review, update, and ensure compliance with these policies.

TAXES AND THE FORM 990

While most nonprofits are tax-exempt organizations, that does not mean they do not have to file returns with the IRS. The IRS requires most nonprofits to file an annual informational return. The return, referred to as the Form 990, provides a mix of financial information with data about corporate governance, policies, and program accomplishments. The board is ultimately responsible for ensuring the 990 is completed correctly, filed on time, and made available to the public. Donors must be able to review how funds were spent, the salaries of the highest-paid employees, who serves on the board, and any remuneration.

Nonprofits that generate income from sources unrelated to their mission (referred to as *unrelated business income*, or UBI) may also have to pay taxes on that income. Examples of unrelated business income would be churches that rent out their halls for functions or the sale of advertising in a newsletter for a nonprofit. There are some exceptions to this rule, and nonprofits should work closely with their accountants to ensure proper identification and filing. In addition, while nonprofits do not necessarily pay taxes on their mission-related income, they are responsible for paying other appropriate taxes, such as employment taxes.

RISK MANAGEMENT

Nonprofits are not immune to risk. One very important role of the board is managing that risk. Boards should spend time identifying and analyzing potential risks and then determining the appropriate methods to mitigate them. A great resource for identifying potential risks is offered by the AICPA in its text *COSO Enterprise Risk Management—Integrating with Strategy and Performance: Compendium of Examples.*[11]

One of the biggest risks nonprofits face is reputational risk. Bad publicity regarding improper actions can lead to a loss of donors and ultimately the demise of the organization.

Board Self-Evaluation

What are potential areas for adverse publicity, and what are we doing to ensure that it doesn't happen?

Reputational risk is very real for nonprofits. Donors have been known to stop donating to organizations that receive adverse publicity. Is the CEO actively managing reputational risk?

REPUTATIONAL RISK

An example of the impact of reputational risk is the Wounded Warrior Project. The Wounded Warrior Project assists veterans and service members who were wounded while serving in the military on or after September 11, 2001.[12]

The project had great name recognition and lots of celebrity endorsements, but in 2016 multiple news stories broke about rampant abuse of funds by executives. A whistleblower provided details on the lavish spending, which ended with the organization seeing donations fall from $373 million in 2015 to $211 million in 2017. The news broke that executive compensation was excessive (CEO salary exceeded $500,000), the nonprofit had a $250,000 budget for candy and soda, and executives were known to hold million-dollar staff meetings at five-star resorts.

Clearly, there was a lack of board oversight in this situation. While the organization later refuted these stories, it would continue to be haunted by them for years to come. Whistleblower retaliation and other poor governance actions would lead to multiple news outlets carrying these stories and many people to this day believing the organization is fraudulent. Donors who thought they were supporting wounded veterans would become disenchanted with the undisciplined spending. Even with a cause as clear and noble as supporting wounded veterans and their families, the organization's reputation was severely tarnished by selfish spending, which ultimately led to a sharp decline in donations and support.

The board, however, is due some credit. As a result of an internal investigation, within six weeks both the CEO and COO were fired. The new CEO, a military veteran, focused on reputation and ensuring public trust. This new accountability did restore some donor confidence, as donations have increased each year since they hit bottom. However, it is important to note they are still not at pre-scandal levels. A failure of governance can be devastating to a nonprofit.[13, 14]

Enterprise risk management is defined by the Committee of Sponsoring Organizations (COSO) as "a process, effected by an entity's board of directors, management, and other personnel, applied in strategy setting and across the enterprise, designed to identify potential events that may affect the entity, and manage risk to be within its risk appetite, to provide reasonable assurance regarding the achievement of entity objectives."[15] The mission of COSO is to help organizations improve performance by developing thought leadership that enhances internal control, risk management, governance, and fraud deterrence.[16] The board of directors plays an instrumental role in determining the risk appetite of the organization and holding the CEO accountable for achievement of the entity's objectives by appropriately managing the organization's risks.

INTERNAL CONTROLS

An *internal control* is defined as "a process, effected by an entity's board of directors, management, and other personnel, designed to provide reasonable assurance regarding the achievement of objectives."[17] COSO identifies three objectives of internal controls: operations, compliance, and reporting. In order to have reasonable assurance regarding the achievement of each of these objectives, organizations have to establish internal controls. These range from segregating duties that are not compatible (to reduce the threat of theft, the person responsible for depositing checks should not be the person who reconciles the bank account) to review and approval (to ensure accuracy and completeness, the work performed by staff should be reviewed and approved by a supervisor or other knowledgeable individual). While these may sound like easy concepts to implement, designing effective internal controls can be very stressful for small organizations or those with limited funds. Sometimes the board has to provide checks and balances. For example, a board member may sign sign checks as a means of reviewing the propriety of invoices.

In financial statement audits, auditors are required to determine whether internal controls have been properly designed and implemented.

In Single Audits, required when a nonprofit expends $750,000 of federal funding in the form of grants or other financial assistance, the auditor tests the operating effectiveness of internal controls in addition to evaluating their design and implementation. This requires the auditor to obtain evidence that the control operates as planned. For review and approval, for example, the auditor would select a sample of invoices and review the sign-off (signature, initials) to ensure they were properly reviewed and approved before payment. For authorization, the auditor may select a sample of checks and ensure the appropriate signatures were on the checks based on signing authority. If the control was not present (i.e., no signature), the auditor would project the ratio of items that lacked the control to the population and potentially report the issue to management or the board in writing.

The board is instrumental in ensuring the organization not only designs appropriate controls but implements them. When auditors (or, even better, the organization) determine controls are either missing or ineffective, the board is responsible for ensuring management takes timely and appropriate corrective action. This includes monitoring management's implementation and having check-ins during board meetings to get status updates.

STRATEGIC FOCUS

When nonprofits are created, they are required to have a mission. It is the role of the board to ensure the organization works toward achieving the mission. Strategic planning requires identifying long-range and short-range goals and then monitoring the achievement of those goals. Identifying the goals requires significant consideration and discussion. Many nonprofits will have a long-term goal (ten years), a mid-range goal (five years), and short-term goals (one year). The organization will then have to periodically reevaluate the long-term goal.

A common way of writing goals is using the SMART mnemonic:

Specific: Vague goals are harder to achieve because there's no clarity about when or how they will be achieved. A goal should target a specific item for improvement. For a person to be motivated to achieve a goal, that person must understand the goal and how the outcome will benefit them.

Measurable: Having measurable goals and consistently checking in to determine if progress is being made toward those goals is a key responsibility of a nonprofit board. When quantifying a goal, it's easier to evaluate whether it has been achieved.

Achievable: We want goals to encourage good behavior without being so lofty that they are unattainable and ruin morale. Aspirational goals that are within reach encourage people to work toward them. Watching the goal inch closer and closer makes people more excited to achieve it.

Relevant: People get behind a vision that shows what the impact can be. Goals have to be worth the effort for people to get behind them. People need to see a direct link between the goal and the mission and understand how the goal will help further the mission.

Time-bound: French writer and pilot Antoine de Saint-Exupéry once said, "A goal without a plan is just a wish." One day is not a goal. Having a clear finish line helps people keep focused. Anything that goes on and on without end will wear people down and lose momentum. A goal with a clear end where people can celebrate the outcome encourages positive behaviors and helps maintain forward momentum.

There are many goal-setting techniques that nonprofits can use to evaluate whether their goal will motivate and help move the organization forward.

KEY PERFORMANCE INDICATORS

Another method of evaluating strategy is the use of key performance indicators (KPIs). While goals are the outcomes you want to achieve, KPIs can help you get there by offering a quantitative method of evaluating progress. KPIs can be identified and reviewed at board meetings to determine if the organization is moving in the right direction. Different subindustries within the nonprofit sector will have different KPIs. Universities, for example, may track things like graduation rates, employment outcomes, and retention rates. Hospitals may track patient satisfaction, wait times, or even death rates. Online fundraising program Donorbox provides a list of twenty generic KPIs that many nonprofits can track, ranging from human resources and financial KPIs to program delivery and fundraising KPIs.[18, 19]

EVALUATING MANAGEMENT PERFORMANCE

The responsibility of hiring, evaluating, and potentially firing the executive director of a nonprofit falls squarely to the board. In order to prevent micromanaging, the board typically stays out of the day-to-day operations of the organization. The chief executive is given responsibility for implementing the strategic plan and achieving the mission while staying compliant with policies and procedures.

Evaluating the competency of the chief executive can be uncomfortable, but it's a necessity. The board sets the direction and leaves management to hire staff, run operations, and execute the mission. Management's failure to execute the mission or run operations effectively can lead to the organization's demise. Boards that tend to ignore poor performance and get involved only when the organization is in dire condition often find the organization is beyond repair, and the nonprofit closes down. Regular review and feedback help ensure things never get that bad.

In 2007, several executives at the Smithsonian quit after excessive personal expenses were revealed. The board was blamed for not enforcing policies and reining in the behaviors of management.[20]

To ensure management is held accountable, the board should identify clear goals for the year. Those goals should be measurable and have clear due dates. In each board meeting, the board should check in with the status of the goals. Some boards use green, yellow, and red color coding in their board packets to indicate whether a particular goal is on target, somewhat behind, or in danger of failing. This way, the board can work to see what the root cause of the issue is and assist management with getting back on track. Boards fail in their oversight role when they simply assume management is achieving their goals and then learn at the end of the year that nothing was accomplished.

If management is not achieving their goals, it may be time to consider a leadership change.

Board Self-Evaluation

What does the CEO see as his or her strengths? What does he or she see as areas for improvement?

There is no one in management above this position. Evaluating the CEO is the responsibility of the board. Proactively engaging the CEO in a self-review can help the board identify areas to assist. This can help the board determine where to provide more support, as well as where to follow up more frequently.

FINANCIAL SUSTAINABILITY

The success of the organization is a board responsibility. The board must ensure the organization is financially sustainable—that it can pay its bills and meet its obligations and that it is bringing in sufficient cash to cover expenses. Boards that shy away from asking the tough questions and evaluating the financial situation can end up with a defunct organization. Being able to read financial statements and ask the right questions of management and the auditor will help ensure financial sustainability.

Often, board members are required to commit to fundraising to help ensure the cash flow of the organization. If the member can't commit personally, they are often tasked with asking others to help meet the goal. Organizations that are heavily reliant on donors can be significantly affected by downturns in the economy.

Setting the organization up for success by ensuring there are sufficient reserves and that funds are being spent prudently is another of the board's responsibilities. Our focus will mostly be on understanding the financial statements and audit reports and making sure you know what questions to ask in your analysis.

CONFLICTS OF INTEREST

IRS Form 1023 is used by charitable organizations to apply for tax-exempt status from the IRS. The form states, "A conflict of interest arises when a person in a position of authority over an organization, such as a director, officer, or manager, may benefit personally from a decision he or she could make." While a conflict-of-interest policy is not formally required to obtain tax-exempt status, the IRS believes the policy is so important that it provides a sample policy for those organizations who may not know where to start. Board members who sell services that may be used by the nonprofit may have a conflict of interest. If the nonprofit hires the child of a board member or other family member, that may be perceived as a conflict of interest. Members who have a conflict should be required to disclose the conflict (actual and potential) and there should be explicit policies explaining how conflicts are to be resolved and whether board members with conflicts can vote on related issues.

SUCCESSION PLANNING AND BOARD SELECTION

Board members often serve for a term that is predefined by the bylaws of the organization. Ensuring a proper mix of board members is incredibly important. When selecting members for the board, it can be easy to select people who are very involved and passionate about the organization. However, having too many insiders can also leave the nonprofit without diversity of thought. In addition, just because a board member is passionate about the mission doesn't mean they necessarily have the insight to be responsible for its governance.

Different factors should be used to select the board based on the mission and strategic plan of the organization. If there are specific targets or goals that have been set, having someone on the board who is knowledgeable about the area of focus is critical. Ensuring geographic diversity is also important for nonprofits that have a particular footprint. For example, Girls on the Run Greater Charlotte tries to ensure that they have board representation from all of the counties in their footprint, which includes Mecklenburg, Gaston, Cleveland, Catawba, and Cabarrus counties in North Carolina. Boards need a mix of backgrounds that cover their major requirements.

The North Carolina Association of CPAs underwent a massive update of their governance structure a few years ago. The board created a governance effectiveness task force to review how it was serving the organization and the gaps in skills and experience among the board members. As part of the update, the association updated its strategic plan. The board then created a list of "board skills" it felt was needed in light of the strategic plan. Some of the skills were obvious, such as experience with governance and consensus building. Others were focused on where the association wanted to go strategically, with a focus on finding individuals who had skills in the areas of IT and cybersecurity and certain service line expertise. The board then evaluated its current members and identified gaps in skills and experience. Thereafter, rather than selecting members based solely on past volunteer experiences, the board would select members based on their ability to fill in the gaps. The association recruited people to the board who had not been active historically but had something to offer in the future. While clearly focused on the state of North Carolina, board members were selected from outside the state when they had the right mix of skills.

Having the right mix of skills can set the nonprofit up for success. Being strategic about having the knowledge required to make the board successful can be difficult. It is often much easier to find a volunteer who has passion than someone who fills a unique need, but ensuring a well-rounded board with the ability to look at issues from different angles is very important.

FINANCIAL KNOWLEDGE NEEDED

Serving on a board is both rewarding and incredibly important. You don't need to be a financial expert to fulfill your fiduciary duties. While having a financial expert on the board is helpful, a board full of financial experts would be missing the diversity necessary for success.

In order to fulfill your responsibilities as a board member, you need basic financial acumen, including understanding the various financial statements and reports and their purposes. Most board members don't need to be able to prepare the financial statements or know the debits and credits of the journal entries, but they all need enough financial knowledge to ask the right questions and sense when something isn't right. It's important that every board member be able to analyze how the actual numbers compare to the original budget and review key ratios to evaluate the overall financial health of the organization.

As the board is ultimately responsible for oversight, each member must also be able to ask probing questions and evaluate whether the responses are appropriate. Identifying negative trends and being able to monitor corrective action from audits is critical.

This book will provide you with the financial basics you need to meet your fiduciary responsibilities and ensure the board is fulfilling its responsibilities.

CHAPTER 2

THE BASIC FINANCIAL STATEMENTS

FINANCIAL REPORTING FRAMEWORKS

There are several different financial reporting frameworks nonprofits can use for financial reporting. We are going to focus on the two most common types: cash basis of accounting and Generally Accepted Accounting Principles (GAAP).

Cash Basis

As the name implies, *cash basis* accounts for transactions when the nonprofit pays or receives cash. Cash basis typically requires the same types of financial statements as the accrual basis or GAAP. The biggest difference is often the timing of recognition and noncash transactions. While this is likely the easier of the two frameworks, it can sometimes misrepresent transactions that have occurred but have not yet been paid for. Transactions are recorded only when cash comes in or out of the organization, not necessarily when the underlying transaction occurs.

For example, if a nonprofit pays their phone bill for the month of May in June (when the invoice is due), then the transaction is recorded in the month of June when the cash payment is made. On the other hand, if a service is performed but the customer doesn't pay until the following month, no revenue is recorded in the period the actual work is performed. The inflow is recorded when cash is ultimately received. This can sometimes make nonprofits look worse off on paper than they actually are. For example, a large donation may have been promised but not yet received, or a substantial project may have been completed but the customer may not yet have paid.

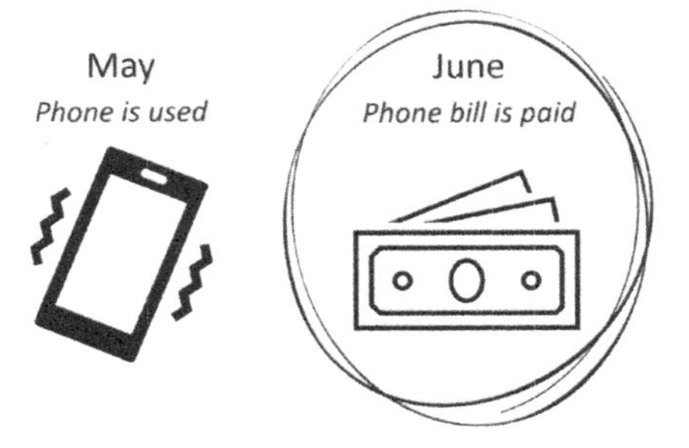

Cash basis is simple and easy to reconcile to the bank statement, which makes it a popular choice for smaller nonprofits. However, it is important to note that noncash transactions are not reported. For example, if a donor contributes supplies for the nonprofit to use, as there is no cash involved, the contribution is missing from the full financial picture.

Accrual

U.S. GAAP is an accrual basis of accounting, meaning transactions are recorded when the underlying transaction occurs, not when cash is impacted. Using the phone bill example, under accrual accounting, May's bill is recorded in May and a payable (a liability account) is recognized. Accountants use the term *recognize* to mean the transaction is recorded in the financial statements. When the bill is paid in June, the payable is reversed and cash is decreased.

Accrual Basis: When Is the Expense Recognized?

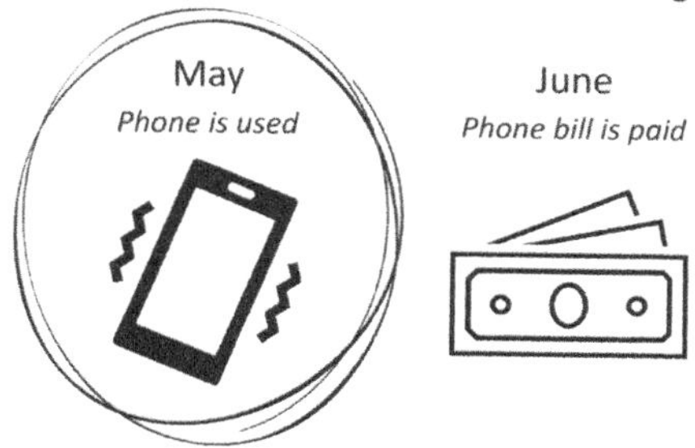

In terms of revenue, nonprofits recognize exchange revenue when the performance obligation has been met, meaning when the good or service has been delivered/performed. *Exchange revenue* is when the customer receives something in exchange for something (e.g., a service in exchange for cash).

Nonexchange revenue (contributions) is recognized when promised unless a condition is attached. Nonexchange transactions are when the other party receives nothing in return (e.g., a donation where the donor doesn't receive any benefits).

GAAP also records noncash transactions. So when a donor contributes a noncash item, the nonprofit records an inflow (revenue) for the donated supplies. While this is clearly more complicated, it helps ensure entities, when reviewing financial wellness, consider transactions that have occurred but have not affected cash.

For example, a cash account may not reflect checks that have been written but not yet cashed or deposits that are en route to the bank. Only looking at cash balances without considering transactions where cash has not yet been affected is like looking at a bank statement online and then bouncing a check because you bought something earlier with a check that had not yet been cashed.

The opposite is also true when someone has worked for ten days but payroll won't hit their bank account for a week. They have to plan for appropriate spending.

While accrual accounting records transactions when they occur, GAAP also recognizes the importance of cash. GAAP requires a statement of cash flows to provide the cash flow information, as concepts like *liquidity*, which is the ease of converting something to cash, are still important.

GAAP financial statements may be required by a bank or grantor. Banks often prefer GAAP, as it both reports the statement of activities using the accrual accounting and also requires the statement of cash flows. It also ensures that they are comparing apples to apples when considering different potential entities when deciding who receives a loan.

Modified Cash Basis

A third option, *modified cash basis,* provides more information for users, as a true cash basis is often difficult to analyze. Usually these organizations know the pure cash method doesn't tell the entire picture, but they may not have the capacity or resources to move to GAAP. Organizations can apply some concepts from accrual accounting and *modify* the cash basis. This method combines elements of both the cash and accrual basis. For example, an entity may recognize *depreciation* (i.e., the cost of an asset spread over its useful life) in the statement of activities in a modified cash basis even though depreciation is a noncash item. Modified cash basis tends to use cash basis for short-term assets and accrual basis for longer-term assets and liabilities.

However, there is no defined standard for what an appropriate modification is when applying modified cash basis. This makes modified cash accounting inconsistent and problematic for comparing organizations. Entities that start making significant modifications are often better off using full accrual accounting for consistency and clarity.

SELECTING A BASIS OF ACCOUNTING

When a nonprofit is organized, the board must weigh the pros and cons of the financial reporting frameworks and select one that makes sense for the organization. As a rule of thumb, larger organizations with employees and diverse revenue streams should use accrual accounting. Very small organizations with no paid staff and minimal revenue should use cash basis.

However, it is not uncommon for a nonprofit to start with cash basis and then switch to an accrual basis when they receive a large grant or negotiate a loan. As an example, a nonprofit could change from cash to accrual basis in order to better comply with federal grants. This gives local and state government financial statement users a better understanding of the organization's financial position. As nonprofits mature or obtain different types of funding, it is not uncommon to see them move to an accrual method either voluntarily or because of the requirements of the funding they receive.

The transition from one basis of accounting to another can be a significant undertaking with significant costs. However, some software actually permits a nonprofit to maintain their books on both a cash and accrual basis. The board should be familiar with the possibilities that the software offers. Finally, the IRS requires entities to use the same accounting method for reporting their income to the IRS (typically on the Form 990) as they use for their books. If a nonprofit wants to switch accounting methods, it will have to ask the IRS for permission. Some requests are automatically approved, while others require review.

U.S. GENERALLY ACCEPTED ACCOUNTING PRINCIPLES

U.S. GAAP is a general-purpose framework of accounting and is issued by the Financial Accounting Standards Board (FASB). The FASB is part of a nonprofit organization, the Financial Accounting Foundation, and is recognized by State Boards of Accountancy, the American Institute of Certified Public Accountants (AICPA), and the U.S. Securities and Exchange Commission as authorized to codify financial reporting standards. The FASB consists of seven full-time members.[1] The FASB is responsible for writing GAAP for commercial entities (public and private for-profit entities) and for nonprofit entities.[2]

GAAP is a general-purpose framework. The AICPA, which is the national standard-setting body for CPAs, defines a general-purpose framework as "a financial reporting framework designed to meet the common financial information needs of a wide range of users."[3] International Financial Reporting Standards is another type of general-purpose financial reporting framework.

Financial reporting standards issued by the FASB are finalized only after they have been through a lengthy due process. Drafts of proposed standards are issued, and stakeholders provide feedback during the comment period. Those comments are then used to issue a final standard. Accounting Standard Updates (ASUs) are issued and are used to update the Codification (which is the authoritative GAAP). The Codification is organized topically, and each ASU indicates the paragraphs that are required to be updated. You'll likely hear people refer to Codification topics (like Topic 958 for nonprofits) or even subtopics for a specific issue (958-605 for nonprofit revenue recognition).

In addition to the board, FASB staff are involved in research and outreach. The FASB also has several advisory committees designed to provide perspective and serve as advisers for additional outreach. The Not-for-Profit Advisory Committee, for example, is a standing committee that provides feedback and advice on nonprofit matters. They provide nonprofit perspectives for broader projects, as well as thoughts on standards specific to the nonprofit industry. The committee is diverse and includes preparers of financial statements, users of financial statements, educators, and auditors.

While the Codification provides generic guidance for all entities within scope, a special section of the Codification is set aside for industry-specific guidance. Topic 958 is the section about nonprofit entities. This guidance is unique to the nonprofit industry and is layered on top of the other general Codification sections.

Recent ASUs issued for nonprofit entities addressed

- presentation and disclosures related to gifts in kind;[4]
- the definition of *collection;*[5] and
- accounting for goodwill.[6]

OVERVIEW OF NONPROFIT FINANCIAL STATEMENTS

The FASB requires nonprofit entities to create three financial statements when following GAAP. Each financial statement has a particular purpose. Nonprofits are required to prepare a statement of activities, a statement of financial position, and a statement of cash flows. While these are the terms used by FASB, ASC 958 does permit the use of other titles so long as they are appropriately descriptive, with the exception of the statement of cash flows, which should not be changed. Statements of financial position are sometimes referred to as *balance sheets.*

A fourth financial statement is optional, and the contents can be presented either as a financial statement, as a disclosure in the notes to the financial statements, or as part of the statement of activities. A statement of functional expenses breaks down the expenses of an organization between those spent on the mission (program) and those that support the operations (general and administrative). Other potential types of expenses within supporting activities include fundraising or membership development.

Nonprofits have a choice of how many years of financial information they would like to present. Some provide a single year of information, while others present two. Presenting the current year information alongside information from a prior year is called a *comparative presentation.* Alternately, *single-year presentation* presents only the current year. Single-year presentation is easier to create and can be less time consuming, especially if there have been changes in accounts during the current year. Comparative presentation is helpful for showing trends.

Statement of Activities

The statement of activities helps users evaluate the organization's performance during the year, assess its service efforts and ability to provide services in the future, and evaluate whether management has properly discharged their stewardship responsibilities. The primary elements in the statement of activities are *revenues* and *expenses.*

- *Revenues* are how the nonprofit makes money.
- *Expenses* are the costs related to running the organization.

The equation for the statement of activities is

The statement of activities plays a similar role for nonprofit organizations as the income statement for for-profit entities. Because nonprofits do not have a profit motive, it does not measure net income.[7] Instead, it provides a reconciliation of what was added to (or subtracted from) net assets due to current-year transactions.

You may hear nonprofits talk about funds or fund accounting. While fund accounting may be used internally, the statement of activities tells the story of the organization as a whole.

The statement of activities provides information about transactions during the fiscal period (i.e., throughout the year). The labels on the statement of activities will say *for the year ending* as opposed to *as of* a specific date. We use the term *fiscal year* because some organizations use a date other than December 31 as their fiscal year end. For example, schools may use June 30 or September 30. For a June 30 fiscal year end, the statement of activities will show the results of transactions from July 1 of the prior year through June 30 of the current year.

Statement of Financial Position

The purpose of the statement of financial position is to provide an accounting of the *assets*, *liabilities*, and *net assets* of the organization.

- *Assets* are the items owned by the organization (e.g., cash, buildings, and property).

- *Liabilities* represent the amounts owed to others (i.e., the outstanding debt of the organization).
- *Net assets* are the excess of assets over the liabilities (i.e., whatever is left over).

The equation for the statement of financial position is

$$Assets = Liabilities + Net\ Assets$$

While net assets = assets – liabilities, when flipped for presentation purposes, the equation becomes assets = liabilities + net assets. The statement of financial position is sometimes referred to as a balance sheet because the equation always balances. If an amount goes up on the left side, it either has to be paired with a decrease of the same amount on the left side or an increase of the same amount on the right side.

By reviewing the statement of financial position, users can see the assets owned by the organization, as well as the types of items it owes money for. Unlike for-profit entities, which have owner's equity, nonprofit entities reflect net assets, which are the amount left over after subtracting the liabilities from the assets. Since nonprofits do not have owners, the net assets are available to serve the mission of the organization. Net assets are divided into two buckets: net assets with donor restrictions and net assets without donor restrictions. Donor restrictions allow the entity contributing funds to tell the nonprofit how to spend the contribution (e.g., requiring a school to spend the money on continuing education for their teachers).

The statement of financial position is a snapshot of the organization's financial position. Unlike the statement of activities, the statement of financial position tells the story of the nonprofit at a particular point in time. The statement of financial position reports *as of* a particular date. The date is referred to as their *fiscal year end* and is selected by the nonprofit and used consistently for all external reporting. Many nonprofits in the United States have June 30 or December 31 year ends, although some universities have May 31 year ends to coincide with the end of their school year. An organization's year end is typically found at the top of the statement of financial position.

Statement of Cash Flows

As the name implies, the statement of cash flows provides a description of the inflows and outflows of cash. As the organization is using accrual accounting (recognizing items based on the occurrence of an event—not when cash is received or paid), the statement of cash flows provides insights into the inflows and outflows of cash. It helps users assess the nonprofit's ability to generate cash and its ability to pay its bills.

When we use the term *cash*, we include cash on hand (i.e., petty cash) but also cash in the bank (i.e., checking or savings), so long as the nonprofit can deposit or withdraw cash at any time without notice or penalty. The statement of cash flows also includes cash equivalents that are short term and very near maturity (original maturities of three months or fewer) so that there is very little risk. These funds are readily convertible to cash. Examples of cash equivalents include treasury bills and money market accounts. The statement also includes cash flows related to restricted cash.

Similar to the statement of activities, the statement of cash flows covers all of the activity over the course of the year. It may also present certain noncash activities (i.e., leasing in lieu of buying an asset) to understand its impact on the organization's financial position.

Operating cash flows (statement of cash flows) and operating income (statement of activities) are not synonymous. Because the nonprofit determines how it wants to present its intermediate measure of operations, there is flexibility in the definition of *operating* for the statement of activities. The statement of cash flows is more explicit on what activities belong in each category.

There are three categories of cash flow: *investing*, *financing*, and *operating*.

- *Investing activities* are primarily made up of cash flows for long-term assets. This includes purchasing or selling a building or equipment. It also includes purchases of investments.

- *Financing activities* are primarily made up of cash flows related to borrowing and repaying funds. It includes activities like taking out a loan or paying back a loan. It also includes cash receipts from donors that are required to be used for long-term purchases or investment (e.g., a gift to buy a new building).

- *Operating activities* are anything that doesn't fit into the investing or financing categories. This includes cash receipts from sales of inventory or provision of services and cash receipts from accounts receivables. Common cash flows include payments to suppliers and employees and payments for taxes. The interest portion of a loan payment is an operating activity, and the payment for principal is a financing activity. Interest and dividend revenues also qualify as operating activities.

REQUIRED DISCLOSURES

While the three required financial statements provide a lot of information for the user, they are incomplete without the notes and disclosures to the financial statements. When you look closely at the financial statement, you will see references to the notes. The notes are an integral part of the financial statements. In addition to the required numbers, nonprofits are required to provide additional details in note disclosures (i.e., words and tables). These notes provide additional analysis of the numbers and context for what they mean and how they were computed. The numbers alone would give an incomplete picture of the organization's financial performance and financial standing.

In addition to writing the rules for the financial statements, FASB also writes the requirements for minimum disclosures of material items. FASB provides the disclosure requirements in the "50" section of the Codification. Most nonprofits use a disclosure checklist to prepare the disclosures or engage their auditor or independent accountant to prepare them. Regardless of who prepares the notes, management is responsible for the preparation and fair presentation of the financial statements and note disclosures.

Most disclosures are required for a particular element (e.g., cash, revenue) or for a particular statement (e.g., financial position, cash flows). However, some disclosures are not tied to a particular element or statement. We'll focus on those disclosures that are incremental for nonprofits.

Basic Disclosures

As all nonprofits are unique, organizations are required to inform users about the nature of their activities. This includes information on the major programs the nonprofit offers.

Sometimes, instead of providing complete financial statements for both years in a comparative format, a nonprofit will show the complete information for the current year and only summarize the prior year. The label for the prior year and an accompanying note disclosure should both state that the prior year's information is summarized. The note should also explain where the reader can get the prior year's detailed financial statements.

Some nonprofits like to provide a ratio of fundraising expenses to amounts raised. This can help users understand the increased revenues from fundraising. If the ratio is disclosed, the nonprofit must also disclose how it calculates the ratio.

Liquidity and Availability Disclosures

Nonprofits must also disclose information about liquidity or maturity of assets and liabilities. Liquidity analysis is important because it helps the board assess how easily the entity can pay its bills. Cash is the most liquid asset, as it can readily be used to pay bills. Other assets have to be sold to be converted to cash to be able to use them to pay bills. If there is not enough cash available to pay upcoming bills, the liquidity of other assets will help the board decide how to handle the situation.

One way FASB requires nonprofits to present information about liquidity is by requiring them to provide information about donor restrictions or board designations that limit the use of the items. For example, if a donor promises to give money in the short term but indicates that the funds need to be used to purchase equipment, that receivable is not liquid (i.e., it can't be used to pay other bills in the near future).

Nonprofits must disclose qualitative information (in words) about their liquidity, including how they manage their liquid assets to meet cash needs for general expenditures within one year of the fiscal year end. This includes information about lines of credit, reserves, and other policies ensuring the capacity to make payments as they become due.

In addition to the qualitative disclosures, the nonprofit must also include quantitative information (numbers) to provide information about the availability of the nonprofit's financial assets as of the end of the year to meet cash needs for general expenditures within one year of the statement of financial position date. This is a relatively new disclosure that requires nonprofits to more carefully assess how they want to communicate this information.

First, the nonprofit must identify its financial assets, which include cash and cash equivalents, short-term investments, accounts, interest, and pledges receivable.

Assets excluded from the definition of a financial asset include land, buildings, equipment, and intangible assets like intellectual property and trademarks.

DEFINITIONS

The definition of financial assets in the FASB Master Glossary is this:

- "Cash, evidence of an ownership interest in an entity, or a contract that conveys to one entity a right to do either of the following:
    a. Receive cash or another financial instrument from a second entity
    b. Exchange other financial instruments on potentially favorable terms with the second entity."[8]

Once the financial assets have been identified, the nonprofit has to back out anything not available for general expenditure. The term *general expenditure* is not defined, so each nonprofit must evaluate how they interpret the measure. Assets are deemed unavailable if there are external limits imposed by donors, laws, and contracts with others (e.g., a donor restricting its cash donation for a particular purpose) or internal limits imposed by governing board decisions that limit to purposes other than general use (e.g., a board designation for a capital campaign). In addition, the nature of items can cause them to be unavailable (e.g., pledges due greater than one year).

There are other unusual circumstances that require liquidity disclosures:

- special borrowing arrangements, requirements imposed by resource providers that cash be held in separate accounts, and known significant liquidity problems;

- the fact that the nonprofit has not maintained appropriate amounts of cash and cash equivalents to comply with donor-imposed restrictions;
- and information about significant limits resulting from contractual agreements with suppliers, creditors, and others, including the existence of loan covenants.

Intermediate Measures of Operations

Some organizations present various subtotals—called *intermediate measures of operations*—that can help a user evaluate the organization. These subtotals are not required or defined by GAAP and are used at the nonprofit's discretion. The nonprofit should include in the notes any information that helps the reader understand what is included in the subtotal.

CHAPTER 3

STATEMENT OF ACTIVITIES

Now that we've covered the major financial statements for nonprofits, let's take a deeper dive into the elements that make up the statement of activities. The statement of activities tells the story of the revenue and expense transactions that took place during the year. It helps users understand the performance of the entity in that time frame. The statement of activities can come in many formats and levels of detail. However, it always includes revenues, expenses, and a reconciliation of the change in net assets. Revenues increase net assets, and expenses decrease net assets. The statement of activities provides insight into the types of revenues a nonprofit receives, as well as the types of expenses.

REVENUE

Nonprofits have a variety of revenue streams. Some may come from *exchange transactions*, where each party receives approximately what they pay for. This is also referred to as *commensurate value*. Some revenue can come from contributions. These are often referred to as *voluntary nonexchange transactions*. Each stream has different recognition and measurement rules.

MEET JANE

Jane is the director of finance at the local art museum in her town. She's a licensed CPA and has worked in the nonprofit sector for the past fifteen years. Jane has a staff accountant who works for her, and she works directly with the director of development, who is in charge of fundraising and donor relations. Jane is reviewing year-end financials for the museum and is ensuring that they meet the requirements of GAAP.

Exchange Revenue

An *exchange transaction* is when a good or service is provided in exchange for consideration, oftentimes cash. When you purchase clothing or sporting goods from Target, that is an exchange transaction. You receive approximately equal value for your payment. Many nonprofits sell goods or provide services similar to for-profit entities. These transactions include the sale of mementos by museum gift stores, tuition revenue collected by private universities, and patient service revenues earned by nonprofit hospitals. The nonprofit rules for exchange transactions are the same as for-profit entities.

Regardless of the types of services or goods provided, all exchange revenue is recognized using the same approach, which is referred to as the *performance obligation method*. A performance obligation is a promise to provide a good or service to a customer.[1] It can be oral (e.g., a salesperson promising something to a customer) or in writing (e.g., a formal contract). Revenue is recognized when the performance obligation is met, meaning the good or service is delivered to the customer.

Any cash or consideration paid prior to the performance obligation being met would be a liability (i.e., the nonprofit owes the customer a good or service) and not yet revenue. Once the obligation is met, the nonprofit reverses the liability and recognizes the revenue.

WHAT DOES IT MEAN TO REVERSE A LIABILITY?

We are going to use the term *reverse* frequently. This means to remove an element previously recognized from the financial statements and instead recognize something else. You've likely heard the term *dual-entry bookkeeping*, which means every transaction must have two parts. *Reversing the liability* is the phrase used when something comes off the liability section of the financial statement and then the same amount is added elsewhere in the financial statements. Often when a liability is reversed, cash is paid or revenue is recognized.

Exchange transactions are classified as part of the net assets without donor restrictions. You couldn't buy a shirt at Target and then tell the store how to spend those funds. When buying a good or service from a nonprofit, the same is also true. A parent paying tuition can't tell the university how to spend the funds.

As with for-profit entities, the other party in an exchange transaction is not a donor. The counterparty in an exchange transaction is a customer, and customers cannot usually place limits on how nonprofits use exchange transactions. Occasionally, a government may provide a grant that qualifies as an exchange transaction, and may place limitations on the use of the revenue. As the government is not a donor in this instance, it would still be classified as *without donor restrictions.*

MUSEUM REVENUE

Jane is reviewing the financials in preparation for the upcoming board meeting and is going over the various types of exchange revenue for the museum. Exchange Revenue:

- Admission Revenue
- Membership Revenue
- Retail Revenue

The museum receives the majority of its funding from the exchange revenues of ticket sales. Visitors can purchase tickets up to sixty days prior to their visit. Revenue is recognized when the visitor enters the museum and visits the exhibits.

The second-largest source of exchange revenues is from memberships. Supporters of the arts often buy membership packages that include unlimited visits to the museum for one year. They also get discounts at the museum retail shop. Because members can visit the museum at any time, membership revenue is recognized by dividing the membership dollars by twelve. One twelfth is recognized each month. The unrecognized amount is shown on the statement of financial position as deferred revenue (i.e., a liability).

Assume one membership costs $240 and is purchased on January 1.

	Cash Received *(Statement of Cash Flows)*	**Revenue Recognized** *(Statement of Activities)*	**Deferred Revenue** *(Statement of Financial Position)*
1/1/Yr1	$240	$0	$240
1/31/Yr1	$0	$20	$220
2/28/Yr1	$0	$20	$200
12/31/Yr1	$0	$20	$0

Finally, the museum gift shop offers various souvenirs for visitors, ranging from keychains and holiday ornaments to reference books and prints of the artwork. Retail revenue is recognized when the product is sold.

Jane reviews the revenue and deferred-revenue calculations to ensure the proper amount of revenue was recognized in the fiscal year.

Contribution Revenue

A *contribution* is defined as "an unconditional transfer of cash or other assets, as well as unconditional promises to give to an entity or a reduction, settlement, or cancellation of its liabilities in a voluntary nonreciprocal transfer by another entity acting other than as an owner."[2] Many people use the terms *contribution* and *donation* interchangeably, but there are important accounting qualifications for contributions.

Examples of contribution revenue include the following:

- when a donor writes a check to an organization (i.e., a transfer of cash)
- when an individual pledges to give a certain amount of money at a particular date
- receipt of a grant that is for the public's benefit from a foundation or federal agency
- forgiveness of debt (i.e., "a reduction, settlement, or cancellation of its liabilities"), where entities forgive a loan to a nonprofit as a means of support
- when someone volunteers their time for an organization (i.e., contributed services)
- when a donor provides a nonfinancial asset like supplies or equipment to a nonprofit (i.e., contributed nonfinancial assets)

The types of contributions vary widely, but there are common themes to recognition.

VOLUNTARY

Not all nonexchange transactions are voluntary, but a contribution must be. For example, fines are typically nonexchange (e.g., library late fees) but are usually not voluntary and therefore are not contributions. Typically, the person giving the contribution decides how much they want to give, whereas in an exchange transaction there is typically a stated price, ensuring each party receives about equal value.

NONRECIPROCAL

Nonexchange or *nonreciprocal* means that the person providing the funds is not receiving commensurate value. The definition clarifies, "In a contribution transaction, the resource provider often receives value indirectly by providing a societal benefit although that benefit is not considered to be of commensurate value."[3] So while there may be indirect benefit, that benefit is not the primary consideration. Churchgoers who put money in the offering tray may receive warm fuzzies from giving, but those warm fuzzies are not commensurate value.

UNCONDITIONAL

Another important word in the definition of a *contribution* is *unconditional. Unconditional* indicates that there are no barriers to the resources. A condition imposed by a donor has one or more barriers that must be overcome for the nonprofit to be entitled to the assets and a *right of return* (i.e., you'd have to give the money back if you didn't meet the requirements) or *right of release* (i.e., they wouldn't have to fulfill a promise if you didn't overcome the barrier), which makes the donation conditional. If there is a barrier to overcome that would otherwise prevent being entitled to the contribution, then no revenue is recognized until the barrier is overcome. FASB provides three indicators of a barrier. No one indicator is determinative, and the evaluation of any transaction is based on facts and circumstances.

The first indicator of a barrier is a measurable performance-related stipulation or other measurable stipulation that will prevent the organization from recognizing the funds. For example, if the donor indicates that a certain number of homeless must be served each month, or if the nonprofit has to raise a certain amount of outside resources to be eligible for the funding (often referred to as a *match*), the nonprofit would recognize revenue only when the required number of homeless had been served or the outside funds raised. If the donor gave the funds up front, the nonprofit would recognize a liability (e.g., a refundable advance) until the barrier had been met.

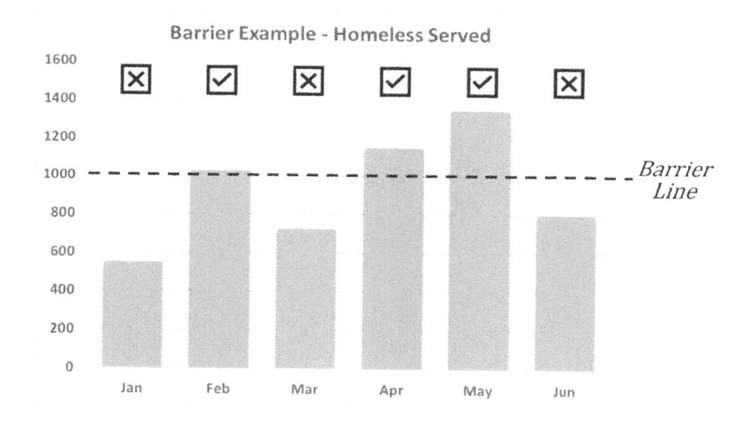

A grantor has agreed to provide $10,000 each month that the nonprofit serves one thousand homeless veterans. The grant is worth up to $120,000 for a grant period that runs from January through December. The organization has a fiscal year end of June 30. Because the grant is conditioned on serving a certain number of individuals, no revenue is recognized upon receipt. In the current year, the organization can only recognize revenue for February, April, and May, when they exceeded the one thousand veterans. Since they served fewer than one thousand homeless veterans in January, March, and June, the entity will not receive funding in those months.

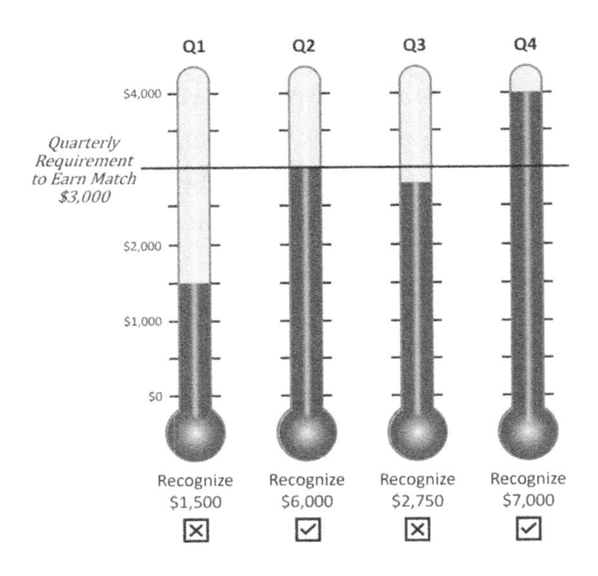

A donor has pledges to match funds received in a quarter (up to $3,000) when the funds exceed $3,000 for that quarter. The nonprofit therefore recognizes the $1,500 received in Q1 but no match. In Q2 the entity recognizes $6,000 ($3,000 in donation and $3,000 in match). In Q3 they just miss the match, so they recognize $2,750. In Q4 they have an excellent quarter and receive the full match. Total revenue recorded in Q4 is $7,000 ($4,000 received plus matched pledge of $3,000).

The second indicator is limited discretion on the conduct of the activity. This includes guidelines about qualifying expenses. For example, many federal grants require the nonprofit to follow the federal regulations in the Uniform Guidance.[4] These regulations provide explicit guidance about what the funds can and cannot be used for. Until the funds are used in compliance with the rules, any funds received in advance are liabilities (called a *refundable advance*). When the funds are used in compliance with the Uniform Guidance, then revenue is recognized, and the liability is reversed.

The third indicator is that the stipulation has to be related to the purpose of the agreement. If the agreement indicates that in order to receive funds "the sun has to come up tomorrow," clearly that has nothing to do with the purpose of a grant to help the homeless. Therefore, that stipulation does not make the contribution conditional. However, if the stipulation requires serving a certain number of homeless, that is related to the purpose and therefore makes the donation conditional. Stipulations not related to the purpose do not impact recognition of the funding, as they are deemed unconditional.

It is important to note that the likelihood of the recipient meeting the stipulation is not a factor when determining whether an agreement contains a barrier. For example, if the nonprofit receives an up-front grant to serve 250 homeless veterans a month but the nonprofit currently serves 1,000 homeless veterans a month, revenue can still not be recognized until the 250th veteran is served.

MUSEUM GRANTS

Jane is reviewing a recently received grant award from the federal government. The grant is specifically designed to support the arts and limits the types of items the funds can be used for by listing qualifying expenses. This is a cost-reimbursement grant, meaning that the museum first has to pay for the items and then request reimbursement from the federal agency. The museum often receives grants from foundations and federal agencies as part of its contribution revenue.

After reviewing the grant, Jane creates a list of items the museum needs that can be paid for by the grant. As it is close to year end, the purchases won't happen until the first quarter of next fiscal year. Jane notices that her staff has already recognized the revenue for the grant in the fourth-quarter financial draft. As a result, Jane enters a correcting entry to reverse the revenue and receivable.

When the funds are spent on the approved items, Jane will create a new entry to recognize a receivable from the federal government and recognize revenue. Jane makes a note to discuss the issue with her staff so that conditional grants are not recognized prematurely.

Accounting for Contributions

RESTRICTIONS

Once a contribution is determined to be unconditional, the transaction should then be evaluated to determine whether there are any donor-imposed restrictions related to either timing or purpose.

Some restrictions are temporary and expire after a period of time. A donor may indicate that funds have to be held for a period of five years before they can be used. After five years, the restriction would expire, and the funds would become unrestricted.

Some restrictions are *purpose related*, which restricts the use of the contributed asset to be more specific than the mission of the nonprofit. For example, a donor might provide funding for the school's athletics department. The athletics department is much narrower than the overall purpose of a nonprofit K–12 school.

Some restrictions are *perpetual* in nature. For example, a donor may provide a very large donation for an endowment and stipulate the original funds (i.e., the corpus) are to never be spent (i.e., held in perpetuity). However, the interest, dividends, and gains from the funds can be used freely. The corpus has a permanent restriction. The other income is unrestricted.

While we use the term *donors*, grantors are also an example of contributors who can restrict funds. However, it is important to note that internal designations by the board are not restrictions. For example, if the board wants to set aside funds for a new project, those funds do not have donor restrictions. Instead, they have board designations, because only external parties (i.e., donors) can restrict.

Restrictions require management to track and carefully monitor resources to ensure the funds are used for the correct purpose or in the appropriate periods. This requires careful accounting. The board should be involved in discussions with management around the internal controls to ensure proper recording of restrictions.

The board should also proactively review the impact of restrictions on liquidity and monitor whether there are sufficient unrestricted donations for general operations. In addition to discussions with finance, the board should meet with individuals from development to discuss fundraising tactics and how they ensure the proper mix of restricted and unrestricted donations. Boards may also consider implementing a gift acceptance policy that limits the types of restrictions or conditions to prevent onerous accounting for small donations.

While conditions prevent recognition of revenue, restrictions do not limit recognition, but they do impact presentation. The statement of activities tracks contributions without donor-imposed restrictions separately from those with restrictions. However, the revenue is recognized in both scenarios, unlike when conditions prevent recognition until the conditions have been met.

Statement of Activities
For the Year Ended June 30, 20XX

	Without Donor Restrictions	With Donor Restrictions	Total
Revenue:			
Revenue Source 1	150,000	50,000	200,000
Revenue Source 2	-	100,000	100,000
Revenue Source 3	30,000	10,000	40,000
Revenue Source 4	25,000	-	25,000
Net assets released from restriction	75,000	(75,000)	-
Total Revenue	$ 280,000	$ 85,000	$ 365,000

RELEASE FROM RESTRICTIONS

When a donor's restrictions have been met (i.e., the funds are used for the correct purpose or the time restriction has expired), the statement of activities shows this as a reduction of the net assets with donor restrictions and an addition to the net assets without donor-imposed restrictions.

Statement of Activities
For the Year Ended June 30, 20XX

	Without Donor Restrictions	With Donor Restrictions	Total
Revenue:			
Revenue Source 1	150,000	50,000	200,000
Revenue Source 2	-	100,000	100,000
Revenue Source 3	30,000	10,000	40,000
Revenue Source 4	25,000	-	25,000
Net assets released from restriction	75,000	(75,000)	-
Total Revenue	$ 280,000	$ 85,000	$ 365,000

Expenses are always unrestricted, so both the revenue and related expenses will show in the "without donor restrictions" column.

A nonprofit can also elect to implement a policy where if a restricted contribution has its restriction met in the same reporting period, the revenue is recognized as net assets without donor restrictions (i.e., without having to show the release from restrictions). If this policy is elected, it must be disclosed to the user.

If a donor pledges to provide funds in the future (common with capital campaigns), any funds due in future periods are donor restricted. Nonprofits cannot spend funds they don't have.

For example, a donor may indicate they will donate $5,000 a year for three years so the nonprofit can start a new program and have enough funding in the initial years. The funds due in future years are restricted until the funds are received. If a donor donates a long-lived asset (e.g., a building) and the donor does not indicate how long the asset must be used, then that would be reported as revenue without donor restrictions. However, if the donor sent cash to purchase a long-lived asset, then those assets are restricted until the asset is purchased and placed into service.[5]

CONTRIBUTIONS FROM DONORS

As part of her financial statement review, Jane reviews the contribution revenue recognized from donors and verifies the restrictions. The museum's policy is to capitalize collection items. The Anderson family, who are large supporters of the museum, have donated $100,000 in cash for the purchase of paintings by female artists. Jane notes that the $100,000 is appropriately recognized as having a restriction (which is temporary in nature). She knows the curator has already identified several amazing female artists and that the museum is planning on creating an exhibit to open sometime next year to display the art. Once the art is purchased, she'll release the funds from restriction.

She also notes that the Gibson donation is for the creation of an endowment. The initial $1 million can never be spent, but the Gibsons permitted any interest or dividends from the fund to be used to purchase art. The initial $1 million is appropriately recognized as restricted due to its perpetual nature. The Gibsons expressly require the art purchased to be of the Renaissance era, so all income generated by the donation has been labeled restricted until the purchases are completed.

The Smith Family Foundation donated $250,000 to be spent for educational purposes. The museum is hoping to use the funds to hire individuals to lead seminars for visitors, including monthly events for children. These funds were appropriately labeled as having donor restrictions due to the purpose restriction.

With everything looking great, Jane is ready to wrap up her review of the cash contributions until she remembers the Donnelly donation. In the third quarter, they donated $150,000 for gallery maintenance. In reviewing the grant, development indicated that most janitorial salaries could be paid for with these funds. In addition, the artifacts exhibit was reorganized, and a complete housekeeping was performed, including all surfaces and exhibit cases. Based on the salary information from payroll and the invoice from the cleaning crew hired to prepare the gallery for reorganization, $75,000 should have been released from restrictions. Jane enters an entry to reduce net assets with donor restrictions and increase net assets without donor restrictions to reflect the spending. She puts a sticky note on her desk to talk to the museum curator about any future plans for deep cleaning.

There is an odd exception to this rule where if the donor explicitly states an intent to support the current period, the funds are without donor restriction. For example, if a donor pledges to give funds in the following month but indicates they want to support an event happening in the current month, the funds are deemed to be without donor restrictions.

FAIR VALUE

Fair value is defined as "the price that would be received to sell an asset or paid to transfer a liability in an orderly transaction between market participants at the measurement date."[6] Any contributions received by a nonprofit are measured at fair value. This is a very complicated and nuanced area of accounting.

Fair value is an exit price (i.e., the price you would receive if you were to sell something). For example, the fair value of your home is not the amount you paid for it (that would be the acquisition value) but the price you could get if you sold it. A real estate agent would likely use comparable sales in the neighborhood to determine the fair value of the home. When applied to contributions, when someone donates their time (contributed services) or supplies (contributed nonfinancial assets), the nonprofit must determine the fair value of the contribution. This can be very subjective. There are disclosures required to assist the reader in understanding how the nonprofit came to its fair-value determinations.

PRESENTATION

While the accounting for various transactions (grants, gifts, etc.) utilizes the concept of contribution accounting, that does not require the nonprofit to use the term *contribution revenue*. Entities can use terms like *grant revenue* or *donations* if they feel that it better describes the transactions for users. The term used does not impact the accounting methodology. While the term *donor* is used throughout this book, grantors, including the federal government, are often large portions of the contribution revenue recognized.

TYPES OF CONTRIBUTION REVENUE TRANSACTIONS

Promises to Give (Pledges)

Oftentimes, donors may pledge to give funds in the future. Accounting for these pledges varies depending on how far in the future the nonprofit expects to receive the funding. Nonprofits that expect to collect the funds within a year should measure the promise at its net realizable value, which is approximately fair value. Net realizable value does not use discounting to value the pledge.

When recording a pledge receivable, nonprofits must consider the likelihood of not being paid. To do so, nonprofits reduce the receivable to the amount they believe they will ultimately receive from the donor, and show that number on the financial statements. Nonprofits use an allowance (referred to as a *contra asset*) to adjust the receivable. Often annual campaigns have a good amount of history to estimate the portion pledged that will not ultimately be collected.

Sometimes the nonprofit will have a multiyear campaign (e.g., a capital campaign) where funds will be received over multiple years. This typically requires the nonprofit to use discounted cash flows (i.e., present value) to determine the value of the pledge. Anytime we deal with a present-value calculation, we need to identify a discount rate to adjust for the time value of money.

When valuing an unconditional promise to give, the nonprofit must consider the timing of collection, the creditworthiness of the donor, past collection experiences, policies regarding enforcement, and any uncertainty about whether the donation will be paid. Over time, as the funds are collected, the discount will be recognized until it equals the full amount of the pledge.

Intentions to Give

There is a very important distinction between a *promise to give* and an *intention to give*. A promise to give (i.e., a pledge) is typically legally enforceable (even if the nonprofit never intends to enforce it). For example, sending in a pledge card or creating an irrevocable trust creates a right for the nonprofit. On the other hand, an intention to give is nonbinding. An example of an intention to give is notifying a nonprofit that they have been included in a donor's will. Until the donor passes, the donor can change their will. In addition, until the will has gone through probate, a family member can challenge the will. Therefore, the inclusion in a will is an intention to give. Other language that indicates the agreement is nonbinding (e.g., "Indicate the maximum you may potentially give; we won't hold you to it") would be an intention. People working in development should ensure the wording on pledge cards does not accidentally convert the pledge into an intention.

MUSEUM PLEDGES

Jane reviews the pledge receivable details from the general ledger. Many donors pledge at the beginning of the year to provide cash on a monthly or quarterly basis. When the pledge is received, so long as there are no conditions attached, Jane recognizes the full amount of the pledge for the year and books a receivable for the full amount. Jane reviews the collections for the quarter and notes all donors have continued to make their payments as promised. When the cash was received, her staffer properly reduced the pledge receivable account for the received amount and recorded the cash. Thankfully, the museum has a very small allowance for doubtful accounts, as donors have historically been very good about making payments.

Jane separately reviews the transactions for the big capital campaign. The museum is hoping to open a new wing to hold a children's exhibit that will engage with the youth of the town. The museum estimates that they will need $10 million to complete the renovation and prepare the space. Thankfully, they have already obtained pledges of $5 million for the project. The pledges are due over a five-year period (to coincide with the preparation and building phases). As one year has passed since the capital campaign kicked off, Jane books an adjusting journal entry to recognize the revenue for the funds. She notes that all expected payments have been received and were properly recorded. Jane looks forward to being able to bring her young daughter to the museum to engage with the exhibit.

Debra, the director of development, had earlier let her know that Sara Johnson—one of the museum's wealthiest donors—has decided to include the museum in her will. A copy of the will was sent by Sara's lawyer to the museum. Debra was excited to add that to the contribution revenue for the year, as it would ensure she hits her revenue budget. Unfortunately, after reading the will, Jane determines that it does not create an irrevocable trust for the funds. As a result, simply being included in the will is not enough to recognize any revenue, as Sara could change her mind at any time and update her will. Jane assures Debra that she will include a mention of the intention to give in the notes to the financial statements, but unfortunately, Debra will need to work on some more last-minute donations if she wants to hit her revenue number.

Contributed Services

For most nonprofits, volunteers are the center of their success. Without them, many organizations would cease to exist. However, accounting for these volunteers is somewhat tricky. The accounting standards recognize only contributed services that are performed by someone with a specialized skill that would otherwise need to be purchased.

Often nonprofits will disclose the number of hours provided by volunteers that were not recognized in the financial statements as a way to thank their volunteers and show the importance of their work. Tracking volunteer hours can also be helpful for nonprofits because they may eventually decide that a full- or part-time paid position is needed. The value of volunteer time continues to grow. In 2021, it was estimated that an hour of volunteer time is worth about $29—up almost 5 percent over the prior year based on data from Independent Sector.[7] For example, if a nonprofit significantly grew its services or simply determined more consistency was needed for a particular position, having an understanding of volunteer hours and efforts would help them know the cost to replace volunteers with paid staff.

Another instance in which a nonprofit recognizes a contributed service is when it creates or enhances a nonfinancial asset (e.g., building a house). Then an asset is recognized for its fair value, and contribution revenue is recognized. Fair value is used for all contributed services whether or not the nonprofit could afford to purchase the service at the specific fair value.

While the general rule for recognizing contributed services is to use the fair value of the service, there is an exception for services from an affiliate. For example, many membership organizations have a related foundation. Often the foundation has no employees, and the membership organization handles the accounting and all the work of the related foundation. When the membership organization does not charge the foundation for the costs of the work performed on the foundation's behalf, GAAP requires that the foundation recognize the value of the services provided by the membership organization at cost (hourly rate of the employee times hours) in its separate financial statements.

VOLUNTEER TIME

Jane is very grateful for all the work of the volunteers at the museum. Without them, the museum would struggle to operate. She reviews the volunteer schedule for the month. The museum has lots of passionate volunteers who staff the information desk and serve as docents. Many spend several hours a week at the museum. Some volunteer so frequently she knows them by name! However, because many volunteer positions do not require a specialized skill, Jane is not permitted to recognize this time in the financial statements. She does, however, total the hours to add to the schedule for when the disclosures are prepared. The museum proudly discloses the number of volunteer hours not recognized each year because of the importance of the work.

At the last board meeting, the treasurer of the board, who is a CPA, presented the completed Form 990 that was due last month. When she received the invoice, she noted that the CPA firm had indicated they were going to forgo payment this year. An accountant donating their time to prepare the Form 990 that the nonprofit had historically paid a public accountant to prepare would meet the requirements for recognition and would be recognized in the financial statements. Jane reviews the invoice and notes that the rate agrees to the engagement letter and the hours appear to be consistent with the prior year. As a result, she recognizes the fair value of the time (normal rate times number of hours) as contribution revenue, and then they would also recognize an expense for professional services for the time equal to the revenue. She leaves herself a note to send the treasurer a thank-you note. This was a really great surprise and will really help the museum preserve cash.

Jane smiles, recognizing how much of an impact these volunteers make on the museum and what a debt of gratitude they all have for their hard work.

Contributed Financial Assets

Financial assets include cash and stock. When a donor gifts stock to a nonprofit (as donors receive tax benefits for these types of donations), the nonprofit measures the contribution at its fair value. For example, if the donor gifts the nonprofit a hundred shares of Apple stock, the nonprofit looks up the value of the stock on the public exchange on the date of receipt to determine the fair value of the contribution. If the donor promises to donate stock, the nonprofit typically bases the value on the projected fair value at the date expected to be received. If it is difficult to determine the future fair value, the fair value at the date of promise can be used.

Contributed Nonfinancial Assets (Gifts in Kind)

Sometimes, rather than cash or stock, donors provide nonfinancial assets or *in-kind donations* to organizations. Donors may provide food to a homeless shelter, art supplies to a nonprofit daycare, or sporting goods to the athletics department of a university. Pharmaceutical companies may donate pharmaceuticals to a hospital. By donating nonfinancial assets, these donors are helping nonprofits preserve cash. If the nonprofit didn't receive these items as donations, they would have to purchase them in order to operate. Sometimes, a donor may provide a nonfinancial asset that the organization may not need but that can be sold to generate cash. This is often the case with donated cars.

These nonfinancial assets are recognized as contribution revenue using the fair value of the asset. Contributed nonfinancial assets are shown on the statement of activities as a separate line from donations of cash or financial assets. There are special disclosure requirements for contributed nonfinancial assets that provide users with information about potential restrictions on the items, whether the assets were monetized (i.e., sold for cash) or utilized, and the valuation inputs (i.e., how the nonprofit determines fair value).

MUSEUM CONTRIBUTED ASSETS

Jane's review is nearly complete. She is quite happy with the draft numbers so far. She plans to send a board package with updated numbers next week. Her last section to review is the contributed assets section of the revenue data.

Consistent with the prior year, several donors made stock donations in the last few weeks. Appreciated stock (i.e., stock that has increased in value since its initial purchase) is taxed when sold. However, if someone donates the appreciated stock, then there is no tax due. Many financial advisers recommend donating stock as a tax strategy for their clients. The museum typically sells donated stock within a few days, and all the donated stock they received was from publicly traded companies, so thankfully valuation was not too difficult. Jane uses Yahoo Finance to look up the stock price on the date of donation and uses that, along with the number of shares, to recognize revenue. When the stock is sold, the investments are removed, and cash is recognized along with a gain or loss on sale.

Looking at the next line item brings a big smile to Jane's face. The Garvey family has donated a beautiful painting that had been in the family's collection for years. Earlier in the day, she noticed that the painting had already been hung and was the perfect addition to that wing. Jane noted that the painting was recently examined by a valuation specialist and was worth over $50,000. As the piece was added to the collection, the contribution revenue increased net assets with donor restrictions.

OTHER REVENUE TRANSACTIONS

Other Income

Other revenues recognized by nonprofits that don't meet the definition of a contribution and are not from transactions with customers fall under the general term of *other income*. An example of other income is investment income. Nonprofits generally do not sit on all the cash they receive. As good stewards of the funds, nonprofits invest the cash to generate interest and dividend revenue.

Changes in the fair value of investments that have not been sold are called *unrealized gains and losses*. They are unrealized as the investments have not been sold, so the value will continue to change while the organization holds the assets. These unrealized gains and losses for debt and equity securities are shown on the statement of activities. Realized gains and losses are also recognized in the statement of activities.

Other income also includes sales of nonfinancial assets for a gain or loss. If the nonprofit decides it wants to sell its building to move to a larger location, any amount of cash received over the carrying value of the building is recognized as a gain on sale and reported in the statement of activities.

OTHER INCOME

Jane is happy with the status of the financial statements, and revenue for the year is looking very strong. As part of the close process, she reviews the brokerage statement from the museum's financial adviser. The museum has a policy to invest excess cash but limits the risk by selecting conservative investments. With the statement in hand, Jane is able to identify the changes in fair value since the last statement. She then records the adjusting journal entries to record the unrealized gains and losses. The museum had sufficient cash during the month, so no investments were sold and no realized gains needed to be recorded.

Due to the conservative nature of the investments, a good portion of them are debt securities that pay interest. Jane records the interest received and compares it to the agreed-upon rates. Finally, she records the dividends reported in the statement. Jane has to wait each month to record this information, as she wouldn't have the information needed without the monthly statement. She's happy to see that the bond and stock market performed well and that the investments provided a good return for the museum. The museum is very happy with the results from the financial adviser, who understands the importance of preserving value.

Agency Transactions

Sometimes the nonprofit is not the ultimate beneficiary and is instead acting as an intermediary or agent. These transactions are referred to as *agency transactions*. The United Way is a nonprofit with name recognition that often acts as an agent. The United Way is known for its fundraising efforts on behalf of other nonprofits.

In an agency transaction, a donor provides cash (or other assets) to a nonprofit with instructions to provide them to another beneficiary that is explicitly indicated. If the donor doesn't allow the recipient nonprofit to change the specified beneficiary, then the nonprofit is acting as an agent (i.e., acting as the middleman in getting the funds from the donor to the ultimate beneficiary). In this scenario, the recipient nonprofit (who received the cash from the donor) does not recognize any revenue. Instead, the cash is recognized, and the offset is a liability. When the cash is ultimately provided to the beneficiary, it is reduced and the liability removed. Agency transactions are a type of exchange transaction. In this scenario, as there is no revenue or expenses, there is no impact on the statement of activities.

There are exceptions: If the donor allows the recipient organization to change the beneficiary (referred to as *variance power*), it is not an agency transaction, because the recipient organization has the right to choose who ultimately receives the money. Variance power must be explicit and give the recipient entity the unilateral right to change the beneficiary without approval. When variance power is granted, the recipient nonprofit recognizes revenue upon receipt of the donated funds. When the funds are then provided to the ultimate beneficiary, an expense is recognized. The net impact on the statement of activities is zero.

Another exception to agency transaction accounting is when the recipient nonprofit and the beneficiary specified by the donor are financially interrelated. For example, if a university has a separate foundation that uses all of its granted funds for scholarships for students of the university, it does not matter if the donor gives the funds to the university or the foundation, because the funds ultimately benefit the university. If the foundation receives the funds with a stipulation they be provided to the university, the foundation recognizes the revenue, as the net assets of the foundation are for the benefit of the university anyway.

Board Best Practices: Revenue

Obviously, revenue is very important to nonprofits. Without sufficient revenue sources, nonprofits close and are unable to provide their services or achieve their mission. The board should play an active role in monitoring revenue and ensuring that there isn't a concentration of revenue from a single source that would leave the organization vulnerable if it stopped providing revenue. While large donors are not uncommon, if a nonprofit is dependent on a single donor for operations, they could be significantly affected if that donor were to pass away and the family decided to not continue donating. The board should discuss the diversity of funding sources with management, and whether any sources are potentially vulnerable. The board should also monitor collections of pledges to ensure the organization is properly recognizing an allowance for bad debt as needed. Additionally, the board should carefully review conditions and restrictions that affect the timing of revenue and limit the use of funds. Too many restrictions may prohibit the nonprofit from paying its day-to-day bills. Finally, a gift acceptance policy can help the organization ensure they do not accept gifts with conditions that cannot be met or that would jeopardize the organization's reputation.

Board Self-Evaluation

What would we do if we stopped receiving grants or a major donor stopped contributing? What are our contingency plans?

Entities need to continue to diversify their donor base. Nothing is promised forever. Management should have a proactive plan to address these types of issues.

EXPENSES

In order to generate revenues and serve the mission of the organization, nonprofits incur certain expenses ranging from fundraising to traditional operating expenses like salaries and utilities. Expenses are reported in the statement of activities as decreases in net assets without donor restrictions. However, nonprofits have a choice in how they present the expenses on the statement of activities. They can choose to display expenses by functional classification or natural classification.

	Without Donor Restrictions	With Donor Restrictions	Total
Expenses:			
Wages	170,000	-	170,000
Rent	30,000	-	30,000
Equipment	20,000	-	20,000
Supplies	40,000	-	40,000
Interest on Loan	5,000	-	5,000
Other Expenses	7,000	-	7,000
Total Expenses	$ 272,000	$ -	$ 272,000

An example of natural classification.

	Without Donor Restrictions	With Donor Restrictions	Total
Expenses:			
Program Activities:			
Program A	120,000	-	120,000
Program B	55,000	-	55,000
Program C	37,000	-	37,000
Supporting Activities:			
Management & General	28,000	-	28,000
Fundraising	32,000	-	32,000
Total Expenses	$ 272,000	$ -	$ 272,000

An example of functional classification.

Natural and Functional Classification

Natural classification entails listing types of expenses, such as salaries, utilities, or rent. Functional classification presents expenses by how they use resources. There are two classes of functional expenses—program services and supporting activities. Program services are the expenses that relate to a particular program. An entity may have multiple programs. A university may have a program related to education and teaching, another related to research, and a third related to a university hospital. Expenses are displayed in total for the program without breaking out the natural classification. Supporting activities are broken into subcategories of *management and general*, *fundraising*, and *membership development*. Expenses are totaled for each major class. Nonprofits are required to present all expenses by both nature and function in one location, but where they display it is at their discretion.

NATURAL AND FUNCTIONAL EXPENSES

As Jane turns her attention from the revenue section of the statement of activities to the expense section, she carefully reviews the functional expense classification.

The first program identified on the statement of activities is research, which is obviously a big portion of the expenses for the museum. This includes expenses related to museum staff, travel, and the research being performed. The second program is curations management, which includes the costs related to caring for the exhibits, as well as storage. The last program is public programs and education, which includes the costs related to programming for the public. At the last board meeting there was discussion regarding adding a new program for auxiliaries. Right now, the costs related to the museum store are included in public programs. The board will vote at the next meeting as to whether they should break out auxiliary expenses separately.

Jane pulls together her slides for the presentation. She is in favor of the change and prepares slides for both three and four programs for board review.

General Expenses

Similar to for-profit entities, nonprofit compensation is on an *accrual basis*. For each day an individual works, an expense accrues with a related liability. When the amount is paid, the liability is reversed, and cash goes out the door to the employee. If the month ends on a Wednesday but the pay period ends on a Friday, the employee's compensation for work performed through Wednesday will be presented in the current period. Thursday's and Friday's pay will be expensed in the following period. For this reason, the statement of cash flows will show a different amount as paid to employees (using the direct method) than the amount shown in the statement of activities.

PAYROLL EXAMPLE

Employees work Monday through Friday and then are paid on the following Friday. In this example, the last day of the month falls on a Wednesday.

Mon	Tue	Wed	Thu	Fri
April... 28	29	30	May... 1	End of Work Week 2
5	6	7	8	Pay Day 9

To ensure that April's expenses are complete, the accountant accrues three days of payroll expenses on April 30. On May 2, they accrue the previous two days so that five days are in the accrual.

continued

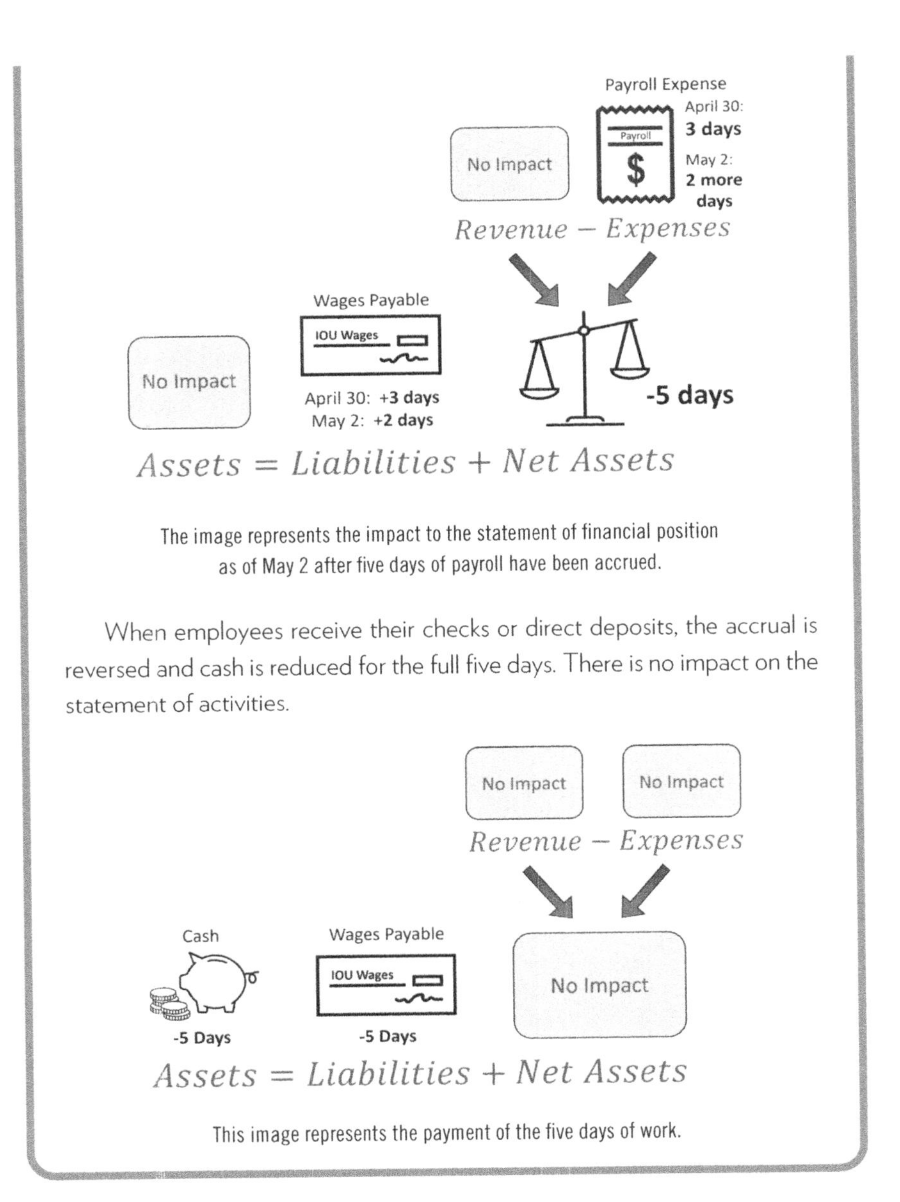

The image represents the impact to the statement of financial position as of May 2 after five days of payroll have been accrued.

When employees receive their checks or direct deposits, the accrual is reversed and cash is reduced for the full five days. There is no impact on the statement of activities.

This image represents the payment of the five days of work.

Nonprofits also have to accrue other expenses on a monthly basis. Many utilities bill for the prior month, so the nonprofit receives the bill for January activity in February. To ensure proper bookkeeping, the nonprofit estimates how much the bill will be for January using an accrual on the last day of the month. Then, on the first of the next month, the entry is reversed. When the bill comes in, the actual is booked. Any difference between the estimate and the actual is corrected in the February financials.

EXPENSE REVIEW

As the statement of activities presents information by functional class, Jane prepares separate schedules of expenses. The board likes to review expenses by natural classification for five years to review trends. Jane breaks out wages between salary and hourly wages. She also provides a separate line for fringe benefits, including health insurance, life insurance, and workers compensation, in addition to payroll taxes. She then combines the general ledger accounts for accountants, lawyers, consulting fees, and professional dues and fees to create a professional services total. Occupancy has been a focus of the board, so she provides a separate schedule of each item that makes up occupancy, including rent, electricity, water, gas, and telephone costs. She also provides a total for postage, printing, and materials and supplies.

Equipment, rental, and maintenance costs are combined to be able to monitor the costs related to the museum collection. A separate line item combines supplies, books, and subscription costs. She recently broke out a separate line item for publications and printing. Marketing, publicity, and advertising are the costs to get the word out about the museum and various exhibits. She keeps a separate line item for cost of sales related to the museum store. She then combines the costs for conferences, travel, and continuing education to provide information about educational costs.

The largest costs related to maintenance and janitorial services are also reviewed at the line-item level by the board. They like to ask questions about trends, so she keeps notes of any noted changes from the prior year in preparation for their questions.

She also uses the "other" category for anything that isn't large enough to stand on its own and doesn't belong to the specific categories, such as bank fees. The reporting package is long and detailed, but the board is very interested in how funds are being spent.

Other potential types of expenses include rent, supplies, and professional services (e.g., legal, accounting). There are also likely costs related to various programs. Some programs will be people intensive, and salary will be the largest expense. Other programs can require significant supplies. All expenses should be booked based on accrual accounting.

Depreciation

Long-term assets can bring value to a nonprofit for many years. When the asset is purchased, cash is reduced and the acquisition cost (amount paid) for the asset will show as a long-term asset on the statement of financial position. Nonprofits using accrual accounting will not leave the long-term asset on the books forever at its acquisition value. Instead, the nonprofit will book depreciation, which is the spreading of the cost of the asset over its useful life. Each time depreciation is recorded, the value of the asset will be shown as a lower amount on the statement of financial position. This may seem counterintuitive, since many buildings increase in actual value (appreciate) over time, but the statement of activities provides performance information, and the use of the asset aligns the expense with the revenue generated. As depreciation is a noncash item, it is not reflected in the statement of cash flows. This is another reason the statement of cash flows doesn't tie to the statement of activities. This example illustrates why it's important to have multiple types of reports to get an accurate understanding of a nonprofit's financial situation.

Interest

Interest, which is the cost of borrowing funds, is another common expense for nonprofits. Like the interest paid on a homeowner's mortgage, there is a cost to borrow funding. Interest is expensed as incurred.

Sometimes nonprofits receive loans that have no interest attached to them. GAAP requires that even if there is no stated interest rate, the nonprofit should impute interest (i.e., calculate interest based on what the prevailing market interest rate would be). The reason GAAP requires imputed interest is to reflect the true economic substance of the transaction in case circumstances change in the future.

EXPENSE REVIEW

Jane is preparing for the board a list of all the fixed assets the museum has, such as property, buildings, and equipment, and each item's useful life (the estimate of how long the asset can be used in operations—for example, many computers are assigned a useful life of five years). Jane's accounting software program automatically calculates the depreciation expense for these items using a straight-line method, where the total book value of the item is divided by the months of its useful life, and then each month that share of depreciation is recorded. So, for a computer that was purchased for $2,400 and has a useful life of five years, the depreciation is split into sixty equal monthly increments of $40.

Glad the software program does the bulk of that work for her, Jane can focus her time on things the computer can't calculate, like checking to see whether there are any assets that may have been retired (i.e., disposed of or removed from use) but not yet removed from the list of fixed assets. She does a quick once-over to ensure the assets appear correct based on her knowledge. Next, her employees will do what is called the *annual fixed-asset inventory*—they will physically find each asset on the list in the museum and report its location and current condition. They will do the inventory at night so as not to interrupt daytime visitors to the museum, and while they are at it, they will also inventory their collections. After her employees report their findings, Jane will update her list and know for certain that all the fixed assets on the list do exist.

It's going to be a busy night at the museum—Jane leaves herself a note to order pizza for the employees and volunteers.

Fundraising

Fundraising expenses are very common for nonprofits. In order to obtain contributions, nonprofits send out mailers and pledge cards and reach out to potential donors. All of these outreach efforts incur expenses, including the salaries of the development team. Fundraising expenses are expensed as incurred and are shown as decreases in net assets without donor restrictions (even if the contributions subsequently received are restricted). The costs related to special events are also an expense in the period the cost is incurred even if the event is being held in the future.

FUNDRAISING EXPENSES

Jane pulls up the email from Debra in the development department to review her comments on the fundraising expenses. Jane prefers to get Debra's thoughts about expenses and explanations for major fluctuations, as she is the closest to the expenses. Debra gives explanations for the drastic increase in fundraising costs. A large event is happening after year end, and they have spent a significant amount in preparation for the event. Debra gives Jane some talking points about the revenue these costs will generate in preparation for the board meeting.

Investment Expenses

One other exception for presentation purposes is investment expenses. Investment expenses are not shown as expenses on the statement of activities or as reductions of net assets without donor restrictions. Instead, investment expenses are netted against investment revenue and therefore presented in the statement of activities in the same net asset class where the investment revenue is shown.

For example, a nonprofit may hire an investment adviser to help select investments and generate the most income from the funds. The fees charged by the adviser should be shown as an offset against the amount that is generated. Therefore, if a nonprofit generates $3,000 in interest revenue and dividends from investments but has to pay the adviser $300 that month, the amount shown on the statement of activities will be $2,700 in investment revenue.

Board Best Practices: Expenses

Monitoring the types of expenses and trends in expenses is very important! While expenses are a normal part of operations, the board should be involved in reviewing expenses as part of their governance oversight. Are expenses in a particular category increasing each period? Is there a reason for the increase? Are unnecessary expenses being incurred? The board should be in frequent conversations with management about expense management. Internal controls over approval of significant unusual transactions can help keep the board apprised of these types of transactions. One way to monitor expenses is to go through an approval process where the person incurring the cost has to get approval from a higher-level employee. Another method is to carefully monitor costs against budgets. When costs are not aligned with budgets, explanations should be provided to explain the misalignment. Controlling expenses and ensuring they properly support the mission of the organization will help the nonprofit remain financially viable.

Board Self-Evaluation

How closely are we tracking to budget? Is our budget process working?

The budget can be an excellent tool to identify problems early. It also can be used to evaluate management. However, the budget development process is often long and cumbersome, only to be ignored until the following year. The CEO should be actively monitoring the budget, and the board should be actively discussing budget-to-actual variances with management throughout the year.

CHANGES IN NET ASSETS

The last piece of the statement of activities is the reconciliation of the prior year's net assets to the current year's net assets. As nonprofits do not have owner's equity, the excess of revenues over expenses in the current year increases the net assets available for the following year. Nonprofits don't pay dividends and don't have retained earnings. Instead, they reconcile the change in net assets. GAAP requires that nonprofits reconcile the change in net assets for total net assets, as well as for net assets with donor restrictions and net assets without donor restrictions. The change in net assets will then flow over to the increase (or decrease) of the net assets shown on the statement of financial position.

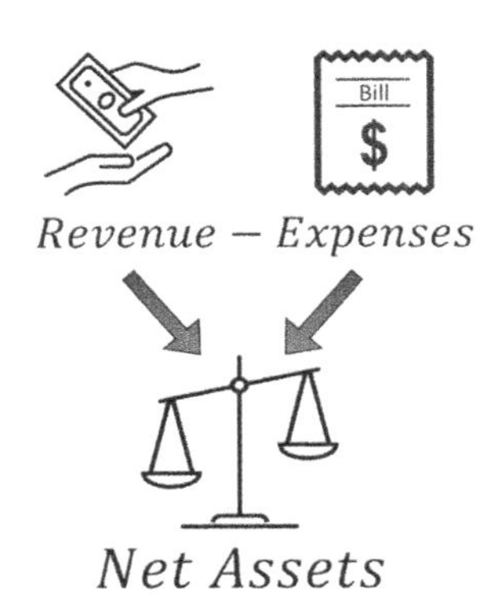

Board Best Practices: Change in Net Assets

Similar to for-profit entities, having expenses greater than revenues can lead to big problems in the long run for a nonprofit's financial stability, particularly when those deficits are unplanned. The board should review the overall change in net assets and evaluate if the revenues being brought in are sufficient to cover expenses. If expenses are trending up and the change in net assets is trending down, the board may need to discuss fundraising ideas with the development department to bring in more revenue.

The board should review the calculation and ensure that the statements properly roll forward. The beginning balance should agree with the prior year's ending balance. The math should work so that the change in net assets plus the beginning balance equals the ending balance for net assets. The board should also look at the change in net assets by net asset class (*with* donor restrictions versus *without* donor restrictions). Simple reviews can help the board spot errors and fraud.

THE ACCOUNTING EQUATION

Now that we've covered the accounting equation for both the statement of activities and the statement of financial position, we can see how they come together to create a balanced equation. Thanks to dual-entry bookkeeping, the journal entries will always keep the equation balanced, with the change in net assets from the statement of activities flowing into the statement of financial position.

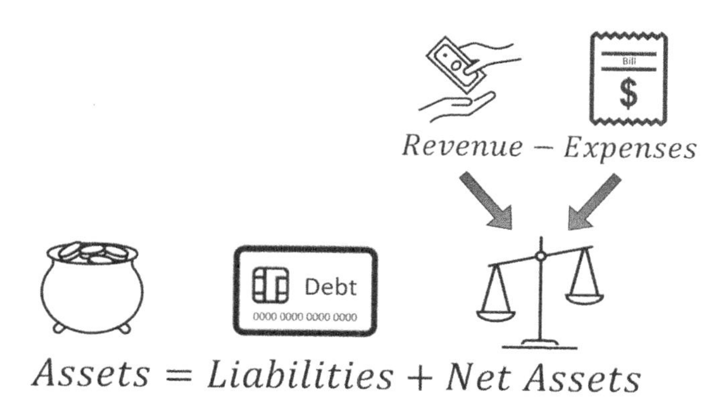

The revenues and expenses of an organization net to the change in net assets. Those changes in net assets update the net assets of the statement of financial position. As a result, the assets will equal the liabilities plus net assets of the organization. With double-entry bookkeeping, any of the elements can be updated to maintain the equation. We'll use this equation throughout the remainder of the book.

DISCLOSURES

Disclosures can help users better understand the numbers reflected in the statement of activities. They can help disaggregate information or provide information about judgments made. For example, while there are no unique requirements for disclosures regarding contribution revenue, other than for contributed nonfinancial assets, entities will often disclose information about the judgments used in determining barriers and how that affects the timing of recognition. Disclosure requirements should be considered the minimum—entities can always provide additional disclosures so long as they help the user understand the financial statements.

General Disclosures

Nonprofits are required to disclose total fundraising expenses. Some may do this on the face of the statement of activities; others will provide the information as a note disclosure. Nonprofits must also disclose the amount of income tax expense incurred and what activities generated the tax. Remember, most nonprofits are not taxed on their mission-related activities, but unrelated business income *is* taxed.

Release from Restrictions

Some disclosures involve accounting policy elections made by nonprofits. When deciding between options, nonprofits need to disclose the option selected. If a nonprofit chooses to show contributions that came in *with restrictions* that were met in the same period in solely the "net assets without donor restrictions" class of net assets (i.e., they chose not to show them as released from restrictions), then the nonprofit must disclose that accounting policy.

Contributed Nonfinancial Assets

Because different nonprofits receive different types of gifts in kind (often referred to as GIKs or *contributed nonfinancial assets*), FASB provides a disclosure requirement to disaggregate the major categories. Each nonprofit will determine its own category list.

For a hospital, the primary categories may be donated pharmaceuticals, donated services from medical professionals, and donated personal protective equipment (e.g., masks). A soup kitchen may receive donated food and serving supplies. A school may receive athletic equipment, art supplies, and books. The number and title of categories is at the discretion of the nonprofit. They may choose to use an "other" category for immaterial miscellaneous items.

Once the nonprofit determines the appropriate categories, they will provide the amount received by category in each year presented. In addition, the nonprofit will have to disclose information about whether the donated gifts in kind were utilized or monetized during the period. For example, if a nonprofit receives a donated car that they later sold to generate cash, the nonprofit has monetized the asset. On the other hand, if donated food is used by a soup kitchen in preparing meals, it was utilized. The nonprofit should indicate which program or activity it was utilized for. If the nonprofit has a policy about monetizing versus utilizing a gift, that policy should be disclosed. (If the nonprofit doesn't have a policy, then there is nothing to disclose.)

Other disclosures related to gifts in kind include a description of any donor-imposed restrictions, a description of the valuation techniques and inputs used to determine fair value, and disclosures of which market (principal or most advantageous) was used to determine fair value when there are donor-imposed restrictions on selling an asset. These types of disclosures help the reader understand how the nonprofit came up with the value of the gifts received.

For contributed services (donated volunteer time), the nonprofit should describe the program or activity that received the donated time. In addition, for those volunteers not recognized on the financial statements, GAAP encourages nonprofits to disclose the fair value of the services.

Revenue from Contracts with Customers (Exchange Revenues)

A few years ago, the rules related to recognizing exchange revenues changed significantly. Instead of a rules-based approach, GAAP embraced a principles-based approach that would require more use of estimates in determining revenue recognition. As a result, there was a significant increase in the needed disclosures to provide users with information about the judgments made in the process of determining recognized amounts.

Many nonprofits can't issue public debt due to state laws. However, some nonprofits can use a governmental entity to have bonds or other debt issued on their behalf. This is referred to as *conduit debt*. If a nonprofit has conduit debt outstanding, it will have even more disclosures, as it will be treated more like a public company for accounting and disclosure purposes.

Nonprofits must disclose the amount of revenue recognized from contracts with customers (exchange revenue) separately from other revenue. Many nonprofits do this on the face of the statement of activities, but note disclosure is permissible. Nonprofits also should disaggregate their revenue into categories that explain the nature, timing, and uncertainty of cash flows. The least amount of disaggregation required would be to break down revenue based on the timing of recognition (point in time versus over time). However, nonprofits can always provide more disaggregation by type of customer, geographic location, and so on.

Nonprofits should also disclose the opening and closing balances of receivables, contract assets (e.g., costs to obtain a customer), and contract liabilities (e.g., unearned revenue) from contracts with customers. However, these are often displayed on the statement of financial position. If not separately called out, they can also be disclosed in the notes. The nonprofit should disclose when the entity typically satisfies its performance obligations, any significant payment terms, the nature of the goods or services that they have promised to transfer, any obligations for returns or refunds, and types of warranties provided.

Revenue recognition requires a lot of judgment. Nonprofits should disclose any judgments (as well as changes in judgments) that affected the amount and timing of revenue recognized so users understand the decisions made by the nonprofit.

Types of judgments include

- the timing of recognition;
- the transaction price for variable revenue; and
- amounts allocated to the performance obligations.

In addition, for performance obligations satisfied over time, a nonprofit should disclose the methods used to recognize revenue (i.e., the input [e.g., cost] or output method [e.g., milestones] used). They should also disclose information about their assessment of whether any variable consideration was constrained.

These disclosures are designed to provide users with a better understanding of how revenue is recognized and the considerations made by management in recognizing that revenue.

Board Best Practices: Disclosures

The board should read the entire set of financial statements, including the disclosures. They should ensure the numbers in the disclosures agree

continued

to the information provided on the face of the financial statements. They should also determine whether the disclosures tell the story that they expect based on the financial updates from management and their understanding of the organization. The board should check that the accounting policies reflect discussions held at board meetings about policy. The board should evaluate whether the disclosures are understandable and whether a reader would be able to comprehend the disclosures. Disclosure checklists are a great tool to ensure disclosures are complete. The board can review a completed checklist to verify the disclosures are complete and accurate. Finally, the board should ask questions of management about anything they don't understand.

PRESENTATION

There is a lot of flexibility in the presentation of the statement of activities.

Operating Measure

The statement of activities provides information about the revenues and expenses of the organization. Revenues can be separated into operating (e.g., related to the purpose of the organization) or non-operating (e.g., unrelated to the purpose). Currently, there is no definition of operating and non-operating, so each organization can define operating and non-operating based on its revenue types. The most common non-operating activities are related to investment revenues and expenses. The FASB does not require a measure of operations to be provided. If an intermediate measure of operations is shown and the definition is not clear from looking at the statement of activities, the nonprofit should include a note disclosure explaining what is included or excluded from the concept of operating revenues and expenses.

Rounding

Larger organizations often round their financial statements. It's not uncommon for financial statements to be rounded to the nearest thousand dollars.

Required Subtotals

The required subtotals for the statement include the change in net assets in total and the change in net assets for each required category (the change in net assets with donor restrictions and the change in net assets without donor restrictions). The level of disaggregation and any other totals or subtotals are at the discretion of the nonprofit.

Order of Presentation

The order of presentation is also at the discretion of the nonprofit. They can choose to put revenues and expenses first and then gains and losses, or to put revenues and gains first and then expenses and losses. They could have certain revenue and expenses at the top and then other revenue and expenses next. In fact, they could even have expenses first. So long as the appropriate subtotals are provided, there are a wide variety of ways to present. Nonprofits use the term *revenue* to describe transactions that are ongoing and central to the operations. Gains are typically used when reporting incidental or peripheral activities. There are judgments to be made as to whether something should be reported gross (revenue) or net (gains).

Release from Restrictions

While most presentation requirements are very flexible, one requirement that is not flexible is this: The amount released from restrictions must be shown separately in the statement of activities as its own line item. During the year, certain restrictions made by donors may be met. For example, the entity may spend funds related to a purpose restriction. Those funds are shown as a negative in the net assets with donor restrictions and then as a positive in the net assets without donor restrictions. The total of these must tie to zero. Columnar formats make it easy to check that they do tie to zero.

Format

Many nonprofits opt to use a columnar format to provide the required subtotals in an easily readable fashion. In comparative financials, sometimes the prior year is summarized (only totals provided), and in other scenarios the full prior year is provided. If the prior year is summarized, it must be clearly marked as such on the financial statements, and there should be a related disclosure explaining that a full set of financials as required by GAAP was not provided. Some nonprofits present separate statements for each year, as the number of columns that are needed can make the statement very wide and overwhelming. The use of columns is not required, and a single-column presentation is permitted so long as all the required elements are presented.

PRESENTATION

Jane reviews the draft financial statements one last time. She verifies that the columns and rows total properly. She reviews the breakdown of entries into operating versus non-operating categories. Operating revenues include contributions, museum admission fees, membership dues, and the bookstore. Non-operating revenues include proceeds from the sale of art and investment return. Expenses are also separated between operating and non-operating, with non-operating expenses including disposal of assets and other one-time expenses. The notes to the financial statements describe this breakout. All operating revenue and expenses are presented at the top of the financial statement with a non-operating section that contains both revenue and expenses below. The financial statements are presented comparatively, so Jane reviews all changes in the presentation from the prior year's financial statements. Most are reclassifications. While a summarized prior year would allow the statement of activities to fit on one page, the board feels strongly about presenting a full set of financial information for the prior year, so each year is presented as its own schedule with columns for each net asset class. Jane feels confident that all required subtotals are included. Now that she's completed her review, she packs up her things. She needs to be back in early to prepare for the board meeting, so she heads out feeling confident about the current financial performance of the organization.

EXAMPLE FINANCIAL STATEMENTS

The easiest way to get comfortable with this financial statement and its flexibility is through examples.

Single Column

The 2020 Goodwill Industries International Consolidated Statement of Activities is a great example of a single-column presentation.[8] In lieu of having a column for net assets with and without donor restrictions, the top half of the statement covers the activities related to net assets without donor restrictions. It shows all the related revenues and expenses. It uses programmatic descriptions of its expenses (program versus support). It also separates the investment return as non-operating before totaling the change in net assets without donor restrictions. It then lists the activities related to the net assets with restrictions. You'll notice the amount released from restrictions appears in the revenues section in the "without donor restrictions" category and again as a negative in the "with donor restrictions" category. The statement then provides the required total for change in net assets with donor restrictions and finally the total change in net assets. This type of presentation makes it easy to present comparative years.

Goodwill Industries International, Inc. and Related Entities
Consolidated Statements of Activities
Years Ended December 31, 2020 and 2019

	2020	2019
Activities without donor restrictions:		
Revenue and support:		
Federal awards	$ 24,828,373	$ 26,467,376
Membership dues	20,477,059	21,565,262
Contributions	20,377,099	236,488
Program service fees	1,137,035	2,522,130
Rental	303,578	294,380
In-kind contributions	150,000	15,727,560
Net investment return – operations	119,903	109,696
Legacies and bequests	88,404	965,755
Other income	16,445	31,779
Net assets released from restriction	9,236,247	7,408,058
Total revenue and support	76,734,143	75,328,484
Expenses:		
Program services:		
Direct services to membership	13,600,020	37,953,779
Sponsored programs and grants	33,787,124	33,257,957
Support services to membership	1,190,052	875,012
Total program services	48,577,196	72,086,748
Management and general services:		
General and administrative	3,439,181	4,103,652
Resource development	634,824	407,273
Total management and general services	4,074,005	4,510,925
Total expenses	52,651,201	76,597,673
Change in net assets without donor restrictions from operations	24,082,942	(1,269,189)
Net investment return – non-operating	365,805	483,983
Change in net assets without donor restrictions	24,448,747	(785,206)
Activities with donor restrictions:		
Contributions	9,511,605	8,715,893
Net investment return – donor restricted	193,737	323,769
Net assets released from restriction	(9,236,247)	(7,408,058)
Cancellation of public service announcement campaign	(1,985,415)	-
Change in net assets with donor restrictions	(1,516,320)	1,631,604
Change in net assets	22,932,427	846,398
Net assets:		
Beginning	24,450,566	23,604,168
Ending	$ 47,382,993	$ 24,450,566

See notes to consolidated financial statements.

Full Comparative

Habitat for Humanity International, Inc., opted to present a full comparative consolidated statement of activities.[9] It shows both 2021 and 2020 with columns for net assets with donor restrictions, net assets without donor restrictions, and total net assets for both years. The financial statement shows revenues and gains together followed by expenses and losses. The "Released from Restrictions" line item shows the amount released into "Without Restrictions" and out of "With Restrictions" and shows a total of zero for both years. Expenses are shown programmatically with program expenses separated from support. Finally, the statement closes with a reconciliation of the change in net assets.

Habitat for Humanity International, Inc.

CONSOLIDATED STATEMENTS OF ACTIVITIES

(In thousands)

	Year ended June 30, 2021			Year ended June 30, 2020		
	Without Donor Restrictions	With Donor Restrictions	Total	Without Donor Restrictions	With Donor Restrictions	Total
Revenues and gains						
Contributions	$ 130,670	$ 129,073	$ 259,743	$ 119,504	$ 80,123	$ 199,627
Donated product, services and advertising	33,901	21,045	54,946	36,859	4,526	41,385
Government grants and subcontracts	17,557	-	17,557	13,802	-	13,802
Other income, net	29,389	-	29,389	32,972	-	32,972
Total revenues and gains	211,517	150,118	361,635	203,137	84,649	287,786
Net assets released from restrictions	124,134	(124,134)	-	98,275	(98,275)	-
Total revenues and gains	335,651	25,984	361,635	301,412	(13,626)	287,786
Expenses						
Program services:						
U.S. affiliates	139,109	-	139,109	115,095	-	115,095
International affiliates	70,489	-	70,489	78,527	-	78,527
Public awareness and education	17,507	-	17,507	19,288	-	19,288
Total program services	227,105	-	227,105	212,910	-	212,910
Supporting services:						
Fundraising	54,309	-	54,309	54,047	-	54,047
Management and general	19,031	-	19,031	19,458	-	19,458
Total supporting services	73,340	-	73,340	73,505	-	73,505
Total expenses	300,445	-	300,445	286,415	-	286,415
Losses on contributions receivable	-	636	636	-	382	382
Total expenses and losses on contributions receivable	300,445	636	301,081	286,415	382	286,797
Change in net assets	35,206	25,348	60,554	14,997	(14,008)	989
Net assets at beginning of year	134,984	109,486	244,470	119,987	123,494	243,481
Nets assets at end of year	$ 170,190	$ 134,834	$ 305,024	$ 134,984	$ 109,486	$ 244,470

Comparative Separate

Capital University presents its statements of activities for each year as a separate financial statement.[10] Entities that want to use a vertical presentation will sometimes present each year separately simply because the number of columns can be a bit overwhelming when combined (see Habitat example). This is still deemed to be comparative, as both years

CAPITAL UNIVERSITY
STATEMENTS OF ACTIVITIES
Year ended June 30, 2021 with comparative 2020 totals

	Without Donor Restrictions	With Donor Restrictions	Total 2021	Total 2020
Revenue, gains and other support				
Student tuition and fees	$ 101,284,886	$ -	$ 101,284,886	$ 104,467,890
Unfunded student financial aid	(52,965,703)	-	(52,965,703)	(54,528,419)
Funded student financial aid	(1,828,609)	-	(1,828,609)	(2,466,328)
	46,490,574	-	46,490,574	47,473,143
Private gifts and grants	1,970,492	2,514,956	4,485,448	4,039,338
Government grants and contracts	208,392	8,521,397	8,729,789	1,990,051
Investment return appropriated for spending	1,062,874	3,738,034	4,800,908	4,776,614
Other	1,412,737	84,716	1,497,453	1,705,701
Auxiliary enterprises	8,920,329	-	8,920,329	12,709,524
Operating net assets released from restrictions	13,225,073	(13,225,073)	-	-
Total revenue	73,290,471	1,634,030	74,924,501	72,694,371
Expenses				
Salaries and wages	32,291,486	-	32,291,486	34,525,675
Employee benefits	10,771,391	-	10,771,391	11,639,360
Services, supplies, and other operating expenses	12,048,256	-	12,048,256	13,690,673
Occupancy, utilities, and maintenance	6,345,780	-	6,345,780	6,979,099
COVID-19 CARES Act Emergency Relief Fund for Students	2,317,984	-	2,317,984	255,000
Depreciation and amortization	8,864,739	-	8,864,739	9,679,715
Interest expense	648,184	-	648,184	789,026
Total expenses	73,287,820	-	73,287,820	77,558,548
Change in net assets before other activities	2,651	1,634,030	1,636,681	(4,864,177)
Other activities				
Investment return, net of spending policy	8,293,143	21,921,388	30,214,531	(3,085,818)
Private gifts restricted for endowment	-	2,869,354	2,869,354	2,780,932
Change in value of split-interest agreements	-	272,410	272,410	310,895
Postretirement benefit obligation related changes other than periodic costs	(85,775)	-	(85,775)	(266,872)
Gain on sale of assets	440,230	-	440,230	2,335,967
Total other activities	8,647,598	25,063,152	33,710,750	2,075,104
Changes in net assets	8,650,249	26,697,182	35,347,431	(2,789,073)
Net assets at beginning of year	114,345,426	107,056,840	221,402,266	224,191,339
Net assets at end of year	$ 122,995,675	$ 133,754,022	$ 256,749,697	$ 221,402,266

The accompanying notes are an integral part of these financial statements.

show full GAAP financials (just on separate pages). They also provide summarized totals for the prior year for easy comparison. The university shows operating revenues first, followed by expenses by natural classification. Then non-operating items (e.g., investment return and gain on sales) are displayed. The line item "Changes in net assets" shows the three required totals in columnar format. Finally, the net asset reconciliation is at the bottom.

CAPITAL UNIVERSITY
STATEMENT OF ACTIVITIES
Year ended June 30, 2020

	Without Donor Restrictions	With Donor Restrictions	Total 2020
Revenue, gains and other support			
Student tuition and fees	$ 104,467,890	$ -	$ 104,467,890
Unfunded student financial aid	(54,528,419)	-	(54,528,419)
Funded student financial aid	(2,466,328)	-	(2,466,328)
	47,473,143	-	47,473,143
Private gifts and grants	2,116,481	1,922,857	4,039,338
Government grants and contracts	180,630	1,809,421	1,990,051
Investment return appropriated for spending	1,066,011	3,710,603	4,776,614
Other	1,425,727	279,974	1,705,701
Auxiliary enterprises	12,709,524	-	12,709,524
Operating net assets released from restrictions	6,422,374	(6,422,374)	-
Total revenue	71,393,890	1,300,481	72,694,371
Expenses			
Salaries and wages	34,525,675	-	34,525,675
Employee benefits	11,639,360	-	11,639,360
Services, supplies, and other operating expenses	13,690,673	-	13,690,673
Occupancy, utilities, and maintenance	6,979,099	-	6,979,099
COVID-19 CARES Act Emergency Relief Fund for Students	255,000	-	255,000
Depreciation and amortization	9,679,715	-	9,679,715
Interest expense	789,026	-	789,026
Total expenses	77,558,548	-	77,558,548
Change in net assets before other activities	(6,164,658)	1,300,481	(4,864,177)
Other activities			
Investment return, net of spending policy	(274,082)	(2,811,736)	(3,085,818)
Private gifts restricted for endowment	599,908	2,181,024	2,780,932
Change in value of split-interest agreements	(487,625)	798,520	310,895
Postretirement benefit obligation related changes other than periodic costs	(266,872)	-	(266,872)
Gain on sale of assets	2,335,967	-	2,335,967
Release of annuity net assets on sale of liability	908,964	(908,964)	-
Total other activities	2,816,260	(741,156)	2,075,104
Changes in net assets	(3,348,398)	559,325	(2,789,073)
Net assets at beginning of year	117,693,824	106,497,515	224,191,339
Net assets at end of year	$ 114,345,426	$ 107,056,840	$ 221,402,266

The accompanying notes are an integral part of these financial statements.

Two Statement Classification

Duke University Health System is another great example of a nonprofit that uses natural classification for their statement of activities.[11] You will notice that they do not use the term *statement of activities*. Instead, Duke uses two statements—a Statement of Operations and then a Statement of Changes in Net Assets—to provide the required information. The

DUKE UNIVERSITY HEALTH SYSTEM, INC.
AND AFFILIATES

Consolidated Statements of Operations

Years ended June 30, 2021 and 2020

(In thousands)

	2021	2020
Revenues, gains, and other support without donor restrictions:		
Patient service revenue	3,967,396	3,669,150
Other revenue	302,102	282,396
Total revenues, gains, and other support	4,269,498	3,951,546
Expenses:		
Salaries, wages, and benefits	2,029,617	1,874,479
Medical supplies	1,147,452	999,746
Interest	24,081	39,334
Depreciation and amortization	176,919	168,406
Other operating expenses	770,720	744,681
Total expenses	4,148,789	3,826,646
Operating income	120,709	124,900
Nonoperating income (loss):		
Investment income (loss)	1,642,016	(10,623)
Nonoperating components of net periodic benefit cost	1,297	16,823
Loss on extinguishment of debt	—	(10,179)
Other	(4,805)	1,302
Total nonoperating income (loss)	1,638,508	(2,677)
Excess of revenues over expenses	1,759,217	122,223
Change in funded status of defined benefit plans	563,080	(301,059)
Net assets released from restrictions for purchase of property and equipment	547	717
Transfers to the University, net	(142,998)	(117,431)
Increase (decrease) in net assets without donor restrictions	2,179,846	(295,550)

See accompanying notes to consolidated financial statements.

Statement of Operations uses an intermediate measure of operations—operating income. The "increase (decrease) in net assets without donor restrictions" total from the bottom of the Statement of Operations carries forward to the Statement of Changes in Net Assets, where the details about the net assets with donor restrictions is found. This type of presentation is common in hospitals.

DUKE UNIVERSITY HEALTH SYSTEM, INC.
AND AFFILIATES

Consolidated Statements of Changes in Net Assets

Years ended June 30, 2021 and 2020

(In thousands)

	2021	2020
Net assets without donor restrictions:		
Excess of revenues over expenses	$ 1,759,217	122,223
Change in funded status of defined benefit plans	563,080	(301,059)
Net assets released from restrictions for purchase of property and equipment	547	717
Transfers to the University, net	(142,998)	(117,431)
Increase (decrease) in net assets without donor restrictions	2,179,846	(295,550)
Net assets with donor restrictions:		
Contributions for restricted purposes	12,795	6,064
Transfers to the University, net	(390)	(335)
Net assets released from restrictions used for operations	(11,261)	(4,937)
Net assets released from restrictions for purchase of property and equipment	(547)	(717)
Net realized and unrealized gains (losses)	14,542	(1,164)
Increase (decrease) in net assets with donor restrictions	15,139	(1,089)
Increase (decrease) in net assets	2,194,985	(296,639)
Net assets, beginning of year	3,483,583	3,780,222
Net assets, end of year	$ 5,678,568	3,483,583

See accompanying notes to consolidated financial statements.

Summarized Prior Year

The Leukemia & Lymphoma Society, Inc., is an example of a nonprofit that chose to show the prior year in summary.[12] It presents a

THE LEUKEMIA & LYMPHOMA SOCIETY, INC.

Consolidated Statement of Activities

Year ended June 30, 2021
(with summarized comparative information for the year ended June 30, 2020)

(In thousands)

	Without donor restrictions	With donor restrictions	Total 2021	Total 2020
Operating revenue:				
Contributions	$ 230,728	30,194	260,922	268,455
Less direct donor benefit costs	(5,868)	—	(5,868)	(19,931)
Net campaign contributions	224,860	30,194	255,054	248,524
Co-pay contributions (note 3)	—	184,417	184,417	176,100
Therapy Acceleration Program contractual returns and royalties	12,544	—	12,544	21,565
Service revenue	12,281	—	12,281	15,997
Donated services, goods and media (note 9)	4,435	—	4,435	8,926
Legacies and other revenue	9,722	1,326	11,048	8,380
Net interest and dividend income	3,701	464	4,165	7,359
Net assets released from restrictions:				
Co-pay assistance (note 3)	119,665	(119,665)	—	—
Satisfaction of other donor restrictions	31,366	(31,366)	—	—
Total operating revenue	418,574	65,370	483,944	486,851
Operating expenses:				
Program services:				
Research	65,402	—	65,402	50,440
Patient and community service (note 3)	171,939	—	171,939	203,547
Public health education	26,994	—	26,994	48,089
Professional education	10,366	—	10,366	16,011
Total program services	274,701	—	274,701	318,087
Supporting services:				
Management and general	46,495	—	46,495	43,757
Fund raising	50,399	—	50,399	46,643
Total supporting services	96,894	—	96,894	90,400
Total operating expenses	371,595	—	371,595	408,487
Change in net assets from operating activities	46,979	65,370	112,349	78,364
Foreign currency translation adjustment and other	681	220	901	(304)
Net increase in fair value of investments	36,803	1,405	38,208	21,402
Change in net assets	84,463	66,995	151,458	99,462
Net assets:				
Beginning of period	255,343	118,188	373,531	274,069
End of period	$ 339,806	185,183	524,989	373,531

See accompanying notes to consolidated financial statements.

column for net assets with donor restrictions, one without donor restrictions, and then a total for the current year. It then shows a total for the prior year. Columns for the net asset classifications are not presented for the prior year. This is not a full GAAP presentation. This presentation election is noted at the top of the statement, where it states, "with summarized comparative information for the year ended June 30, 2020."

It then includes the following note disclosure:[13]

Summarized Financial Information

The consolidated financial statements are presented with 2020 summarized information. With respect to the consolidated statement of activities, such prior year information is not presented by net asset class and, in the consolidated statement of functional expenses, 2020 expenses by object are presented in total rather than by functional category. Accordingly, such information should be read in conjunction with LLS's 2020 consolidated financial statements from which the summarized information was derived.

The Leukemia & Lymphoma Society, Inc., also presents its contributions separate from its other revenues and its in-kind contributions (goods, services, and media). It then presents its expenses in programmatic format. Finally, it totals its change in net assets and provides the reconciliation of prior year to current year.

Overall

All of these examples meet the requirements of GAAP despite looking very different. This demonstrates the flexibility the FASB provides to nonprofits to tell their story to the users of the financial statements. The level of detail and the order of elements are all used to help financial statement readers.

CHAPTER 4

STATEMENT OF FINANCIAL POSITION

The statement of financial position reflects a nonprofit's financial status by way of its assets, liabilities, and net assets at a given point in time (generally the end of the fiscal year). The statement of financial position provides information about what would be left over after all the liabilities were subtracted from the assets, which is useful in helping users understand the nonprofit's ability to pay its obligations.

For-profit entities tend to use the term *balance sheet*, which is also acceptable for nonprofit organizations. The term *statement of financial position* is also acceptable for for-profit entities. The purpose of the statement of financial position is very similar for both for-profit and nonprofit organizations.

FASB recently updated its Concept Statements to redefine the terms *assets*, *liabilities*, and *equity*. This was part of a larger project to ensure consistency in the elements of the financial statements. While the Concept Statements are not GAAP, they do assist the board in writing GAAP. In fact, they are often thought of as the theory that underlies GAAP.

MEET AALIYAH

Aaliyah is the director of finance for a private university. The university has a teaching and research focus but also has a teaching hospital and related foundation that are consolidated in their financial statements. Aaliyah is preparing for the first-quarter board meeting for the board of trustees. She is reviewing the balance sheet reconciliations of her staff, as well as preparing the board reports. She was recently promoted to the director role, so this will be her first board meeting in this position. She is excited but nervous, as she wants to make a good first impression.

ASSETS

Assets are the things the nonprofit owns. FASB defines *assets* as "a present right of an entity to an economic benefit." Nonprofits have many of the same assets as corporations and even individuals (e.g., cars and bank accounts), but there are some unique assets reported by nonprofits (e.g., endowments and collections). Assets are reported in homogeneous groups like cash, accounts receivable, and property, plant, and equipment. This means, for example, that a single cash line item will be reported on the face of the statement of financial position, instead of a list of every cash account.

TYPES OF ASSETS

Cash

Cash is one of the most common assets of a nonprofit. Whether kept in a savings account, a checking account, or a money market, cash is a liquid asset that can be used to purchase other assets, pay off debts, or pay for expenses.

Because of its liquidity, cash is often the first line item on the statement of financial position. Liquidity of assets is important to nonprofits because if all of the assets were tied up in illiquid items, paying for day-to-day costs would become problematic.

On the other hand, holding on to excessive amounts of cash that provide very little return on investment through dividends or interest is also not in the best interest of the nonprofit. Since most checking and savings accounts provide very little interest, nonprofits with significant excess cash should consider developing an investment policy that considers liquidity but provides better returns.

BANK RECONCILIATIONS

The university Aaliyah works for, which has multiple operating accounts, considers all highly liquid investments with a maturity of three or fewer months to be cash equivalents. In addition to accounts for each of the colleges in the university (graduate school, college of arts and science, business school, and law school), it also has separate bank accounts for athletics and various auxiliary services. Each account is reconciled on a monthly basis, and each staff accountant is assigned a number of accounts to reconcile.

When completing a bank reconciliation, the staff starts with the balance per the general ledger. They then review the bank statement for bank fees and interest revenue and book adjusting entries to update the financials.

Once all entries are posted, the accountant compares the amount per the general ledger to the amount on the bank statement. The amount on the bank statement doesn't reflect outstanding checks (i.e., checks that have been mailed but not yet cashed). Therefore, the accountant makes a list of all outstanding checks and adjusts the bank balance to reflect the updated amount.

If the account still doesn't reconcile, they compare the transactions per the bank statement to the transactions in the general ledger software. In the past, the accountant has identified instances where the amount of a deposit was entered incorrectly (e.g., $15.21 instead of $12.51), and checks have occasionally bounced. While the amounts were deposited, the bank knew of the

continued

bounced check and removed the funds per the bank statement. Therefore, the accountant will book an adjusting entry to remove the deposited cash from the ledger.

At this point, the cash balance per the books will equal the adjusted cash balance per the bank. All adjustments and corrections are noted on the reconciliation. Aaliyah reviews each reconciliation for the types of adjustments made and verifies that the reconciliation does tie out. Any unusual adjustments are reviewed in more detail. If a number of errors are noted, she will review the original transactions to see who booked the transaction. If there is a pattern of errors from an individual, she will schedule time with them to discuss the errors.

The board typically doesn't review the cash reconciliations unless it's the end of the year. Aaliyah's goal is to make sure errors are minimal and most adjustments are timing related (outstanding checks or insufficient funds). She's pleased to see that all accounts were reconciled within ten days of the end of the month and minimal adjustments were needed.

Receivables

Receivables are another common asset for nonprofits. Trade receivables are created when the nonprofit provides a good or service (i.e., exchange transactions) but does not require payment at time of sale and instead bills the customer. These are typically short-term thirty- or forty-five-day receivables.

Nonprofits should evaluate the credit quality of customers that will have large balances to ensure they have the ability to pay the bill. Credit quality can be very helpful in evaluating a customer. Like mortgage companies evaluate the ability of a potential client to repay the loan by reviewing tax returns and bank statements, nonprofits should evaluate the ability of customers to pay. Sometimes entities will provide financial statements of an organization. If the customer is an individual, a FICO score can be used.[1]

Nonprofits should evaluate any past-due balances and determine if they are at risk of not being paid for the good or service. The term used for the amount that may not be received is called the *allowance for doubtful accounts* or simply *allowance*. The allowance is a *contra asset*, which means it is shown with the related asset (in this case accounts receivable), and it reduces the receivable to the amount that the nonprofit expects to receive on the financial statement. For example, if a nonprofit was owed $50 but only expected to be repaid $45, the accounts receivable is $50, the allowance is $5, and the amount shown on the statement of financial position is the net $45.

In accrual accounting, nonprofits should not wait until the receivable goes bad (e.g., the other entity goes bankrupt). Rather, they should evaluate and recognize a credit loss (bad debt) as part of their regular accounting. Performing these types of adjustments is part of what is often referred to as *closing the books*. Nonprofits should consider developing a policy for write-offs and allowances in order to report the allowance consistently.

ACCOUNTS RECEIVABLE RECONCILIATIONS

Student receivables for tuition are recognized at net realizable value and are typically unsecured. The university uses an allowance method to evaluate the bad debt. Aaliyah runs an aging report that shows the days outstanding for each receivable in buckets. The buckets are current, one to thirty days past due, thirty-one to sixty days past due, sixty-one to ninety days past due, and over ninety days past due.

All accounts that are over ninety days past due are reviewed individually. The collections department leaves notes for each about the contacts with the individuals and the current status. Some students are waiting for scholarship funds to be received; others are experiencing financial difficulties and have requested the financial aid department grant them a hearing. The notes are an important part of the financial statement review.

Each bucket is assigned a bad debt percentage based on historical

continued

experience. The percentage ranges from 1 percent to 50 percent. The staff accountant meets with the collections department each month to evaluate whether the percentages are appropriate and whether there are identified accounts that will definitely not be collected. When all collection efforts have been exhausted, the accounts are written off against the allowance. As an account moves between buckets, the amount of allowance increases.

Aaliyah provides the board with a list of all accounts that are over ninety days past due with an explanation of the last contact and the status of expectation of collection. She also provides a list of accounts that were written off during the period. Thankfully, the number of accounts is very small, and the collections department has been reliable in its estimates.

Promises to Give

Promises to give or *pledge receivables* are a unique element for nonprofits. Individuals or entities can promise to give money to a nonprofit in the future. Promises to give can be oral or written (although large oral pledges should be followed up with a confirmation letter to document the agreement).

When unconditional, a pledge is booked as a receivable until the nonprofit is paid in cash. Revenue is recognized when the pledge is made. Then, when the cash comes in, the receivable is reversed. Conditional pledges are not recorded until the condition has been met (i.e., the barrier is overcome).

If the promised cash will be received in the future or over a span of several years, the entity has to use present-value techniques that take into consideration the time value of money. A dollar today is worth more than a dollar in the future, since that dollar today can be invested to increase its value. In addition, inflation generally reduces purchasing power. Therefore, nonprofits discount cash flows to consider the time value of money. Unconditional pledges where the donor will pay in less than a year are recognized as their net realizable value.

Nonprofits should evaluate the likelihood that the receipt of cash from the pledge will occur. For the amount not expected to be received, the nonprofit recognizes an allowance similar to trade receivables.

As mentioned earlier, intentions to give (i.e., wording on the document where the donor indicates the pledge amount is for budget purposes only, or that explicitly allow the donor to rescind the pledge) are not reported as receivables, and no revenue is recognized.

PLEDGE RECONCILIATIONS

Annual Fund

The university has been very successful in engaging its alumni, and many pledge annually to provide scholarships for the next generation of students. Volunteers complete a telephone campaign each year to call alumni and ask for pledges. If an alumnus agrees to donate, the amount is recorded, and the date and name of the student who called is documented. The development department then sends a confirmation email to the alumnus that details the amount pledged. Alumni have until the end of the school year to send the funds. As funds are collected, the receivables are reversed.

As it's close to the end of the year, most pledges have been collected in full. Aaliyah reviews the list of outstanding pledges. If the alumnus has historically pledged and the amounts have been received, Aaliyah provides a list to the development department, and the school sends a reminder email. On the other hand, if this is a new donor or one with very little history of participation, an allowance is created based on historical averages of amounts that ultimately did not get collected.

Capital Campaign

The university is planning to construct a new building for the science department. The current facilities are in need of an upgrade, and they have determined it would be easier to construct a new building than to retrofit the current one that does not have sufficient space.

The school has identified five alumni who are interested in funding the cost of the capital campaign. The pledge agreements have been signed by the alumni and indicate that the funds must be used for this particular building. The funds are due in annual increments over a five-year period. The

continued

campaign is in its third year. Aaliyah reviews the accounts and verifies that year-three funds have been collected from all pledges. She also recalculates the discount amortization and verifies that the appropriate income was recognized in year three.

The staff accountant that is responsible for this account has always been very good at identifying issues. Before the pledge agreements were sent, they reviewed the agreements and verified the terms to ensure that they would qualify as pledge receivables and not intentions to give. They also verified that the wording was unconditional and that the funds were only restricted. Review of documents is a key responsibility of staff accountants to ensure proper accounting and notes are left when wording is unusual.

Inventory

Inventory is another possible asset of a nonprofit. Organizations with bookshops or stores can have inventory that they sell. These are part of the organization's exchange transactions. When the inventory for the store is purchased, the items are recorded on the statement of financial position as assets. Upon the sale, the amount paid to obtain or make the inventory item, which is called the *cost of goods sold*, is recognized on the statement of activities.

For example, assume a nonprofit purchases a book from a publisher for $10.

- First, the nonprofit would reduce cash by $10 and then recognize an inventory asset of $10 when the asset is purchased.

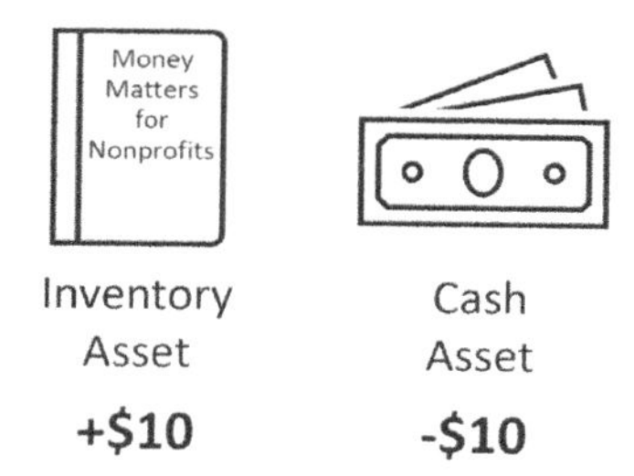

- Then, when the book is sold for $12, cash is received of $12, and revenue is recognized for $12.

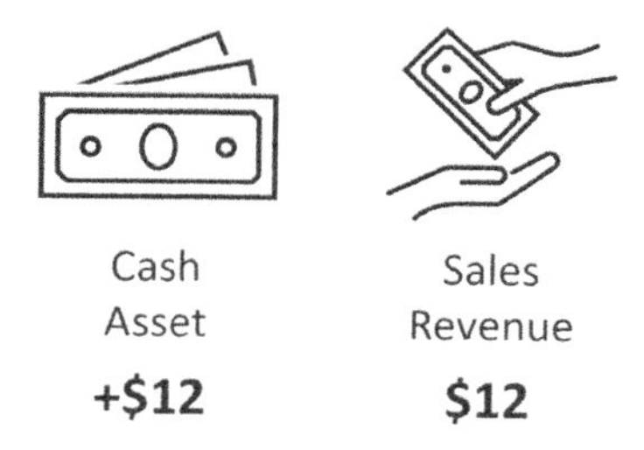

- Finally, as the book is no longer the property of the store, the nonprofit would recognize the cost of goods sold ($10) as an expense on the statement of activities, and inventory would be reduced by $10.

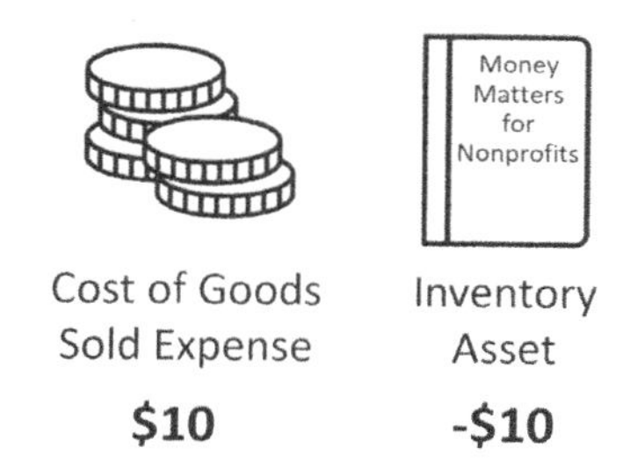

Here is a visual of the transactions, once completed, in the financial statements:

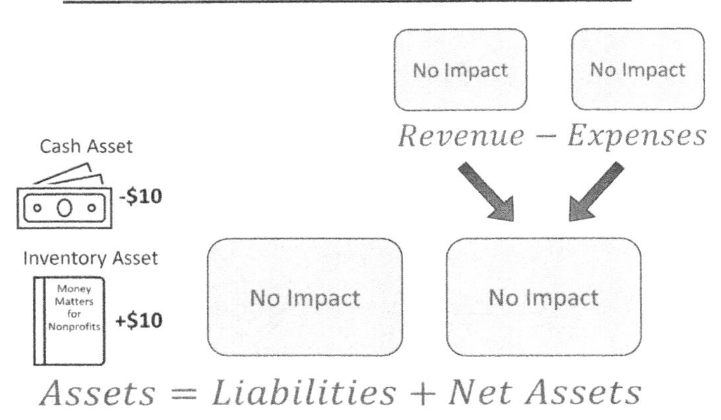

As you can see, the purchase of the inventory reduces an asset account (cash) and increases an asset account (inventory). There is no impact on the rest of the equation.

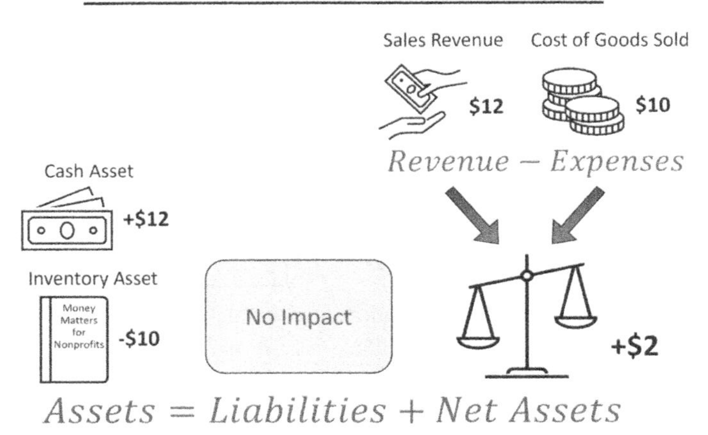

When the book is sold, the inventory is removed (at cost) and cash is received from the customer (at the price sold). In addition, revenue is recognized for the book (at the price sold), and the cost of goods sold is recognized as an expense (at cost), to provide an increase in net assets. As a result, the equation remains in balance.

INVENTORY COUNTS

The university has minimal inventory. Most of the inventory is books held for sale in the bookstore. The bookstore manager is responsible for doing monthly inventory counts of the books. Theft is minimal, as the books have asset tags and all entrances and exits to the bookstore have machines that alert to unsold items. The school also protects inventory by prohibiting students from carrying large bags or backpacks in the store. Students can store their book bags in lockers if needed while shopping.

Aaliyah reviews the inventory counts from the current period and notes only minor adjustments. Each year, the school will also review inventory for obsolescence when texts are updated and the older editions can no longer be sold.

Prepaids

The term *prepaids* refers to when a good or service is paid for in advance of receiving the benefit. Prepaids are another type of asset a nonprofit may recognize on their statement of financial position. The use of accrual accounting indicates that if a purchase has a future benefit, that benefit should be spread over the period receiving the benefit.

For example, if the nonprofit pays up front for a three-year subscription to an industry magazine, they are entitled to three years of magazines.

When they make the initial payment of $120 for the three-year subscription, they would reduce cash by $120 and recognize a prepaid asset for $120.

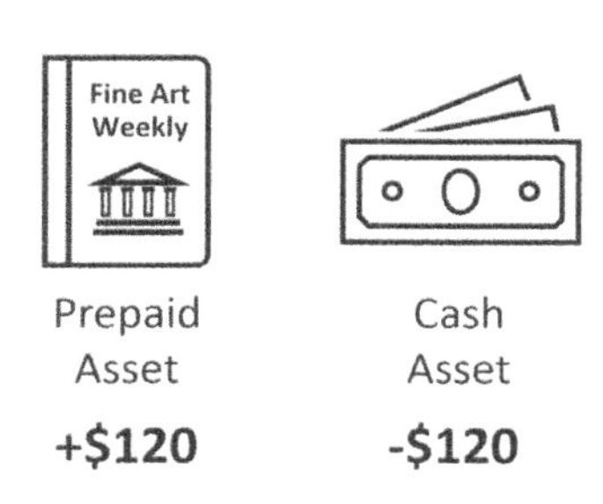

For each of the three years, they would reduce the prepaid by $40 ($120/3) and recognize an expense in the statement of activities.

As a result, the cost of the periodicals is spread over the three years of benefits.

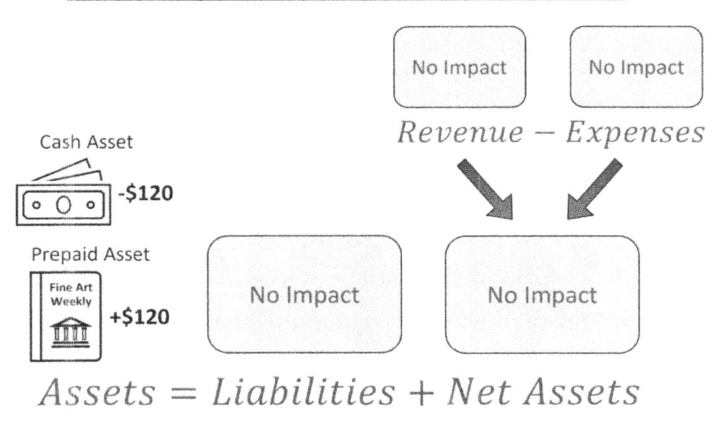

As you can see, cash is initially reduced in the same amount the prepaid asset is recognized. The remainder of the equation is not impacted.

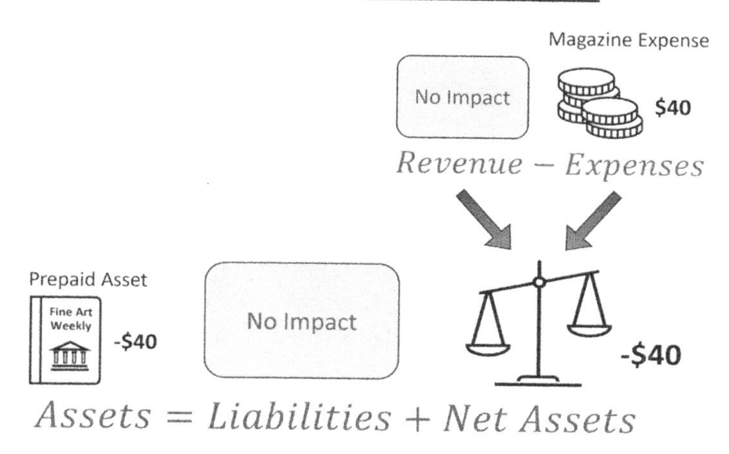

Each year that the benefit of the prepaid is used up, an expense is recognized that reduces net assets, and an equal amount is shown as a reduction of the asset.

This is a great example of why the statement of cash flows does not tie to the statement of activities.

Year	Statement of Cash Flows	Statement of Activities
1	$120 Cash Outflow	$40 Expense
2	No Impact to Cash	$40 Expense
3	No Impact to Cash	$40 Expense

Prepaids are presented on the statement of financial position at the amount remaining that has not yet been expensed. For example, at the end of year one, the statement of financial position would show the prepaid at $80 ($120 paid less the $40 expensed in year one).

PREPAID RECONCILIATIONS

The university has few prepaid accounts. The general ledger system is equipped to handle the *amortization* (i.e., periodically lowering the book value of the asset over time) of prepaids. When an accounts payable specialist enters an invoice for a prepaid, it is sent over to the general accounting group. The accountant there sets up a recurring entry by providing the start date and end date of the service or good that automatically runs on its own each month. The system then allocates the expense evenly to the expense code provided. Aaliyah is grateful for modern technology that reduces the likelihood of error and allows her team to focus on the more analytical aspects of their job.

As part of the reconciliation process, the accountants calculate the months remaining on the item and then calculate the amount that should still be shown as prepaid. This is then compared to the general ledger. The accountants rarely find issues. Most issues are due to keying errors when entering start and end dates into the system.

Aaliyah reviews all the reconciliations and notes no major issues that would warrant the attention of the board.

Investments

Nonprofits often invest excess cash in investment accounts to generate a return (e.g., interest, dividends, etc.). When a nonprofit purchases debt or equity securities, these securities are initially measured at cost (excluding brokerage and other transaction fees). If a nonprofit receives a donated security, it is measured at fair value, and the nonprofit recognizes contribution revenue.

Each subsequent reporting period (for most nonprofits, these are annual), the fair value of the asset is determined, and an unrealized gain or loss is recognized in the statement of activities. Accountants refer to an increase or decrease that is calculated for accounting purposes only but hasn't generated cash as an *unrealized gain* or *unrealized loss*.

Assume a nonprofit receives a donation of ten shares of Apple stock, and each is worth $40 at the date of contribution. The nonprofit recognizes $400 in an investment account and then contribution revenue of $400.

At the end of the year, when the nonprofit makes their financials, the finance person looks up the stock price of Apple stock. If Apple is trading at $50, then the nonprofit has a $100 ($10 in appreciation multiplied by ten shares) gain.

However, the price of Apple stock will continue to fluctuate, so this gain is not permanent. Therefore, the nonprofit in this example books an unrealized gain of $100 in the statement of activities and adjusts the related asset value by $100. This transaction has no impact on actual cash, as the stock was not sold.

If at the end of the second year, Apple stock is now worth $55 per share, the nonprofit recognizes an additional $50 of appreciation ($55 current value subtracted by $50 prior value multiplied by ten shares). They then recognize an unrealized gain of $50 and adjust the asset account.

If midway through year three, the nonprofit sells the stock for $60 per share (an actual cash transaction), they have a realized gain of $20 per share, or $200 ($60 current value subtracted by the $40 original price). This is an actual gain, as the entity is receiving $60 for shares that were worth $40 when they were donated. At this point, the nonprofit reverses the unrealized gains and recognizes a realized gain. The actual cash flow is $600.

For publicly traded stock, fair value is very easy to determine. Sometimes nonprofits invest in investments that do not have readily determinable fair values, which makes valuation far more difficult.

		Statement of Financial Position	Statement of Activities	
Date	Value of Stock	Investment Account	Unrealized Gain	Realized Gain
1/1/Y1	$40	$400	$0	$0
12/31/Y1	$50	$500	$100	$0
12/31/Y2	$55	$550	$50	$0
6/30/Y3	$60	$0 (sold)	-$150	$200

INVESTMENT RECONCILIATIONS

The university has a sizeable investment portfolio, and it uses investment pools, which act similarly to mutual funds, to track assets. There are multiple accountants assigned to these accounts to ensure transactions are properly recorded. Investments are recorded at fair value, and those with readily determinable prices are updated monthly to record unrealized gains and losses. The university invests in assets in a prudent manner to achieve a long-term rate of return. It keeps a diversified investment portfolio with the help of its vice president of investments and the board's investment committee. For liquidity purposes, a portion of the investments are in money market accounts with quoted prices. The university also invests in equity securities and fixed-income investments.

For investments with a readily determinable fair value, the accountant obtains an investment statement from the trustee. The accountant then books an adjusting journal entry to record any unrealized gains or losses and any investment fees. The investment fees, as well as internal salaries of the VP of investments, are netted against the return. These are typically not known until the statement is received. Investment returns are carefully tracked, and the VP of investments often presents updates on investment strategy. The staff also reviews the statement for purchases and sales to ensure they are properly recorded.

Investments are subject to liquidity, currency, interest rate, and credit risks. These risks are carefully managed by the investment team. Risk summaries are drafted for each board meeting. The board carefully reviews the investment return, as well as the types of investments. The investment committee meets more frequently than the board to discuss positions with the VP of investments, Indira.

Aaliyah reviews the reconciliations, which show that the ending balance per the investment statements ties to the investment accounts. She'll meet with Indira to ensure the rest of the board presentation will be ready in time for the meeting.

Property, Plant, and Equipment

Before PPE stood for personal protective equipment, PP&E stood for property, plant, and equipment. These are long-term assets like buildings, equipment, computers, and land. Another term for PP&E is fixed assets. A list of fixed assets is often referred to as a fixed-assets inventory.

PURCHASED PP&E

When purchased, PP&E is recognized at the acquisition price (i.e., the amount paid to purchase). However, as these assets will be of benefit to the nonprofit for many years, GAAP requires the cost to be spread out over those years and recorded as long-term assets and then depreciated over their useful lives.

Upon purchase, the nonprofit recognizes an asset at acquisition value (e.g., a building worth $400,000). They then book the other side of the entry based on how the building was purchased (perhaps recognizing a mortgage payable or even cash if it was a cash transaction). These accounts are all on the statement of financial position.

Because the building will likely continue to provide benefit to the nonprofit over many years, the nonprofit estimates the useful life of the asset. For ease of calculation, let's assume the building has a forty-year life. Each year the nonprofit recognizes a depreciation expense of $10,000 in the statement of activities. This is not a cash transaction. It is simply spreading the value received from the building over its useful life.

The offset to this depreciation entry is called *accumulated depreciation*. This is another contra asset account. It simply reduces the value of the asset. Now while the building likely will increase in value each year, GAAP requires the nonprofit to depreciate the building, since depreciation is a spreading of the cost to the periods benefited, not a means of tracking current market value. As a result, the net book value of the building will decrease each year on the financial statements.

	Statement of Financial Position			Statement of Activities
Date	Asset	Accumulated Depreciation	Net Book Value	Depreciation Expense
1/1/Y1	$400,000	$0	$400,000	$0
12/31/Y1	$400,000	$10,000	$390,000	$10,000
12/31/Y2	$400,000	$20,000	$380,000	$10,000
12/31/Y3	$400,000	$30,000	$370,000	$10,000
12/31/Y40	$400,000	$400,000	$0	$10,000

When assets are sold, the asset is removed from the books, the accumulated depreciation is removed, and then the cash received is recognized. Any difference between the net book value (historical cost subtracted by the accumulated depreciation) and cash would be a gain or loss (realized).

In our example, if the building was sold on 12/31/Y3 for $500,000, we would do the following:

1. Remove the $400,000 from the financial statements, since we don't own the building anymore.
2. Remove the accumulated depreciation ($30,000) from the financial statements.
3. Receive in cash of $500,000.
4. Book a gain on sale of $130,000 ($500,000 cash less $370,000 net book value).

Depreciation is a noncash item and a reconciling item on the statement of cash flows when using the indirect method of cash flow.

Date	Statement of Cash Flows	Statement of Activities
1/1/Y1	-$400,000	$0
12/31/Y1	$0	$10,000
12/31/Y2	$0	$10,000

Depreciation applies to assets such as buildings, equipment, computers, and so on. The exception to depreciation is land. Because land doesn't reduce in value and is permanent, GAAP does not require nonprofits to depreciate land, as we expect the earth to be around for a really long period of time.

FIXED-ASSET RECONCILIATIONS

Property, plant, and equipment are stated at cost at the date of acquisition. They are then depreciated over their useful lives. The useful lives of buildings range from ten to eighty years. Software ranges from three to ten years. Equipment and motor vehicles range from three to twenty years. Depreciation is calculated on a straight-line basis. Depreciation is not recorded for purchases of land. Buildings are by far the largest asset for the university. Thankfully, it is pretty easy to ensure that the buildings are still there! Land is the third-largest category, and its tracking is also pretty easy.

All other assets that are the property of the university are issued a fixed-asset tag, which shows the fixed-asset number. Each piece of fixed assets is logged, and the location is tracked. When an asset is transferred, the appropriate department is supposed to inform finance; however, that does not always happen. The university tracks assets by major division (e.g., athletics, classroom, housing, libraries, research).

Purchased assets are recorded within the fixed-asset system. The estimated useful life is selected based on university policy. The computer system automatically calculates depreciation. There is very little risk with respect to the calculation; however, Aaliyah does review useful lives periodically to ensure they are reasonable.

Aaliyah is most concerned with the existence and classification of the second-largest fixed-asset group, which is equipment, furniture, and motor vehicles. If they are not transferred, sold, or disposed of properly and in accordance with policy, it can lead to incorrect accounting. As a result, her team periodically performs counts of the fixed assets. They review the fixed-asset register and physically observe the fixed asset. This can be a cumbersome process, but it is often the only way to ensure fixed assets

continued

are properly recorded. Some departments, like the library, perform periodic counts of their fixed assets (i.e., library books) regularly. Other departments rely on finance to perform the counts.

Aaliyah reviews the reconciliation of the fixed assets and notes that some athletic equipment was disposed of but not recorded until the physical count. She puts a note in her calendar to send an email with the policies and related forms over to the athletic department.

DONATED PP&E

Donated PP&E is a type of *contributed nonfinancial asset* or a *gift in kind*. The assets are recognized at fair value. The nonprofit recognizes contribution revenue for the same amount.

Sometimes donors will stipulate the period of time that the PP&E must be used (i.e., can't be sold). In those scenarios, the transaction is deemed as having donor restrictions. When the period passes, the restriction is reclassified into net assets without donor restrictions. If a donor does not stipulate a holding period, the contribution is deemed to be without donor restrictions.

Some donors state assets must be used in a specific way, like for a particular program. This is called a *purpose restriction*. Once the asset is used the way the donor required, the amount of the asset changes from "with donor restrictions" to "without donor restrictions" on the statement of activities. The exception would be if the donor placed restrictions on how the asset would further be used.

If a donor contributes cash for the purchase of a long-term asset (purpose restriction), when the asset is placed into service (i.e., used in operations), the restriction is deemed to be released.

Some grants may indicate whether depreciation or the full asset should be expensed in a particular year as an allowable cost. The grant instructions do not impact financial reporting. They only impact reporting for that grant to the grantor. In this scenario, the full asset is shown as an expense in the reporting to the grantor, but in the financial statements it shows as a fixed asset. Therefore, when trying to tie the grant reporting to the financial statements, there are important differences that need to be reconciled.

DONATED FIXED ASSETS

The McDonald family recently donated a new mass spectrometer for the research lab. It was a very welcome donation, as the school continues to grow its research program. The McDonalds restricted the asset's use to the research center. The donation was recorded at fair value. Aaliyah was able to find the same model for sale online and used the price for estimating fair value, as it was brand new and could theoretically be sold for the amount of purchase.

The Jones family has donated property adjacent to the university that includes a building, and they indicated that the building must be used by the university for at least ten years. Aaliyah recorded the land and building at fair value using comparable sales in the neighborhood. Thankfully, the price per square foot is pretty similar for the three other comparable sales, so Aaliyah feels pretty good about the valuation. The building is shown as restricted due to the time restriction.

The Smith family has donated a significant amount of money to build a new building for the business school. The university is excited to be able to offer a modern building for the growing school. Aaliyah reviews the construction-in-progress account and notes that the funds used have been properly released from restrictions. The Smith family did not provide a time restriction for the use of the building.

The board carefully reviews all donations of property, plant, and equipment, as well as any construction in progress. The board members take turns calling the donors to thank them for their generosity.

Right-of-Use Lease Assets

Almost all organizations have assets that they use but don't own. Common equipment rented by nonprofits includes buildings, cars, copiers, and office furniture. For cash flow purposes, nonprofits may choose to lease or rent an asset in lieu of purchasing it. A newly created asset type for nonprofits is the right-of-use asset created for leases. They recognize the ability to use the asset as a right-of-use asset, but they cannot recognize the asset itself (e.g., the machinery that they leased). GAAP requires nonprofits to recognize a right-of-use asset and a lease liability when entering into most leases that exceed twelve months. GAAP requires a discounted cash flow calculated to determine the valuation of the asset account at inception. Similar to the rules for PP&E, the right-of-use asset should generally be expensed over the term of the lease. The expense is referred to as *amortization.*

A change in how nonprofits account for leases was issued in 2016, which led to certain assets being recognized that were historically not recognized on the statement of financial position.[2]

It is important to note leases that are less than one year are not required to be presented in the statement of financial position. They can just be expensed over the appropriate period.

LEASES RECONCILIATION

The new lease standard took a lot of effort to implement. Aaliyah and her team had to use their professional judgment to determine things like lease term, stand-alone selling prices, and discount rates.

The board took a keen interest in the adoption of the standard, as several million dollars of leased assets were recorded that had been in existence for many years. Aaliyah attended several continuing-education classes to learn about the lease standard and how it would apply to the university's leases of equipment, cars, and buildings.

For the most part, the capital leases that were previously on the books had very little change outside of additional disclosures. However, the operating leases required significantly more effort. Several of the leases had options to extend, and Aaliyah had to evaluate the likelihood of making the decision to extend. Almost none of the leases had a stated interest rate. As a result, Aaliyah had to estimate the incremental borrowing rate for most leases.[3] The university elected to use the risk-free rate alternative for small leases like vehicles and machinery, but it did not elect the private company alternative for larger assets like buildings. For those leases, she had to estimate the rate.

The university purchased software to track the leases and to perform the lease accounting. The initial setup of the software was tedious, but now that it is up and running, Aaliyah's team is able to run detailed reports that she uses for writing up her board presentation.

The board was very involved with reviewing the judgments and asking questions throughout the process of adopting the standard. Now that the standard is fully implemented, Aaliyah is excited to share her insights into the process and some lessons learned. She has drafted the proposed note disclosures that provide information about adoption and details about types of leases, average lease terms, discount rates, and other important information. The board will review the disclosure at the upcoming meeting.

Intangible Assets

Intangible assets are a type of *nonfinancial asset* that lacks physical substance. Examples of intangible assets are goodwill, trademarks, and software.

Some intangible assets have finite lives. Therefore, in lieu of depreciation, intangible assets are amortized, and nonprofits recognize amortization (similar to depreciation). On the other hand, some intangible assets (like goodwill) don't have a finite life and are instead tested for *impairment*. *Impairment* is the term used to describe a situation in which the value on financial statements is more than the fair value of the asset. In such a case, the intangible is adjusted down to reflect the change in fair value. If the value of an intangible asset increases, GAAP prohibits recognizing the increase. Only the impairment (reduction) of the asset is permitted.

Collections

Some nonprofits, such as museums, may also have collection items. There is special accounting if the items meet the definition of a collection per GAAP.

DEFINITION

GAAP defines *collections* as "works of art, historical treasures, or similar assets that meet all of the following criteria:

a. They are held for public exhibition, education, or research in furtherance of public service rather than financial gain.
b. They are protected, kept unencumbered, cared for, and preserved.
c. They are subject to an organizational policy that requires the use of proceeds from items that are sold to be for the acquisitions of new collection items, the direct care of existing collections, or both."[4]

If the work of art meets the definition of a collection, then the nonprofit qualifies for specialty accounting. If a donor contributes an item to a collection, GAAP does not require that to be recognized in the financial statements. Nonprofits can choose to elect the accounting alternative, or they may choose to capitalize all collection items. Selective capitalization is not permitted. If a nonprofit does not capitalize its collection items, the statement of financial position will have a line item for collections but will not have any values provided. There will be a disclosure in the notes about the collection items.

The Smithsonian, for example, is a nonprofit with a significant collection that has chosen not to capitalize its collection items.[5]

SMITHSONIAN INSTITUTION
Statements of Financial Position
September 30, 2020 and 2019
(Dollars in millions)

		2020			2019		
		Trust	Federal	Total Funds	Trust	Federal	Total Funds
Assets:							
Cash, cash equivalents, and U.S.Treasury balances	$	173.8	713.0	886.8	139.9	645.3	785.2
Accounts receivable and other assets, net		65.8	1.8	67.6	77.3	3.2	80.5
Pledges receivable, net		179.1	—	179.1	167.9	—	167.9
Investments		2,179.1	—	2,179.1	1,946.2	—	1,946.2
Property and equipment, net		981.6	1,759.1	2,740.7	730.6	1,710.3	2,440.9
★Collections		—	—	—	—	—	—
Total assets	$	3,579.4	2,473.9	6,053.3	3,061.9	2,358.8	5,420.7

As you can see, although the Smithsonian has many of America's treasures, it reflects no value in its statement of financial position. Instead, a note disclosure provides information about the collection items.

Nonprofits that do not recognize their collections in the statement of financial position report the cost of collection items purchased as a decrease in the appropriate class of net assets, and any proceeds from sales of collection items are reported as increases in net assets.

Nonprofits that capitalize their collections also include a separate line called "collections" to denote the collections separate from other assets.

If a work of art is not part of a collection, it must be recognized as an asset in the financial statements. The amount capitalized is either presented separately on the financial statement or disclosed in the notes.

Endowments

Endowments are set up by motivated donors who want to have a long-term impact.

Types of endowments include the following:

- Endowments with donor restrictions are reflected in net assets with donor restrictions and are referred to as *donor-restricted endowment funds*. A donor may restrict the endowment for a period of time (a temporary endowment) or in perpetuity (a permanent endowment). An endowed chair at a university would fall into this category.

- Sometimes a board may establish an endowment fund (e.g., the launch of a big capital campaign). They can set aside funds to kick off the campaign. As the assets are designated by the board and not a donor, the assets are reflected in the net assets without donor restrictions. These are often referred to as *quasi-endowments.*

DEFINITION

An *endowment fund* is defined as "An established fund of cash, securities, or other assets to provide income for the maintenance of a not-for-profit entity (NFP). The use of the assets of the fund may be with or without donor-imposed restrictions. Endowment funds generally are established by donor-restricted gifts and bequests to provide a source of income in perpetuity or for a specified period."[6]

In most states, there are special rules for permanent endowments that allow the organization to spend a small percentage of the endowment (called a *spending policy*). The spending policy predefines what percentage of the endowment can be set aside to be spent by the governing board based on prior returns from investments. The states that follow this policy follow the Uniform Prudent Management of Institutional Funds Act of 2006 (UPMIFA). UPMIFA treats the funds as donor restrictions until the funds are appropriated for expenditure (set aside for spending) by the governing board. The goal is to ensure the longevity of the endowment fund while allowing nonprofits to budget for spending.

Typically, the nonprofit has to retain the original gifted amount, any additional gifts to the endowment fund, and a portion of the investment return. Donors can provide explicit guidance on the different components of investment return. For example, the donor may indicate that the fund must be kept in perpetuity, but any gains, dividends, or interest revenue can be spent. Donors can indicate that they have to be spent for a particular purpose (impacting net assets with donor restrictions) or that they can be used for any purpose (net assets without donor restrictions).

As most endowments invest the cash received in debt or equity securities, sometimes when there is a bad economy, the dip in fair values results in an *underwater endowment* (i.e., the fund balance dips below the amount given). The position of the endowment is still displayed in net assets with donor restrictions with a note disclosure to indicate the amount underwater.

ENDOWMENT REVIEW

The university has over a thousand funds in its endowment, each set up for a different purpose. All but two of the endowments are donor restricted. The board has an endowment fund set aside for the new business school building capital campaign. They also have a liquidity reserve (for any unexpected liquidity issues) that is outside of the endowment and is intended for more short-term considerations. The board-designated endowments are shown as net assets without donor restrictions. The remaining funds are shown as net assets with donor restrictions. The endowment is carefully tracked by the VP of investments. Endowment yield (interest and dividends) and appreciation (realized and unrealized) are important figures that the board carefully reviews. The board reviews the roll forward from the prior period to the current period with an explanation of all movement at each board meeting.

The university uses UPMIFA, which permits the university to spend below the original gift value. Fortunately, the endowment has had

continued

amazing returns lately, and no funds are underwater. Most of the assets are merged into one investment pool, and the university utilizes the total return concept in allocating the endowment income. The university's spending policy permits the appropriation of 5 percent of a twelve-quarter average of the fair value of the endowment investments. The board periodically reviews and updates the endowment payout as part of its strategic initiatives. If income generated by the endowment is in excess of the amount appropriated per the spending policy, the balance is reinvested in the endowment. Much of the endowment is spent on providing financial aid.

The board package includes a ten-year rate of return for the endowment, as well as a detailed breakdown of the endowment spending distribution. The board typically has a lot of questions about these graphs and charts, so the accountants assigned to these areas provide detailed breakdowns of the movements as part of their reconciliation. Copies of investment sheets are also provided.

Board Best Practices

Review and approval of balance sheet reconciliations are a key control for most nonprofits, as they can help identify errors in journal entries, missed transactions, and so on. The board can add value in smaller organizations by periodically reviewing balance sheet reconciliations. The board likely wouldn't review each one every month, but periodically providing a second set of eyes and looking for trends in unreconciled items can be helpful. Asking questions about why an item was unreconciled for an extended period or why numerous large-value items went unreconciled can help identify areas of potential fraud or error.

For larger organizations where there is sufficient segregation of duties, reviewing disaggregated data about types of assets, significant additions, and so on can provide excellent oversight. Boards can also add value by evaluating whether investments appear to be in line with the investment policy, or whether a significant addition to PP&E was made that may have required board approval but did not obtain it.

There is a fine line between management oversight and micromanaging. Management is responsible for the day-to-day operations, so it's important the board evaluate the organization's abilities and provide the appropriate level of oversight.

LIABILITIES

A *liability* is "a present obligation of an entity to transfer an economic benefit."[7] If you pay for something on a credit card, you owe the credit card company a payment. If you borrow money for a mortgage to buy a home, you owe the bank repayments. Nonprofits have many of the same liabilities as corporations and individuals, including mortgages.

To provide users with information about liquidity, nonprofits can order their liabilities on the statement of financial position according to the nearness of maturity. For example, something due this month would be a current liability, while a mortgage on a building would be a noncurrent liability. Ranking them in order of when they come due helps users understand if they have sufficient assets to pay their liabilities as they become due.

Liabilities are settled through transfer of assets (typically cash) or other financial assets (like stock). However, a liability can also be settled through delivery of goods or services (e.g., to reverse unearned revenue).

TICKET SALES EXAMPLE

In this scenario, the university is hosting a famous speaker on campus. Tickets are sold in advance for the discussion. When payment is received, unearned revenue (sometimes referred to as *deferred revenue*) is recorded.

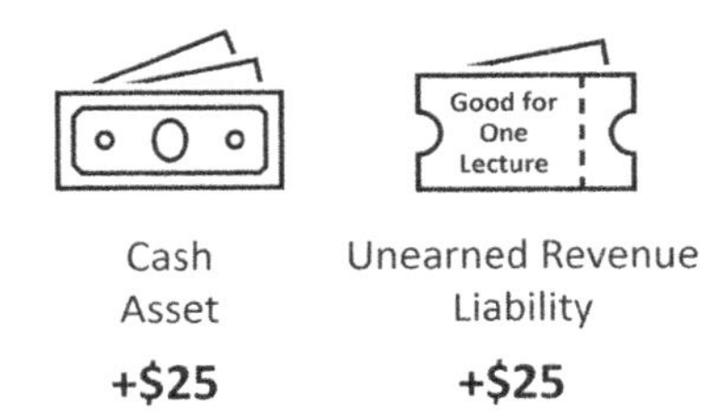

When the event is held, the unearned revenue is reversed, and revenue is recognized.

The impact on the financial statement is as follows:

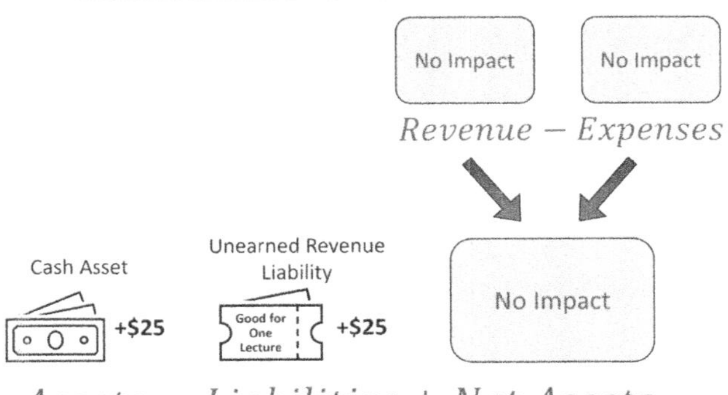

In this scenario, as the university has yet to admit the ticket buyer to attend the lecture (delivery of a service), the university will increase the cash account. The liability (unearned revenue) is recognized for the same amount. The liability will be outstanding until the event happens.

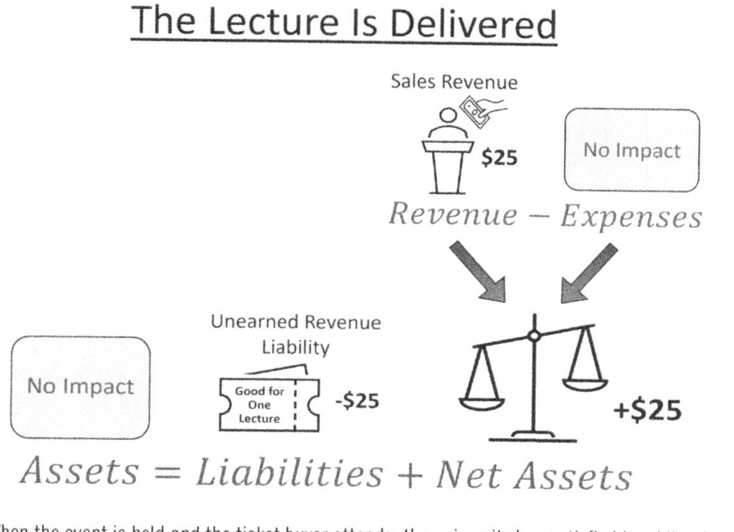

When the event is held and the ticket buyer attends, the university has satisfied its obligation to the ticket buyer. As a result, the liability is reversed and revenue is recognized. The increase in revenue will increase net assets, which keeps the equation balanced.

TYPES OF LIABILITIES

Accounts Payable

Accounts payable (AP) is a common liability for nonprofits. Many nonprofits will purchase goods and services on credit, typically with relatively short due dates (fifteen to thirty days). When the item is purchased, no cash is paid, and instead accounts payable is recognized. When the nonprofit performs its check run, it will reduce cash and reverse the accounts payable. Typically, AP does not accrue interest due to the short-term nature of the liability.

ACCOUNTS PAYABLE

Treasury does their weekly check runs on Fridays. This period ended on a Thursday, which means there was considerably more in accounts payable than in the previous period, which closed on a Tuesday. The accountant that oversees accounts payable reviews the outstanding accounts and investigates payments that are more than thirty days past due. The goal is to identify why these haven't been paid yet. Often, they were not submitted to accounts payable on time for processing. The school carefully monitors late fees and interest. As such, any invoices that incur these types of fees are identified, and the individual who submitted them is asked to provide an explanation for the delay in submission. They are often asked to negotiate with the vendor to reduce or eliminate the late fees and interest, especially if the delay was caused by a disagreement about the invoice.

Accrued Liabilities

Because GAAP requires the use of accrual accounting, sometimes there is a difference between when a benefit is received and when cash is paid. As we discussed in earlier chapters, most utility bills (e.g., telephone, electric) work this way. In order to ensure matching of the benefit to the right time period, an *accrued liabilities* account is commonly used. At the end of the month, nonprofits will look for any bills that have not yet been received and estimate the amount by booking the expense and related accrual.

Typically, these entries are reversed at the beginning of the next month, and when the bill comes in, the actual amounts are recognized in the financial statements. Any difference between the estimated amount and the actual amount is corrected when the bill is received.

ACCRUED LIABILITIES

Aaliyah carefully reviews the reconciliation for accrued liabilities for June. Trying to ensure that all liabilities have been captured can be difficult. For the first five days of July, her team enters any invoices that are received for work done in June back into the June accounts payable. The invoice date is entered, but the transaction date is backdated to the last day of the month. This helps capture actuals for as many invoices as possible.

Then the very detailed work of verifying all expenses comes in. For each expense account, the accountant reviews the current balance to its historical average. If an invoice was not received, often the account shows as well below the average. Then the accountant reviews the movement in the account and reviews the invoices received. If it's a weekly or monthly invoice that has not been received, the accountant will enter an adjusting entry to accrue for the expected amount of the invoice. The entry will auto reverse at the beginning of the next period so that when the invoice is entered, the amount of expense will not be overstated.

Aaliyah reviews each accrual to ensure the estimate is reasonable and all expenses have been accrued for.

Deferred Revenue

Deferred or *unearned* revenue is when a nonprofit is paid in an exchange transaction before the good or service has been delivered. Revenue cannot be recognized until the entity has performed or satisfied the performance obligation.

When payment is received up front, cash has to be recognized. Until they have performed, the nonprofit can't recognize revenue, so they recognize a liability. If they don't perform, they will have to give the money back, so a liability is an appropriate response. When the good or service is delivered, then the deferred revenue account is reversed, and revenue is recognized.

DEFERRED REVENUE

As the university is at the end of its fiscal year, most deferred revenue has been recognized. However, summer school tuition was billed this period and isn't eligible for revenue recognition, as the performance obligation is satisfied when classes are offered. As a result, all revenue was booked as deferred revenue and will be recognized over the two months that summer school takes place.

The accountant verifies that all deferred revenue for the academic year has been appropriately booked and that only revenue related to the summer semester is left. Aaliyah reviews the reconciliation and notes no adjusting entries are needed.

Refundable Advances

Nonprofits cannot recognize revenue when the contribution has conditions (i.e., a barrier and right of return or right of release). If a contribution is conditional but the donor provides the cash up front, as with deferred revenue, cash will be recognized in the statement of financial position. In order to balance, a refundable advance will also be recognized, which is a liability until the condition is met. Refundable advances are used for nonexchange transactions the way deferred revenue is used for exchange transactions. When the condition is met, the advance will be reversed, and contribution revenue will be recognized.

REFUNDABLE ADVANCES

Aaliyah reviews the listing of refundable advances and notes most are related to federal grants subject to qualifying expenses. All initially received funds are recorded as refundable advances. As the expenses are paid, the amounts are released (the refundable advance reversed), and revenue is recognized. The schedule identifies the key terms of the conditions. The schedule is completed by the staff accountant for grants, but the head of grant management reviews and approves it. Aaliyah reviews the notes left by the grant manager.

Employment Liabilities

Nonprofits also have employment-related liabilities. Pensions, other post-employment benefits, and general payroll expenses are liabilities. These liabilities can be very long term in nature (e.g., pensions or 401k plans) and require actuaries to assist the determinations of the amounts due. These typically have significant estimates for which management will have to determine inputs and assumptions to determine the appropriate accounting.

Notes Payable

Nonprofits may borrow funds for various purposes. When nonprofits borrow larger sums of money for longer periods, the bank will issue a contract called a *note payable*. Notes payable are more formalized liabilities. These are typically long-term contracts that incur interest.

Nonprofits follow the same accounting for these long-term debts as for-profit entities. Interest is recognized, and the debt is reduced on the statement of financial position as payments are made or when legally released (e.g., if the bank forgave the debt).

Some nonprofits issue tax-exempt debt through various governmental entities (conduit debt). Because the governmental entity is acting as an intermediary and ultimately the nonprofit is responsible for the payment of the debt, the debt should be recognized as a liability of the nonprofit and not the governmental entity.

When interest is below market, the entity will need to recognize the effective interest rate and may recognize contribution revenue for the difference between the interest rate charged and a market rate.

Lease Liability

As mentioned earlier, there were significant changes made to lease accounting recently.[8] All leases greater than one year are recognized on the balance sheet. Lease liabilities represent the present value of all the payments the nonprofit expects to make over the lease term. The lease term is an estimate based on the period that the nonprofit is locked into the lease, which is referred to as the *non-cancellable period*, but also takes into consideration lessee and lessor options to extend or terminate the lease.

The liability includes not only fixed payments but also variable payments that depend on an index or rate, option prices for renewals or purchases (if the nonprofit expects to exercise such options), penalties for lease termination, and so on.

It is important to note that if a lease is significantly below market value (e.g., one dollar per year for a building), it doesn't fall within the scope of the Leases section of the Codification (Topic 842). Instead, these leases are subject to the rules for contribution accounting and the disclosure requirements for gifts in kind.

Agency Transactions

Finally, *agency transactions* are when a donor provides funds to a recipient organization with instructions to provide the funds to the ultimate beneficiary.

In this scenario, if the nonprofit is the recipient organization, the general rule when acting as an agent or intermediary is that when funds are received, the nonprofit will recognize cash and then a liability to the ultimate beneficiary. The liability is typically labeled "amounts held for others." When the funds are provided to the beneficiary, the liability will be reversed, and cash reduced. There is no statement-of-activities impact for agency transactions (e.g., revenue is not impacted).

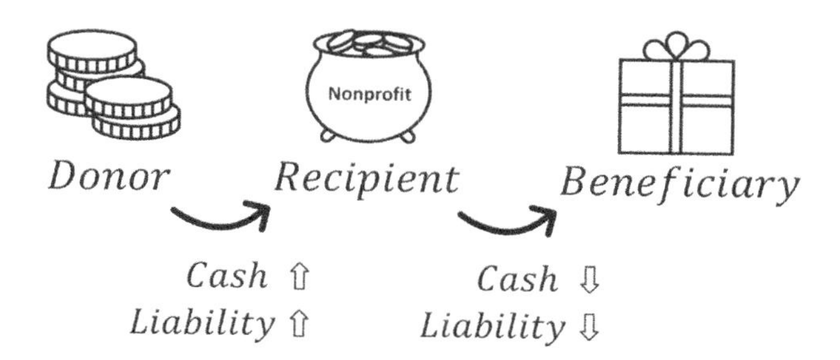

Board Best Practices

It is important to note that because a balance sheet is a snapshot of a point in time, a balance may be unusually high one year due to timing, and in other years it may be unusually low. For example, if a check run was recently performed before the end of the month, accounts payable may be significantly lower than the prior year. On the other hand, long-term debt can be pretty consistent, and unless a debt is paid off or new debt taken off, there is typically much less variability. The board should review financials each period to ensure the balances in the liabilities look reasonable. They should also evaluate whether debt is growing so quickly that liquidity is becoming an issue.

Having consistent discussions with management about short- and long-term liabilities and trends can be very important so that the board is aware of any changes. The board should ensure debt payments are being made and that employment-related liabilities are properly remitted. Nonprofits can get in a lot of trouble with the government for failure to remit employment taxes. Careful tracking by the board about the reasonableness of liabilities is vital to ensuring all liabilities are being properly treated and paid.

There are two exceptions to the agency accounting—when the recipient organization and beneficiary are financially interrelated, and when the donor grants the recipient organization *variance power*. Variance power is the explicit unilateral right to change the beneficiary.

When variance power is granted, the recipient organization determines the ultimate beneficiary. In such an instance, revenue is recognized by the recipient organization. Then, when the funds are provided to the beneficiary, an expense is recognized.

AGENCY TRANSACTIONS

Aaliyah is responsible for the university's accounting and also for the accounting of its legally separate foundation, which provides scholarships for students. Donors who would like to support deserving students often send checks to the foundation and restrict the use of the funds to the university for scholarships. Because the donor stipulates an entity other than the foundation, the transaction looks like an agency transaction. However, the university influences the foundation's financial and operating decisions by appointing the board of the foundation. It also has an ongoing economic interest in the other entity's net assets, as the bylaws indicate that all net assets revert to the university. As such, these entities are financially interrelated, and the foundation recognizes the revenue in lieu of a liability to the university.

Aaliyah provides detailed analysis of the foundation's financials, which are much simpler than the university's. The balance sheet only has cash, contributions receivable, and investments for assets. The foundation has no liabilities. Net assets are segregated between those with donor restrictions and those without. The foundation's only revenue is contributions and investment earnings. The expenses include scholarships and professional services (primarily for the independent audit).

NET ASSETS

Nonprofits do not recognize owner's equity. Instead, the statement of financial position calculates net assets (i.e., assets minus liabilities). The net assets are the excess of assets over liabilities.

Net assets are reported in two categories—*with donor restrictions* and *without donor restrictions*. The only thing that impacts classification is whether there are any donor-imposed restrictions. For example, if a board were to designate funds for a particular purpose, those funds would still be displayed in net assets without donor restrictions, as there are no donor restrictions for those funds.

While GAAP only requires nonprofits to use these two categories, nonprofits can choose to further disaggregate their net assets if they so desire. For example, nonprofits can choose to show those net assets that are expected to be held in perpetuity separately from those that are restricted only temporarily. The most common types of restrictions are those related to purpose and those related to timing. The nature and amounts of the donor-imposed restrictions are important to users. Nonprofits can choose to provide this information within the statement of financial position or in the note disclosures.

Nonprofits can also choose to show the amounts designated by the board on the face of the financials as a subcategory of the *without donor restrictions* category. If not disclosed on the statement of financial position, the nonprofit will provide both the purpose and amount of any board designations in the note disclosures.

NET ASSET REVIEW

Net assets without donor restrictions include the board-designated endowment fund and liquidity reserve. It also includes contributions from donors that did not indicate a purpose or time restriction. Aaliyah verifies that all expenses reduced net assets without donor restrictions and all exchange revenues increased net assets without donor restrictions. The reconciliation includes a total for unrestricted contributions, which increased net assets without donor restrictions. Many of these donations come in the form of a check to the university's development or alumni services departments. Aliyah reviews the schedule to ensure that the line item for the amount released from restrictions ties to zero.

She prepares a separate schedule for the board of the net assets with donor restrictions that will later be used in the financial statements for

continued

disclosure. It shows the major types of restrictions in comparative format. The largest restrictions relate to the endowment, student loan funds, and capital restrictions. Some of the endowment restrictions are temporary in nature, while others are permanent and subject to the university's spending policy. This schedule is reviewed carefully by the board to ensure the university is appropriately liquid and that restrictions are not hampering the university's ability to pay its bills.

DISCLOSURES

There are many disclosures related to the elements in the statement of financial position. Sometimes, nonprofits are given the option of presenting information within the financial statements or in the note disclosures. As a result, the disclosure content is not always the same for nonprofits who choose to present the required information within the financial statement instead of in the note disclosures.

GAAP requires disclosures about the nature and amount of limitations on the use of cash and cash equivalents, as well as contractual limitations on the use of assets. Nonprofits also provide information about the nature and amount of the types of restrictions that impact how and when (if ever) net assets can be used. They also provide information about the nature and types of board designations.

Nonprofits typically show releases from restrictions as a separate line in the statement of activities. If a nonprofit has a policy of reporting restrictions met in the same period in which they're received as *net assets without donor restrictions*, they must disclose this policy.

Endowment Disclosures

Nonprofits must disclose very specific information about endowment funds, including net asset classification, net asset composition, any changes in net asset composition, and the nonprofit's spending and investment policies. Nonprofits must describe the board's interpretation of the laws regarding net asset classification (including whether the nonprofit can spend from underwater endowments). If an endowment is underwater (i.e., below its original gift amount), the nonprofit must provide details of the current fair value of the fund, the original gift amount, and the amount of deficiency. Nonprofits must also describe the policy for appropriating endowment assets. This is frequently referred to as a *spending policy*.

To help users understand the nonprofit's investment policies, the nonprofit must disclose its return objectives and risk parameters, how return objectives relate to the spending policy, and the strategy for achieving the return objectives. The nonprofit will also disclose the composition of the endowment by net asset class (i.e., donor restricted as opposed to board designated).

Finally, nonprofits also disclose the beginning and ending balance of the endowment to show the impact of investment returns, contributions, amounts appropriated for expenditure, and any other changes. This helps users understand what impacted the endowment balance.

Board Best Practices

Obviously, the endowment is a very important asset to a nonprofit's ability to sustain itself. As economies often go through peaks and valleys, the board must ensure its spending policy is appropriate and endowments are being used for their intended purposes. Carefully reviewing the disclosures for the endowment and checking on investment returns and spending can help a nonprofit proactively weather a storm by adjusting spending. Maintaining proper liquidity reserves is key.

Policies are a key area of governance for a nonprofit board. Ensuring that policies are meeting the needs of the organization and are up to date is vital. All policies should be reviewed at least annually.

Promises to Give

Nonprofits are required to disclose unconditional pledges that are receivable in less than one year, in one to five years, and in more than five years to understand the timing of the cash receipts. They also must disclose any allowance related to un-collectability of these receivables. When recognizing the pledge receivables due in more than one year, present-value technique recognizes the impact of the time value of money, and as such, a discount reduces the amount of the receivable. If the net amount of the pledge is shown on the financials, nonprofits will disclose the amount of the discount in the notes.

If a promise to give is conditional, the nonprofit will disclose the total amount promised, group the promises with similar characteristics, and disclose the description and amount of the grouped promises, including the types of conditions.

Investments

Nonprofits are required to disclose the carrying amount of investments by type (e.g., equity, debt) for each period presented in the statement of financial position. For the current year, the nonprofit will also disclose any significant concentration of market risk (e.g., all investments being from a particular industry or geography).

PP&E

Nonprofits should disclose their *capitalization threshold* (i.e., the threshold over which items are capitalized versus expensed) and the method of valuing PP&E.

Collections

Finally, nonprofits should describe their capitalization policy regarding collection items (capitalization, prospective capitalization, or no capitalization). For items not recognized on the face of the statement of financial position, nonprofits must report the amount capitalized for items such as works of art that do not meet the definition of collection and therefore require capitalization. If the nonprofit elects not to capitalize its collection, it should describe the collection and its significance, as well as the nonprofit's stewardship policies.

Nonprofits should also disclose their organizational policy for the proceeds from items sold or otherwise *deaccessioned* (i.e., used for the purchase of new items for collection, used for direct care, or both). If it permits the funds to be used for direct care, then the nonprofit should disclose its definition of direct care.

PRESENTATION

In preparing reports for a board presentation, it's important to consider the sequence and grouping of assets. Assets are reported either by sequencing them in terms of liquidity or by classifying current and noncurrent assets. Additional relevant information about liquidity, maturity of assets, and any related restrictions can be provided in the notes, which helps the user better understand the financial flexibility of the nonprofit.

As a general rule, restrictions from donors apply to the net asset accounts only. However, to assist the user in understanding the restrictions, cash or other assets that have donor-imposed restrictions that limit their use to long-term purposes should not be classified as assets without restrictions. Assets do not need to be disaggregated on the basis of donor restrictions if available for current use (i.e., cash available for current use does not have to be separate from cash that has restrictions that is also available for current use).

A typical balance sheet contains a list of the major classes of an organization's assets and a total of all the organization's assets. Some organizations will provide more detailed subtotals, like current versus noncurrent assets (differentiating the period of time the assets will be used). But the minimum subtotal will be total net assets followed by all of its major liabilities. This is typically done in order of maturity, with those due sooner at the top and those due many years in the future at the bottom. Again, these can have a number of different subtotals, but the standards require a total of all liabilities.

The liability section is followed by the net asset categories. The minimum classification for net assets is *net assets without donor restrictions*, *net assets with donor restrictions*, and *total net assets*. Many organizations voluntarily choose to present more detailed information. Some nonprofits will break down net assets between those that cannot be spent by the organization due to donor stipulation and those not currently available for the nonprofit to use because of a donor stipulation related to using the funds for a particular purpose or activity or because of a timing restriction. Net assets without donor restrictions can be further disaggregated into undesignated net assets and net assets with board designation. This further disaggregation is not required but provides additional information for users.

The final total required is the *total liabilities and net assets*. This total should equal the total amount of the total assets. The equation for the statement of financial position is *assets – liabilities = net assets*. Reorganized, the equation could also read *assets = liabilities + net assets*. If the statement of financial position doesn't balance, we know there is an error in financial reporting.

EXAMPLE FINANCIAL STATEMENTS

Classified

Here is an example of the Financial Accounting Foundation's (FAF) statement of financial position.[9] The FAF is the parent organization of the FASB.

Statements of Financial Position

For the years ended December 31 (dollars in thousands)	2020	2019
Current assets:		
Cash and cash equivalents	$ 7,097	$ 4,605
Short-term investments (Note 5)	9,278	9,250
Accounting support fee, publishing, and other receivables (net of allowance for doubtful accounts of $101 and $56)	7,303	6,273
Prepaid expenses and all other current assets	1,144	1,278
Total current assets	24,822	21,406
Noncurrent assets:		
Reserve Fund investments (Note 5)	62,595	60,925
Assets held in trust (Note 6)	3,167	2,517
Operating lease right-of-use assets (Note 8)	1,922	2,994
Furniture, equipment, software, and leasehold improvements, net (Note 7)	5,862	3,824
Total noncurrent assets	73,546	70,260
Total assets	$ 98,368	$ 91,666
Current liabilities:		
Accounts payable and accrued expenses	$ 3,005	$ 1,656
Accrued payroll and related benefits	1,460	1,066
Operating lease liability—current (Note 8)	1,648	1,657
Unearned publication and other deferred revenues	6,501	6,766
Total current liabilities	12,614	11,145
Noncurrent liabilities:		
Accrued pension costs (Note 6)	575	646
Accrued postretirement health care costs (Note 6)	1,001	1,138
Operating lease liability—long term (Note 8)	1,211	2,797
Other liabilities (Note 6)	3,167	2,517
Total noncurrent liabilities	5,954	7,098
Total liabilities	18,568	18,243
Net assets—without donor restrictions		
Designated by the Board for Reserve Fund (Notes 3 and 5)	62,595	60,925
Undesignated	17,205	12,498
Total net assets without donor restrictions	79,800	73,423
Total liabilities and net assets	$ 98,368	$ 91,666

See accompanying notes to these financial statements.

As you can see, they have a December 31 year end. They have chosen to issue a classified balance sheet, which means they segregate their assets and liabilities between *current* and *noncurrent.* FASB does not have any net assets with donor restrictions, but they do choose to disaggregate their net assets without donor restrictions between *designated* and *undesignated.* You can also see the note at the bottom that informs the reader to read the related notes to the financial statements.

Unclassified

Here is an example of Elon University's financial statements.[10] As a private university, Elon is required to follow nonprofit GAAP.

ELON UNIVERSITY
CONSOLIDATED STATEMENTS OF FINANCIAL POSITION
May 31, 2021 and 2020

	2021	2020
ASSETS:		
Cash and cash equivalents	$ 45,900,225	$ 39,017,777
Accounts receivable, net	6,549,098	4,477,634
Prepaid expenses and other assets	4,223,812	4,830,777
Deposits with bond trustee	47,800,270	-
Contributions receivable, net	3,309,492	6,462,194
Investments	476,893,373	365,748,368
Loans to students, net	1,671,941	2,082,805
Construction in progress	11,973,187	2,739,179
Property and equipment, net	455,598,987	468,810,550
Total Assets	$ 1,053,920,385	$ 894,169,284
LIABILITIES:		
Accounts payable	$ 6,203,529	$ 2,767,656
Accrued liabilities	19,576,540	17,802,657
Student deposits	6,552,845	13,588,651
Deferred revenue	8,314,659	7,497,764
Other liabilities	19,070,828	18,222,343
Obligation under capital leases	10,563,801	10,933,404
Notes payable	-	1,100,000
Bonds payable, net	205,893,294	170,068,089
Obligation under interest rate swap agreements	1,880,538	3,650,995
U.S. Government advances for student loans	1,823,259	2,262,461
Total Liabilities	279,879,293	247,894,020
NET ASSETS:		
Without Donor Restrictions		
Undesignated	410,317,723	369,001,639
Designated by the Board for endowment	121,176,514	95,537,037
With Donor Restrictions	242,546,855	181,736,588
Total Net Assets	774,041,092	646,275,264
Total Liabilities and Net Assets	$ 1,053,920,385	$ 894,169,284

The accompanying notes are an integral part of these consolidated financial statements.

Like many universities, Elon has a May 31 fiscal year end. Elon chooses not to provide a classified balance sheet. Instead, assets are listed in order of liquidity (ease of converting to cash), and liabilities are listed in order of maturity. The net asset classes report on the required totals.

Both examples provide users with information, and the note disclosures provide more detailed information about the elements in the financial statement. The FASB tries to provide enough flexibility so that nonprofits can report financial information in the most meaningful way for their intended users.

CHAPTER 5

FUNCTIONAL EXPENSES

FUNCTIONAL EXPENSES

One unique area of accounting for nonprofits is the requirement to report *functional expenses* (i.e., expenses grouped according to the purpose for which costs are incurred). Because nonprofits are mission driven, donors often like to see how the funds they donate are being spent. To help donors and other users assess service efforts, GAAP requires nonprofits to provide details of expenses by both nature and function.

Nonprofits have a choice in how this information is displayed. Some nonprofits create a statement of functional expenses and display the required information as a separate financial statement with the statement of activities, statement of cash flows, and statement of financial position. Others elect to show the required information as a note disclosure. In some scenarios, nonprofits with fewer programs may elect to provide the additional information on the statement of activities. The information provided is the same regardless of the format of presentation.

MEET JAYDEN

Jayden has been the controller at the local homeless shelter for five years, during which time the downturn in the economy has really stretched the organization. Prior to working at the homeless shelter, Jayden worked in public accounting as an auditor who specialized in nonprofits. He was so moved by the work of his clients that he accepted a role at the homeless shelter when the previous controller retired. He is passionate about the nonprofit's mission and works closely with the development department and others. The shelter does not have a lot of resources, so in addition to supervising the staff accountant, named Kai, Jayden is also responsible for overseeing IT and operations.

Natural vs. Functional Classification

Natural classification is grouping expenses by the kinds of economic benefits received. Natural classifications often look like general ledger categories. Examples of natural classifications include salaries, supplies, utilities, and depreciation.

The same expenses are also shown by functional classification, where they are grouped according to the purpose for which the cost is incurred. The primary classifications are *program* (i.e., expenses incurred related to the mission of the organization) and *supporting activities* (i.e., costs related to overhead and fundraising).

Some expenses might be shown in the statement of activities in a category other than their natural classification. For example, the cost of renting a facility may be shown as a direct benefit to donors for a special event. When reporting in the analysis of functional and natural expenses, those costs should be shown in their natural classification (rental costs).

Some expenses are never shown in the statement of functional expenses. For example, the investment expenses that are netted against investment return, which are shown in the revenue and gains in the statement of activities, are therefore not included in the statement of functional expenses. In addition, unrealized gains and losses from available-for-sale debt securities and several pension-related gains and losses that are reported in the statement of activities for nonprofits are excluded from the functional expense analysis.

USE OF SOFTWARE

Jayden has been asked to set up an additional general ledger account to track expenses related to a new fundraising event. The event will include a silent auction and meal. The shelter tracks the costs related to each event in a separate ledger account. The ledger has accounts and sub accounts in order to be as granular as possible. Expenses have a first-level disaggregation between operating and non-operating. Then, within operating, they are broken down into salaries, employee benefits, payroll taxes, professional fees, and so on. Then within these groupings, the general ledger further disaggregates employee benefits (e.g., medical insurance, dental insurance, life insurance, long-term disability, and workers compensation). When coding invoices, each invoice must be coded to the most disaggregated category.

In addition, the general ledger software uses classes to track functional expense classification. There is a code for each program, as well as the different supporting activities. The person who purchased the good or service codes all the invoices, and their manager approves them. The accounts payable staff will flag invoices that appear to be miscoded or missing coding. However, the payroll system will automatically charge some costs, such as salaries to salary expense. When financial statements are prepared, Jayden reviews the different line items and reclassifies the salary into the cost of the event for presentation and evaluation purposes. This helps the nonprofit to evaluate the profitability of the event by reporting all costs, including salaries, in the expenses. However, when he creates the functional expense statement, he will leave those costs in salaries expense.

Tracing vs. Allocation

Some costs can be directly traced to a particular category. For example, a worker who only works in one program and spends 100 percent of their time working with program beneficiaries will have 100 percent of their salary charged to program activities. If a counselor who works for a nonprofit that focuses on programs for youth works only for a particular after-school program, then 100 percent of their pay will be charged directly to that program.

However, when preparing the analysis to show expenses by both function and nature, some of the costs will need to be allocated between functional expense classifications. For example, if a staff person spends 25 percent of their time on fundraising, 25 percent of their time on accounting, and 50 percent of their time serving program recipients, their salary would be allocated 25 percent to fundraising, 25 percent to management and general, and 50 percent to program services.

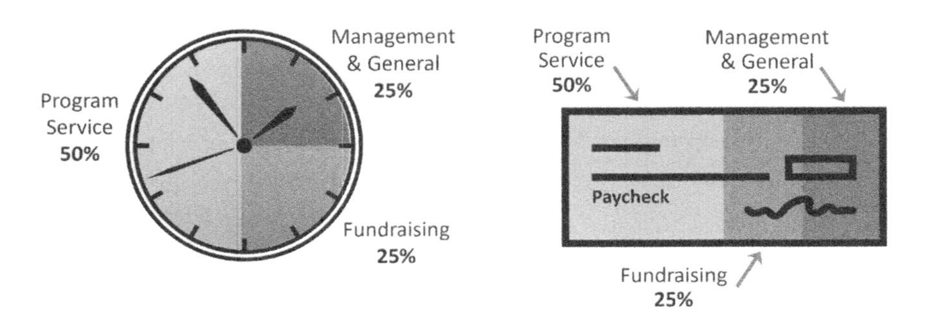

There are many ways to determine these percentages. A nonprofit might have employees track their time by function so they can directly trace their hours to the correct classification, allowing the analysis to be exact. In a given workweek, as the individual's time fluctuates between focus, their time would be accurately reported. For some organizations, tracking time at this level is not feasible. As a result, they will estimate the time based on time studies or interviews with staff. When tracking is not cost prohibitive, it is the preferred method because it offers organizations the most accurate way to trace the costs to the correct function.

Other costs, such as utilities, also need to be allocated. Often, nonprofits use square footage to make this allocation. The use of estimates to determine functional expense categories requires the nonprofit to have sufficient evidence to support the categories. Reporting information about the functional classification of expenses may require the allocation of costs that benefit two or more functions.

Entities that use allocation percentages for their estimates should regularly review the estimates to ensure they are still accurate. For example, if there is a new employee that increases the headcount or a space is rearranged, the old percentages might no longer be accurate. A common audit finding for nonprofits is using percentages for which there is no reasonable basis.

ALLOCATION

Jayden encourages all invoices to be coded with an expense class, which makes it easy for him to prepare the statement of functional expenses. As there are very few employees at the shelter, employees track their time by program in an excel spreadsheet. The spreadsheet has the days of the week as columns and rows for each program, as well as supporting activities. Most professional services, postage, printing, food, and housing costs are directly chargeable to the related program. On the other hand, costs such as insurance, utilities, and telephones have to be allocated. Utilities are allocated based on square footage of the headquarters building. Insurance and telephone costs are allocated based on head count. Each year Jayden updates the percentages for changes in headcount.

Board Best Practices

For many nonprofits, the allocation of functional expenses is one of the significant risks frequently identified by an auditor. Because of the importance of the functional expenses to users and the inability to trace these items, the auditor will often spend time understanding management's methodology for tracking expenses and how estimates are determined.

The board should be equally concerned about the accuracy of the functional expense allocation. It is important that the allocation percentages are valid and have a methodology to support them. The board should regularly make evaluations to see if there are better ways to track or determine allocation percentages. Having strong internal controls to prevent management bias in estimating functional expense allocation is very important. If the head of finance is the one determining the allocation, the board should review the allocation and methodology to ensure that there is no management bias and there is proper support for the expenses and the allocation. If management changes methodology frequently without good explanation or has little support for the percentages, this could be an indicator of error or even fraud.

In organizations that are receiving an annual audit, it's important to have a conversation with the auditor about the methodology and how management tracks expenses. You may learn best practices that will help improve financial reporting. In organizations that are not receiving an annual audit, the board is the oversight function, and functional expenses should be carefully scrutinized.

PROGRAM SERVICES

Program services are defined as "The activities that result in goods and services being distributed to beneficiaries, customers, or members that fulfill the purposes or mission for which the not-for-profit entity (NFP) exists. Those services are the major purpose for and the major output of the NFP and often relate to several major programs."[1]

University programs may include instruction, academic support, research, and hospital services. Colleges that do not have related hospital or research focuses may just have instruction and academic support.

Some organizations use geographic locations to look at their programs. The number of categories of programs is at the discretion of the organization. Most organizations have more than one program, but it is possible to have only one program.

Displaying expenses by program allows donors and other users to understand how the entity spends their resources at the program level. You can also see the types of expenses each program generates. Trend analysis can also be interesting to donors who wish to see which programs are receiving an increasing share of expenses over time.

Number of Programs

Nonprofits often struggle with determining the number of programs to identify. They may consider quantitative factors, but internal measures and budgets can be very helpful as well. How does the nonprofit measure its impact? How does it evaluate its programs? These questions can help an organization identify the number of programs. When a new program is started, it can be added to the functional expense breakout.

Nonprofits have a lot of discretion in determining their programs. However, they should understand that users of the financial statements consider this information to be a key way to evaluate the effectiveness and efficiency of a nonprofit.

When identifying programs, nonprofits must consider their objectives: who is being served, whether there are multiple geographies, different services being offered, and so on. Often, looking at fundraising materials or programmatic promotional materials (i.e., information for individuals who use the nonprofit's services) can be helpful in identifying programs. The last consideration is how the organization budgets and who has ultimate responsibility for programs.

Board Best Practices

The determination of the number of programs and identification of programs is important for ensuring users have a good understanding of the work of the nonprofit. The board should annually review the program identification with management and determine if there are any changes needed to the programs identified. They should also review the disclosures related to the programs to ensure they clearly describe the purpose of each program and its impact.

PROGRAM SERVICES

When Jayden first joined the shelter, there were only three programs: advocacy, housing, and food services. Housing and food services relate to how the shelter helps meet the immediate needs of the homeless, including providing temporary housing, while advocacy includes the executive director's work with state and local officials on policies affecting the homeless, including advocating for access to housing, jobs, schools, and support services. However, two years ago there was an uptick in youth staying at the shelter. As a result, the shelter expanded its services to provide a children's program for those who were not yet school aged so their parents could look for work. During the summer, there is a full summer program for all children that is primarily funded through grants. This past year, the shelter added a job-training program. Many of the shelter's residents were actively looking for work but lacked the skills needed in the current economy. The job-training program includes courses on résumé building, technology, financial literacy, networking, and workplace communication. These courses are primarily facilitated by volunteers. Because of the importance of the program, the board voted to create a separate program for tracking purposes. Jayden is very proud of how the organization continues to grow and address the needs of the homeless.

SUPPORT

While many donors may wish all of their funds would go directly to support the mission of the nonprofit, nonprofits could not operate without their supporting activities. Supporting activities are all other activities that are not program services. Nonprofits need support in areas such as development and accounting in order to operate. While nonprofits do not exist to generate profit, they do have to operate like a business and meet regulatory and legal requirements.

Having an executive director that is excellent at organizing programs, generating donations, and motivating staff helps ensure the survivability of the organization. Organizations that invest too little in supporting activities may over-rely on volunteers and eventually run out of steam. Entities that have antiquated systems that require significant effort of the staff are not using staff time in the best way possible. However, investing in the proper software would increase depreciation charged to support, so the nonprofit continues to use staff in a way that doesn't bring about the best results and often leads to turnover. There are many studies on what is referred to as "the starvation cycle."[2] Routinely being so lean that you are inefficient or create an unfriendly environment can be very damaging to an organization. While the nonprofit should focus on its mission, supporting activities play an important role.

Supporting activities are typically lumped into three categories—*management and general activities*, *fundraising activities*, and *membership-development activities.*

Management and General

Management and general activities are defined as "Supporting activities that are not directly identifiable with one or more program, fundraising, or membership-development activities." They are basically the catch-all and include costs for the accounting department, running payroll, and general overhead, such as the human resources function.

Management and general activities include salaries and expenses of management and governance (including the board). Again, some staff may split their time between program and support.

MANAGEMENT AND GENERAL

The board carefully monitors the management and general bucket to ensure funds are being used as efficiently as possible. Half of the executive director's salary is charged to management and general. The other half is split between fundraising and advocacy. Jayden's and Kai's salaries are charged to management and general, as is the salary of the human resources manager. The cost of the annual audit is directly charged to management and general. On the other hand, utilities and telephone costs are allocated based on head count.

The board reviews the head count and allocations each year prior to the board meeting to approve the financials. Jayden provides detailed explanations for each allocation and summarizes the key items in each natural classification.

Fundraising

Fundraising activities are defined as "Activities undertaken to induce potential donors to contribute money, securities, services, materials, facilities, other assets, or time."[3] As many nonprofits are primarily supported by donations, having a development team who can work on activities like identifying potential donors and planning special events allows the organization to generate more revenue in the long term.

Fundraising costs include fundraising materials, maintaining donor lists, and grant-writing functions. GAAP requires that nonprofits disclose total fundraising expenses. A common question asked around fundraising activities is whether a nonprofit is *required* to have fundraising expenses. While it is unusual for a nonprofit, there are those who do not incur significant costs for fundraising.

- Many churches do not have significant costs to fundraise because members automatically provide regular funding.
- Some nonprofits, such as the American Red Cross, have excellent name recognition and may receive regular donations from the public without significant fundraising costs.
- Some nonprofits use volunteers to call prospective donors. My daughter's school asks parents to call other parents (and grandparents and alumni) each year for the annual campaign. This significantly reduces the costs of fundraising for the school.

TRACKING FUNDRAISING

Jayden works carefully with the development manager to track fundraising expenses. As the shelter wants to ensure that any funds that are spent on fundraising generate a significant return, Jayden tracks each fundraiser with a separate general ledger code and then even further disaggregates by types of costs. The funds generated by each fundraiser are also tracked separately so that an analysis of effectiveness can be performed.

Membership Development

The third type of activity that falls under supporting activities applies to nonprofits that have members. Associations that exist to support a particular membership will track the costs related to membership separately. *Membership-development activities* "include soliciting for prospective members and membership dues, membership relations, and similar activities."[4] Nonprofits should carefully evaluate whether there is a significant benefit connected to membership, and whether an expense might actually qualify as fundraising instead. For example, if a zoo were trying to sell memberships by printing flyers and T-shirts, the costs would be classified as fundraising, as there would be no real membership benefit. On the other hand, the salaries for membership-services individuals who are responsible for assisting members with questions about their membership or supporting members would be classified as a membership-development activity.

Nonprofits can choose to have more categories to describe their supporting activities. For example, some nonprofits will segregate out facility rental costs in the costs of direct benefits to donors.

Board Best Practices

Because of the value that the functional expense classifications bring to the user, the board should review the overall allocation for reasonableness and to identify trends that may indicate that the organization has started to spend in ways inconsistent with its purpose or mission. The amounts should reflect the board's understanding of the organization.

EXAMPLE FINANCIAL STATEMENTS

Single Program

Here are some examples of how to present functional expenses. Birmingham Zoo, Inc., presents their functional expenses in a stand-alone financial statement.[5] As you can see from the financial statement, they show only a single program, then they show their support (fundraising and management and general). In this scenario, the nonprofit shows the functions along the top and the natural classifications as rows.

BIRMINGHAM ZOO, INC.
STATEMENTS OF FUNCTIONAL EXPENSES
FOR THE YEAR ENDED DECEMBER 31, 2020

	Program Services	Management and General	Fund Raising	Total
Salaries and wages	$ 3,978,025	$ 163,301	$ 256,007	$ 4,397,333
Administration	-	64,677	-	64,677
Animal acquisitions	10,766	-	-	10,766
Animal exhibits	789	-	-	789
Animal management	437,384	-	-	437,384
Animal tracks	4,308	-	-	4,308
Bank and credit card processing fees	116,853	19,168	-	136,021
Computer	73,020	7,565	53,034	133,619
Conservation	98,693	-	-	98,693
Continuing education/conventions	6,184	579	578	7,341
Depreciation and amortization	1,969,786	-	-	1,969,786
Dues and subscriptions	52,340	302	1,201	53,843
Employee benefits	409,182	29,207	17,589	455,978
Equipment expense	22,725	-	-	22,725
Equipment rental	7,240	2,440	2,440	12,120
Insurance	219,061	3,388	3,388	225,837
Interest	38,521	-	-	38,521
Legal and accounting	-	23,471	-	23,471
Marketing	38,182	-	-	38,182
Miscellaneous	352	200	12,391	12,943
Payroll taxes	282,126	12,539	18,808	313,473
Postage and printing	24,122	1,838	8,523	34,483
Professional consulting	67,110	-	-	67,110
Repairs and maintenance	356,643	-	-	356,643
Security	108,351	-	-	108,351
Signage and graphics	4,201	120	3,573	7,894
Social and special events	112,070	-	59,623	171,693
Summer camps and other programs	52,600	-	-	52,600
Supplies	104,073	9,630	3,312	117,015
Taxes and licenses	29,269	20,715	-	49,984
Travel and meals	4,931	1,824	881	7,636
Uniforms	2,954	-	-	2,954
Utilities	811,539	13,512	12,808	837,859
Volunteers	2,413	-	-	2,413
Total Expenses	$ 9,445,813	$ 374,476	$ 454,156	$ 10,274,445

BIRMINGHAM ZOO, INC.
STATEMENTS OF FUNCTIONAL EXPENSES
FOR THE YEAR ENDED DECEMBER 31, 2019

	Program Services	Management and General	Fund Raising	Total
Salaries and wages	$ 4,124,776	$ 174,299	$ 450,683	$ 4,749,758
Administration	-	73,159	-	73,159
Animal acquisitions	120,679	-	-	120,679
Animal exhibits	10,837	-	-	10,837
Animal management	510,513	-	-	510,513
Animal tracks	33,245	-	-	33,245
Bank and credit card processing fees	166,410	23,402	-	189,812
Computer	95,922	8,773	65,851	170,546
Conservation	150,376	-	-	150,376
Continuing education/conventions	26,300	2,284	5,198	33,782
Depreciation and amortization	1,803,793	-	-	1,803,793
Dues and subscriptions	24,311	24,950	1,638	50,899
Employee benefits	436,390	40,061	18,712	495,163
Equipment expense	47,030	-	2,776	49,806
Equipment rental	6,684	2,332	2,332	11,348
Insurance	190,661	2,948	2,948	196,557
Interest	87,070	-	-	87,070
Loss on disposal of fixed assets	5,996	-	-	5,996
Legal and accounting	-	26,004	-	26,004
Marketing	161,880	-	14,902	176,782
Miscellaneous	2,219	7,824	9,769	19,812
Payroll taxes	303,935	13,974	31,441	349,350
Postage and printing	45,251	2,650	30,829	78,730
Professional consulting	70,257	-	-	70,257
Repairs and maintenance	516,517	-	-	516,517
Security	80,937	-	-	80,937
Signage and graphics	10,035	-	5,404	15,439
Social and special events	349,488	-	168,300	517,788
Summer camps and other programs	106,921	-	-	106,921
Supplies	195,957	17,897	2,560	216,414
Taxes and licenses	26,095	22,372	125	48,592
Travel and meals	15,133	6,239	4,169	25,541
Uniforms	8,455	-	-	8,455
Utilities	1,179,930	16,280	15,875	1,212,085
Volunteers	5,178	-	-	5,178
Total Expenses	$ 10,919,181	$ 465,448	$ 833,512	$ 12,218,141

See independent auditors' report and accompanying notes to financial statements.

Separate Financial Statement

Ronald McDonald House Charities also uses a separate financial statement to display their expenses categorized by function and nature.[6] They show their four program activities and then a total for all programs, followed by their supporting activities as columns along the top. They show a complete set of information for the current year and then show the prior year below in a separate table with a complete set of information.

RONALD MCDONALD HOUSE CHARITIES, INC.
STATEMENTS OF FUNCTIONAL EXPENSES
YEARS ENDED DECEMBER 31, 2020 AND 2019

(In Thousands)

Year Ended December 31, 2020	Ronald McDonald House	Ronald McDonald Family Room	Ronald McDonald Care Mobile	RMHC Local Chapter Grants and Support	Total Support of RMHC Local Chapters	Other Programs	Total Program Services	Management and General	Fundraising	Cost of Direct Benefits to Donors	Total
Grants	$ 3,271	$ 654	$ 70	$ 35,964	$ 39,959	$ -	$ 39,959	$ -	$ -	$ -	$ 39,959
Professional fees	-	-	30	2,800	2,830	-	2,830	1,065	2,026	-	5,921
Donated services and occupancy	-	-	-	2,532	2,532	-	2,532	1,836	1,211	-	5,579
Meetings, education, and training	-	-	-	48	48	-	48	1	58	-	107
Travel, meals, and entertainment	-	-	-	145	145	-	145	24	31	-	200
Advertising	-	-	-	-	-	-	-	35	1,150	-	1,185
Other	-	-	40	3,757	3,797	-	3,797	346	1,583	-	5,726
TOTAL EXPENSES	$ 3,271	$ 654	$ 140	$ 45,246	$ 49,311	$ -	$ 49,311	$ 3,307	$ 6,059	$ -	$ 58,677

(In Thousands)

Year Ended December 31, 2019	Ronald McDonald House	Ronald McDonald Family Room	Ronald McDonald Care Mobile	RMHC Local Chapter Grants and Support	Total Support of RMHC Local Chapters	Other Programs	Total Program Services	Management and General	Fundraising	Cost of Direct Benefits to Donors	Total
Grants	$ 6,035	$ 916	$ 1,047	$ 25,957	$ 33,955	$ 2,018	$ 35,973	$ -	$ -	$ -	$ 35,973
Professional fees	-	-	20	2,259	2,279	50	2,329	692	1,452	-	4,473
Donated services and occupancy	-	-	-	2,145	2,145	-	2,145	1,675	1,022	-	4,842
Meetings, education, and training	-	-	-	270	270	-	270	33	384	563	1,250
Travel, meals, and entertainment	-	-	-	1,091	1,091	3	1,094	103	123	477	1,797
Advertising	-	-	-	398	398	-	398	76	684	-	1,158
Other	-	-	40	4,339	4,379	-	4,379	520	1,821	-	6,720
TOTAL EXPENSES	$ 6,035	$ 916	$ 1,107	$ 36,459	$ 44,517	$ 2,071	$ 46,588	$ 3,099	$ 5,486	$ 1,040	$ 56,213

Footnote

The Bill & Melinda Gates Foundation opts to present their analysis in a footnote. They use geographic analysis for their functions, separating the United States from their global programs.[7] They also show a category for programmatic support (salaries for individuals involved in programs).

Analysis of Expenses

The Foundation's functional expenses, displayed by natural expense classification, for the years ended December 31, 2020 and 2019 are summarized in the tables below. The tables list all expenses on an accrual basis.

	Program expenses					
December 31, 2020	Global programs	U.S. program	Other charitable programs	Programmatic support	Management and general	Total expense by natural classification
Grants	$ 3,294,035	546,840	84,430	-	-	3,925,305
Direct charitable contracts	455,767	73,565	30,221	-	-	559,553
Total	3,749,802	620,405	114,651	-	-	4,484,858
Compensation and benefits	291,328	43,730	23,385	39,993	83,524	481,960
Other support and administrative	34,014	2,227	5,004	23,423	155,612	220,280
Total	$ 4,075,144	666,362	143,040	63,416	239,136	5,187,098

Unique Presentation

Another unique presentation that has been used for the statement of functional expenses is to invert the rows and columns. The natural classification shows as columns, and the functional classification is shown as rows. GAAP does not prescribe how the information is presented. It just requires nature and function in one place, as seen in this hypothetical nonprofit's statement of functional expenses here.

Wonderful World Giving Group
CONSOLIDATED STATEMENT OF FUNCTIONAL EXPENSES
For the year ended December 31, 20XX
(In thousands of U.S. dollars)

	Salaries, Benefits, & Taxes	Professional Services	Conference, Travel, Staff Development	Grants	Occupancy, Shipping, & Supplies	Total Expenses
Program Services						
Program A	$3,800	$1,600	$385	$12,000	$180	$17,965
Program B	$2,500	$2,400	$420	$9,780	$20	$15,120
Program C	$30,000	$2,050	$1,950	$55,000	$800	$89,800
Program D	$1,500	$7,550	$215	$16,500	$200	$25,965
Other Programs	$1,300	$1,000	$330	$1,220	$100	$3,950
Total Program Services	$39,100	$14,600	$3,300	$94,500	$1,300	$152,800
Support Services						
General & Admin.	$4,500	$4,000	$500	$0	$900	$9,900
Fundraising	$3,800	$250	$300	$0	$800	$5,150
Total Support Services	$8,300	$4,250	$800	$0	$1,700	$15,050
Total Expenses	**$47,400**	**$18,850**	**$4,100**	**$94,500**	**$3,000**	**$167,850**

ALLOCATION

Natural expenses can often be used for multiple functional categories. The general rule is to allocate those costs across the functional categories. However, as we often say in accounting, for every rule there is an exception. This rule specifically applies to costs of activities that include fundraising. When fundraising activities are conducted along with other functions, we refer to those as *joint costs.*

JOINT COSTS

Joint costs (i.e., costs that include fundraising and another function) are required to be charged entirely to fundraising and not allocated unless the organization can meet three criteria—purpose, audience, and content. If the three criteria are met, then costs that are identifiable with a particular function are charged to that function.

Joint costs that meet the three criteria but can't be directly traced are allocated between fundraising and the other function. If even one of the three criteria is not met, then all of the cost of the joint activity is charged to fundraising.

Purpose

The purpose criterion is met if the purpose of the joint activity includes accomplishing program or management and general functions. Sometimes an organization has a special event that serves its program or management and general functions, such as an annual meeting. If at the annual meeting they were to include envelopes at every seat to ask for a donation, the nonprofit would have to evaluate the combined function to determine if the purpose criterion was met.[8]

Audience

The second criterion is the audience. When the audience is selected based on ability or likelihood to donate (e.g., the audience is made up entirely of donors or only wealthy individuals), then the audience criterion fails, and the entire cost is allocated to fundraising.

- If an annual report (management and general and fundraising) is sent to only past donors or individuals over a certain income, then the cost of the annual report should be charged entirely to fundraising, even if most of the cost of the annual report is for general and administrative use.

- On the other hand, if the annual report is sent to everyone in a certain zip code or individuals who are likely to benefit from the services of the organization, then the audience criterion is met.

Content

The final criterion is content. This is met if the joint activity calls for specific action by the recipient that will accomplish the organization's mission or fulfill a management and general responsibility. For example, if a nonprofit wants the United States Congress to pass a law that would positively affect those who are served by their mission, and as part of the joint activity, there is a letter-writing campaign to Congress that provides the names and addresses of the representatives from that state, along with sample verbiage that is a call for specific action, the content criterion is met.

Allocation

Joint costs should be allocated using a reasonable methodology that is consistently applied. Nonprofits need to closely analyze joint costs to determine if they have been properly disclosed.

DISCLOSURES

If a nonprofit allocates joint costs, it is required to disclose the activities for which joint costs have been incurred. This must include a statement indicating that the costs were allocated and providing the total amount allocated during that period, as well as the portion allocated to each category. Nonprofits are encouraged (but not required) to disclose the amount of joint costs for each kind of joint activity.

Here is an example disclosure created by the AICPA's Not-for-Profit Section.[9] It comes from the Section's Illustrative Financial Statements for a fictious nonprofit, "Save Our Charities." The Section offers excellent benefits, including sample financial statements and disclosures like this one.

Note 13 - Joint Costs of Activities That Include a Fund-Raising Appeal

We produce a monthly newsletter that includes programmatic and administrative information, together with a request for contributions in support of our mission. During the years ended December 31, 20X1 and 20X0, the costs of producing the newsletter included joint costs not directly attributable to any single function. Those costs were allocated among the following functional expense categories as follows:

	20X1	20X0
Advisory Program	$ 29,912	$ 27,126
Training Program	7,043	-
Management and general	9,751	10,647
Fundraising and development	41,238	52,311
	$ 87,944	$ 90,084

To learn more about the membership, visit https://us.aicpa.org/membership/sections/not-for-profit-section.html.

Fundraising

If a nonprofit discloses a ratio of fundraising expenses to amounts raised (which is optional), the nonprofit must then also disclose how it computed the ratio.

CHAPTER 6

STATEMENT OF CASH FLOWS

The statement of cash flows is designed to provide users with information about the entity's ability to generate positive cash flows, as well as its ability to pay its bills and debt. The statement explains the change in cash—as well as cash equivalents and restricted cash—during the fiscal year.

When determining whether an investment qualifies as a cash equivalent for inclusion in the statement of cash flows, nonprofits should identify short-term highly liquid investments. Nonprofits must also evaluate if there are any restrictions on even highly liquid short-term investments that would require holding the asset as a long-term investment. In that scenario, if restricted for long-term use, they are not included in the statement of cash flows.

The statement of cash flows segregates cash flow by three categories—operating, investing, and financing.

MEET SEBASTIAN

Sebastian is the director of finance for the City of Anywhere Animal Shelter. He has been with the shelter for five years and enjoys his work. The shelter focuses on finding homes for thousands of animals every year. They also run a foster program. The shelter uses nearly a hundred volunteers throughout the course of the year. In addition, several local veterinarians provide free services for the animals at the shelter. Sebastian loves his job and has the opportunity to work with the shelter staff, which consists of Camila, who is the executive director; Harper, who is the medical director; Zoe, who is the adoptions and operations manager; and Isaiah, who is the volunteer engagement and grants manager. Without the use of volunteers, the shelter wouldn't be able to operate its programs.

Sebastian is preparing for an upcoming board meeting and has been asked to discuss a potential change to the statement of cash flows. The shelter has historically prepared the statement using the indirect method, and the board has asked Sebastian to determine what the additional time and effort would be to prepare the statement of cash flows using the direct method.

Thankfully, the statement of cash flows is currently pretty straightforward. The shelter considers any highly liquid investments with an initial maturity of three months or less to be cash equivalents. Cash is held at the local bank, and the staff keeps $250 in petty cash on hand for emergencies. The petty cash box is locked in Sebastian's office, and anyone who takes funds is required to provide him with a receipt.

OPERATING CASH FLOWS

Common operating cash flows include cash receipts from sales of goods or services. For example, if a museum has a gift shop, cash received from sales from the gift shop is an operating cash flow. Cash paid to purchase materials from suppliers and cash paid to employees are both operating cash flows as well.

While sometimes counterintuitive, receipts of interest and dividends are also operating cash flows—however, consistent with the application restrictions for long-term use, interest or dividends that are restricted by donors for long-term purposes are reported in financing activities.

Other common operating cash flows are payments for taxes and fees, interest, and sales of donated financial assets. When a donor contributes stock that is immediately sold to generate cash, that falls under operating cash flows. But again, if the donor restricted the stock to long-term purposes, the sale would be classified as a financing activity due to the long-term nature.

Cash paid and received in agency transactions is also treated as an operating cash flow. When a donor provides funding to the intermediary organization, for example, that inflow is treated as operating. When the intermediary organization provides the funds to the ultimate beneficiary, that outflow is also operating.

Presentation

Nonprofits can present the operating section of the statement of cash flows using either a direct method or an indirect method. The direct method reports classes of cash receipts and payments. The indirect method is a reconciliation of the change in net assets from the statement of activities under the accrual accounting method to cash flows from operating activities.

The first presentation option, the direct method, looks similar to the presentation for investing and financing activities. It shows the cash inflows and outflows by category, is much easier for the reader to understand, and can help users who are less sophisticated understand the cash flows. The direct method requires tracing of cash flows and can be more difficult to prepare if the computer system is not sophisticated enough to trace the cash flows.

The second presentation option, the indirect method, reconciles the change in net assets by adding back (or subtracting off) any noncash activities and then adjusting for the change in short-term balance sheet accounts. Nonprofits must also reclassify items that should be presented as investing or financing activities that are included in the change in net assets. This method is typically easier to prepare, as it doesn't require tracking cash. The amounts are calculated using the statement of activities and statement of financial position. However, the indirect method is often difficult for the reader to understand. Because it is a reconciliation, less sophisticated users may not understand the results of the reconciliation and therefore may not be able to make informed decisions.

OBTAINING THE OTHER FINANCIAL STATEMENTS

Sebastian has already prepared the statement of activities and the statement of financial position for the year. It's time for him to work on the statement of cash flows.

The draft statement of activities looks as follows:

City of Anywhere Animal Shelter
Statement of Activities
For the Period Ending June 30, 20X2 with Summarized 20X1

	Without Donor Restrictions	With Donor Restrictions	Total	Summarized 20X1
Revenues & Other Support				
Contributions & grants	$1,000,000	$250,000	$1,250,000	$1,000,000
Governmental exchange revenue	$750,000		$750,000	$700,000
Special events	$175,000		$175,000	$150,000
Program service revenue	$250,000		$250,000	$250,000
Gifts in kind	$575,000	$10,000	$585,000	$550,000
Net assets released from restrictions	$200,000	-$200,000	$0	$0
Total Revenues	$2,950,000	$60,000	$3,010,000	$2,650,000
Expenses				
Program	$1,980,000		$1,980,000	$2,000,000
Support				
Management & general	$109,500		$109,500	$125,000
Fundraising	$186,000		$186,000	$175,000
Total Expenses	$2,275,500	$0	$2,275,500	$2,275,500
Other Income/Expenses				
Investment gains (unrealized)	$10,000	$5,000	$15,000	$10,000
Interest expense	-$20,000		-$20,000	-$40,000
Increase in Net Assets	$664,500	$65,000	$729,500	$344,500
Net Assets Beginning of Year	$2,000,000	$395,500	$2,395,500	$2,051,000
Net Assets End of Year	$2,664,500	$460,500	$3,125,000	$2,395,500

The statement of financial position looks like this:

City of Anywhere Animal Shelter
Statement of Financial Position
As of June 30, 20X2 & 20X1

	20X2	20X1
Assets		
Cash	$1,000,000	$900,000
Short-term investments	$215,000	$225,000
Accounts receivable	$10,000	$25,000
Grants receivable	$50,000	$45,000
Refundable advances	$250,000	$120,000
Prepaid expenses	$50,000	$75,000
Inventory	$15,000	$10,000
Property plant & equipment, net	$2,000,000	$2,012,500
Total Assets	**$3,590,000**	**$3,412,500**
Liabilities		
Accounts payable	$10,000	$72,000
Accrued liabilities	$125,000	$245,000
Long-term debt	$330,000	$700,000
Total Liabilities	$465,000	$1,017,000
Net Assets		
Net assets without donor restrictions	$2,664,500	$1,920,500
Net assets with donor restrictions	$460,500	$475,000
Total Net Assets	$3,125,000	$2,395,500
Total Net Assets & Liabilities	**$3,590,000**	**$3,412,500**

DIRECT METHOD

When electing the direct method, entities must have the following subtotals at minimum:

- cash collected from customers
- interest and dividends received
- other operating cash receipts
- cash paid to employees and other suppliers of goods or services
- interest paid
- income taxes paid

- other operating cash payments

However, entities can continue (and are actually encouraged) to provide more detailed categories that are useful to the reader.

Unlike for-profit entities, if a nonprofit elects the direct method, it does not have to provide an indirect reconciliation.

OPERATING CASH FLOWS

Sebastian is reviewing the cash flows of the organization to determine what categories he would use if they switched to the direct method. Based on his initial analysis, he believes the cash flow categories for cash inflows would be cash received from customers for adoptions and medical services, cash received from grants, and cash received for special events. Cash outflows would include cash paid for supplies, employees, interest, and operating expenses. Based on the current financial reporting system, each vendor would need to be tagged with one of these cash flow categories if they were to switch to the direct method.

INDIRECT METHOD

For entities that elect the indirect method, GAAP requires the nonprofit to reconcile the change in net assets back to operating cash flows. Regardless of the methodology used, the total of cash from operating cash flows should be the same.

The indirect method starts with the change in net assets (from the statement of activities). Entities then reconcile the change in net assets by adjusting for changes in short-term assets and liabilities. For example, if accounts receivable increased from the prior year by $100, then the nonprofit recognized $100 more in revenue than it received in cash. In order to reconcile back to cash, the nonprofit reduces change in net assets by $100.

The general rule of thumb is that *increases* in short-term assets are subtracted back and *decreases* in short-term assets are added back. The opposite is true for liabilities—*increases* in short-term assets are added back and *decreases* in short-term assets are subtracted out.

Rule of Thumb		
Short-Term Asset	Increase ↑	**Subtract**
Short-Term Asset	Decrease ↓	**Add**
Short-Term Liability	Increase ↑	**Add**
Short-Term Liability	Decrease ↓	**Subtract**

Now, the changes in net assets are reconciled. Short-term liabilities include accounts payable, payroll liabilities (outside of long-term ones like pension or other post-employment benefits), deferred revenue, and so on. Short-term assets include accounts receivable, some pledges receivable, inventory, and prepaids.

EXPECTATIONS

Note: As the goal of this book is to provide nonprofit board members with financial information to understand the financial statements and ask the right questions, we do not expect most board members to be able to prepare the statement of cash flows. But one of the most common issues CPAs have is that the board can't read the statement of cash flows when prepared on an indirect basis. For this reason, this case study walks you through the process of preparing the statement in hopes of helping it make more sense. Plus, who doesn't want to spend some extra time looking at how animal shelters support cute furry animals?

In addition to changes in short-term assets and liabilities, nonprofits must also add back noncash items like depreciation and amortization that are recognized in the accrual basis. They also add back any gains and losses on sale of PP&E. The full amount received in cash is recognized in the investing section of the statement of cash flows.

INDIRECT METHOD

Sebastian is now ready to prepare the statement of cash flows using the indirect method. He starts by finding the increase in net assets from the statement of activities of $729,500. He then scans the draft functional expenses footnote and statement of activities for noncash items.

The draft functional expense footnote for the current year shows the following:

Note 11: Functional Expenses

	Program	Management & General	Fundraising	Total
Salaries, wages, payroll taxes	$400,000	$50,000	$25,000	$475,000
Food for animals	$200,000			$200,000
Veterinary services	$600,000			$600,000
Medical supplies	$250,000			$250,000
Spay/neuter surgery	$50,000			$50,000
Cost of sales	$10,000			$10,000
Depreciation	$100,000	$10,000	$2,500	$112,500
Dues and licenses	$10,000	$500		$10,500
Advertising	$10,000	$4,000	$75,000	$89,000
Event expenses	$0		$75,000	$75,000
Insurance	$25,000	$7,500	$1,000	$33,500
Occupancy costs	$250,000	$25,000	$5,000	$280,000
Office supplies	$25,000	$5,000	$2,500	$32,500
Professional services	$50,000	$7,500		$57,500
Total Expenses	**$1,980,000**	**$109,500**	**$186,000**	**$2,275,500**

Sebastian notes that he has to add back depreciation expense of $112,500 and the unrealized gain of $15,000.

Next, he focuses his attention on the changes in the statement of financial position. He notes that the investments decreased by $10,000, but he knows that this change includes the unrealized gain. Therefore, the true change in the account is a decrease of $25,000. As a result, Sebastian adds $25,000 to the increase in net assets. He keeps a note on his desk that says, "Increase in short-term assets = subtract, and decrease in short-term assets =

add." The statement has always been an odd one to prepare, and often the board doesn't understand the information provided.

He then goes through each change in short-term assets and adds the decrease in accounts receivable of $15,000 ($25,000 - $10,000), subtracts the increase in the grants of $5,000, subtracts the change in the refundable advance ($130,000), adds the change in prepaids ($25,000), and subtracts the change in inventory ($5,000).

PP&E is a long-term asset, so he'll address that in the investments section. Next, he looks for his short-term liabilities, noting only two accounts payable and accrued expenses. Now that he's dealing with liabilities, he adds increases and subtracts decreases. As both accounts decreased over the prior year, he subtracts $62,000 and $120,000, respectively.

Now it's time to total the operating cash flows, and he notes that operating activities increases a hefty $570,000. The shelter has done well this year, and he is very proud.

City of Anywhere Animal Shelter
Statements of Cash Flow
Year Ended June 30, 20X2

Cash Flows from Operating Activities	
Increase in net assets	$729,500
Depreciation	$112,500
Unrealized gain	-$15,000
Change in investments	$25,000
Change in account receivable	$15,000
Change in grants receivable	-$5,000
Change in refundable advance	-$130,000
Change in prepaids	$25,000
Change in inventory	-$5,000
Change in accounts payable	-$62,000
Change in accrued liabilities	-$120,000
Net Cash Provided by Operating Activities	$570,000

INVESTING CASH FLOWS

Investing cash flows focus on long-term assets and investments. Examples of cash flows from investing activities include buying and selling available-for-sale debt securities, as well as cash received from loan receivables. Other inflows include cash from selling PP&E. Cash from buying PP&E would be an investing outflow. Disbursements for loans made by the nonprofits, payments to buy equity instruments, and cash flows from unrecognized (uncapitalized) collection items are also all investing cash flows.

While operating cash flows can be presented using either the direct or indirect method, the investing section must be presented using the direct method. Investing cash inflows are reported separately from investing cash outflows. Inflows and outflows for each type of cash flow must be presented separately and cannot be netted.

INVESTING ACTIVITIES

The shelter has a very conservative gift acceptance policy. They currently don't accept any gifts that are restricted to long-term use. This helps keep the investments liquid and available as needed. All investments are currently short term and are reported in the operating section. The shelter's only long-term assets are PP&E and include the building and various equipment. During the year, PP&E decreased by $12,500. However, depreciation expense was $112,500. Sebastian notes that there was a purchase of a new X-ray machine during the year of $100,000, so the PP&E increased by $100,000 and then had a noncash decrease of $112,500. Therefore, the true cash flow for investing activities was for the purchase of the X-ray machine, which he records as an outflow of $100,000.

Cash Flows from Investing Activities	
Purchase of PP&E	-$100,000
Net Cash Used by Investing Activities	-$100,000

FINANCING CASH FLOWS

Financing cash flows are linked to how entities finance themselves through long-term borrowings. When a nonprofit pays back amounts borrowed, that is a financing cash flow (any interest is operating). Interest and dividends that are donor restricted for long-term purposes are also financing. Cash from the sale of donated financial assets (e.g., stock) that are immediately sold but the donor restricted the use of the contributed resources to a long-term purpose are reported as financing activities. Principal payments for finance leases are also treated as financing activities.

Nonprofits should recognize proceeds from issuing bonds, notes, mortgages, and any other short-term or long-term borrowing as a financing activity. Receipts that are restricted by donors for long-term purposes of acquiring, constructing, or improving PP&E or establishing a true endowment are also financing activities.

Similar to investing cash flows, the financing section is presented using the direct method. Financing cash inflows should be reported separately from financing cash outflows.

FINANCING CASH FLOW

Sebastian reviews the debt section of the balance sheet and notes that a balloon payment of $370,000 was paid this year, along with interest of $20,000. The interest is recorded in the operating cash flows, so Sebastian records the debt payment of $370,000 as a financing cash outflow.

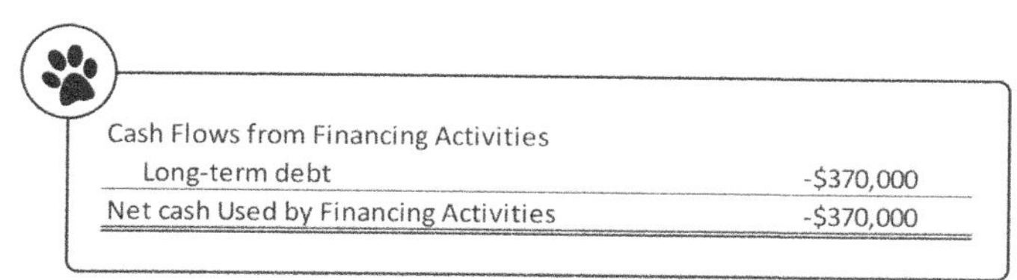

Cash Flows from Financing Activities	
Long-term debt	-$370,000
Net cash Used by Financing Activities	-$370,000

The last step for the statement of cash flows is to reconcile beginning-of-year cash to end-of-year cash. Sebastian notes that at the beginning of the

continued

year, the cash balance was $900,000. He then totals the operating cash inflows of $570,000 and the cash outflows for investing and financing activities of $100,000 and $370,000, respectively. He notes that this ties to his balance per the general ledger for the current year of $1,000,000. It's great to see another year of positive cash flows for the organization and a reduction of debt.

Increase in Cash Flows	$100,000
Cash & Cash Equivalents Beginning of Year	$900,000
Cash & Cash Equivalents End of Year	$1,000,000

Sebastian now has a completed cash flow to provide for the board.

City of Anywhere Animal Shelter
Statements of Cash Flow
Year Ended June 30, 20X2

Cash Flows from Operating Activities	
Increase in net assets	$729,500
Depreciation	$112,500
Unrealized gain	-$15,000
Change in investments	$25,000
Change in account receivable	$15,000
Change in grants receivable	-$5,000
Change in refundable advance	-$130,000
Change in prepaids	$25,000
Change in inventory	-$5,000
Change in accounts payable	-$62,000
Change in accrued liabilities	-$120,000
Net Cash Provided by Operating Activities	$570,000
Cash Flows from Investing Activities	
Purchase of PP&E	-$100,000
Net Cash Used by Investing Activities	-$100,000
Cash Flows from Financing Activities	
Long-term debt	-$370,000
Net cash Used by Financing Activities	-$370,000
Increase in Cash Flows	$100,000
Cash & Cash Equivalents Beginning of Year	$900,000
Cash & Cash Equivalents End of Year	$1,000,000

USAGE

Board Best Practices

The statement of cash flows can be used to look at trends related to where cash is coming from. For example, if the only way a nonprofit is generating cash is through borrowing funds or by selling its headquarters building, that can be very telling of a future issue. If operating cash flows are consistently negative, that is also not a great sign. The board should actively evaluate how the organization is generating cash. Doing so will reveal a lot about the financial health of the organization. If there has been a negative trend in operating cash flows, the organization may need to consider how they will reduce expenditures to compensate. It can also be useful to review the investment policy for liquidity if cash generation is an issue. If an organization's board is proactive, when they see a concerning trend, they can immediately start with a fundraising campaign or adjust spending. Failure to look at how cash is generated can lead to organizations being unable to pay their bills.

DISCLOSURES

Because of the diversity in types of cash equivalents, nonprofits should disclose which items are treated as such. If nonprofits use the indirect method, they should still disclose the amount of interest paid and income taxes paid (if any) during the period.

Sometimes nonprofits finance a purchase of a large item in lieu of using cash. Any investing or financing activities that affect assets or liabilities but do not result in cash receipts or disbursements should be disclosed. For example, if they used a lease agreement to finance the acquisition of equipment, there should be a disclosure—either narratively or in a summarized schedule. Obtaining the right to use a building through a lease is an example of a noncash activity that would be disclosed. This can be presented on the face of the statement or in the notes. Often this is displayed on the same page as the statement of cash flows, but it can also be in the note disclosures.

If a transaction is part cash and part noncash, only the cash portion is displayed in the statement of cash flows.

As the statement of cash flows includes restricted cash and restricted cash equivalents, nonprofits need to disclose information about the nature of restrictions on the use of the cash.

PRESENTATION

While the statement of cash flows works much like a checkbook monitoring cash in and cash out, there are two different options for presentation for operating cash flows. Luckily, there are no differences for investing and financing activities. The nonprofit can choose which method it would like to present.

EXAMPLE FINANCIAL STATEMENTS

Let's take a look at two examples of the statement of cash flows using each method.

Indirect Method

The Foundation for the Carolinas utilizes the indirect method.[1] It starts with the change in net assets from the statement of activities and then adds back noncash items (depreciation, unrealized gains and losses, and noncash contributions). It then adjusts for changes in short-term assets and liabilities.

FOUNDATION FOR THE CAROLINAS
CONSOLIDATED STATEMENTS OF CASH FLOWS
YEARS ENDED DECEMBER 31, 2020 AND 2019

	2020	2019
Cash flows from operating activities:		
Change in net assets	$ 307,457,859	$ 260,447,176
Adjustments to reconcile change in net assets to net cash flows from operating activities:		
Depreciation	425,748	424,306
Realized and unrealized gains on investments	(242,783,591)	(337,179,266)
Contributions and income restricted for investments in endowments	(3,501,268)	(13,126,914)
Noncash contributions - investments	(203,129,083)	(138,975,634)
Noncash contributions - property and equipment	(39,500)	(228,600)
Changes in operating assets and liabilities:		
Accounts receivable	(2,681,401)	(3,162,758)
Contributions receivable, net	5,287,015	20,792,163
Prepaid expenses and inventory	7,400	41,882
Beneficial interest in trust	(1,024,757)	(32,299)
Contributed securities held for sale	(125,011,447)	(4,985,863)
Cash surrender value of life insurance	(145,925)	(205,939)
Fund obligations	1,266,479	(57,489)
Deferred revenue	695,329	(12,979)
Grants payable	8,716,536	(2,837,550)
Amounts held on behalf of others	52,314,916	75,720,199
Annuity obligations	307,288	(536,414)
Net cash flows from operating activities	(201,838,402)	(143,915,979)
Cash flows from investing activities:		
Purchases of property and equipment	(7,182,163)	(8,673,537)
Net sales of investments	179,683,982	89,552,212
Issuance of notes receivable	(7,500,000)	-
Collections of notes receivable	331,559	1,231,388
Net cash flows from investing activities	165,333,378	82,110,063
Cash flows from financing activities:		
Contributions restricted for investment in endowment	3,501,268	13,126,914
Net change in cash and cash equivalents	(33,003,756)	(48,679,002)
Cash and cash equivalents, beginning of year	82,825,077	131,504,079
Cash and cash equivalents, end of year	$ 49,821,321	$ 82,825,077

The accompanying notes to the consolidated financial statements are an integral part of these statements.

Direct Method

On the other hand, the Bill & Melinda Gates Foundation utilizes the direct method.[2] The operating section starts with cash received from the trust and donors and then the cash paid for grants and other expenses.

BILL & MELINDA GATES FOUNDATION

Consolidated Statements of Cash Flows

Years ended December 31, 2020 and 2019

(In thousands)

	2020	2019
Cash flows from operating activities:		
Cash received:		
Contributions from the Trust	$ 6,755,163	5,851,675
Contributions from donors, without restrictions	8,536	6,666
Contributions from donors, with restrictions	156,227	20,455
Other cash received	67,248	55,097
Cash paid:		
Grants	(5,362,313)	(4,686,654)
Direct charitable support	(541,821)	(423,328)
Compensation and benefits	(479,620)	(433,439)
Other expenses	(177,626)	(227,344)
Excise taxes	(1,111)	(485)
Net cash provided by operating activities	424,683	162,643
Cash flows from investing activities:		
Cash received:		
Proceeds from sale of program-related investments	103,131	18,002
Cash paid:		
Funding of program-related investments	(390,914)	(103,335)
Purchases of property and equipment	(53,596)	(39,979)
Net cash used in investing activities	(341,379)	(125,312)
Net increase in cash	83,304	37,331
Cash, beginning of year	75,342	38,011
Cash, end of year	$ 158,646	75,342

See accompanying notes to consolidated financial statements.

Both examples present the investing and financing activities utilizing the direct method as required. Then there is a reconciliation of cash from the beginning of the year to the end of the year, which should tie to the statement of financial position.

While the statement of cash flows focuses on cash, it also requires the nonprofit to present certain noncash transactions at the bottom if applicable. Investing and financing activities that impact assets or liabilities but that do not result in cash receipts or cash payments are disclosed.

CHAPTER 7

RATIOS, TRENDS, AND ANALYSIS

Now that we've covered the basics of the financial statements, the big question is: What story are the statements telling? Individually, each statement tells a piece of the story. With the use of ratios and benchmarking, nonprofit boards can use information in the financial statements to assess the organization's financial stability and determine areas of focus. Ratios can help assess financial health today and also help with strategic planning and budgeting to improve areas of concern. Trends can be evaluated over time to see improvements.

Board Best Practices

It is important that boards evaluate which ratios, KPIs, and other data they want to track. Some boards spend so much time tracking data they lose sight of the mission. This chapter will provide a variety of different ways a board can actively evaluate the organization. Some may be more relevant than others, and over time what gets tracked will need to be changed.

continued

An organization in its infancy may be very focused on cash. As it becomes more stable and has consistent cash flow, other metrics are more appropriate to track. Looking at leading and lagging information is also important. If we look only at information after the fact, all we can do is react. Incorporating leading indicators can help predict changes that can affect the organization and allow the organization to address issues more proactively.

The board should meet regularly and ask management to prepare the ratios or other analysis, as determined by the board, with explanations as to trends, misses, or issues. The board should spend time reviewing these items and carefully considering the appropriate response.

MEET ZARA

Zara is the head of finance at the local hospital. She's been here for just over three years. She's always worked in the healthcare field, but this is her first time working for a hospital that also has a free clinic. She is responsible for the full consolidated financial statements of the hospital. Levi is the accounting manager for the hospital. The hospital is a nonprofit and provides a variety of services for the people in the community. Luna is the accounting supervisor for the free clinic. The free clinic serves the uninsured through grants. Most of the services at the clinic are performed by doctors and nurses from the hospital, who volunteer their time at the clinic. A large number of volunteers assist with the office-related functions as well. Free legal services are provided by a local law firm, and free printing and computer services are provided by a local company. Zara is meeting with Luna and Levi to review their submissions for the board package. Each quarter, they prepare various ratios and KPIs to assist the board in understanding the operations of the two organizations. While they are presented in a consolidated financial statement, the board reviews the analyses separately.

Here is the statement of financial position for the clinic:

Free Medical Clinic
Statement of Financial Position

		As of December 31 20XX
Assets:		
Cash & Cash Equivalents	$	850,000
Contributions Receivable	$	500,000
Inventory	$	10,000
Prepaid Expenses	$	25,000
Investments	$	575,000
PP&E, net	$	5,000,000
Total Assets	***$***	***6,960,000***
Liabilities & Net Assets:		
Accounts Payable	$	100,000
Accrued Wages	$	25,000
Line of Credit	$	120,000
Total Liabilities	**$**	**245,000**
Net Assets:		
Without Donor Restrictions	$	5,750,000
With Donor Restrictions	$	965,000
Total Net Assets	**$**	**6,715,000**
Total Liabilities & Net Assets	***$***	***6,960,000***

This is the statement of financial position for the hospital:

Hospital
Statement of Financial Position

		As of December 31 20XX
Assets:		
Cash & Cash Equivalents	$	150,000,000
Patient Receivables	$	450,000,000
Other Receivables	$	40,000,000
Inventories	$	125,000,000
Other Assets	$	850,000,000
Investments	$	3,000,000,000
PP&E	$	2,000,000,000
Total Assets	***$***	***4,615,000,000***
Liabilities & Net Assets:		
Accounts Payable	$	200,000,000
Accrued Salaries & Wages	$	230,000,000
Estimated Third Party Payor Settlements	$	300,000,000
Other Liabilities	$	32,000,000
Long Term Debt	$	1,250,000,000
Total Liabilities	**$**	**2,012,000,000**
Net Assets:		
Without Donor Restrictions	$	1,750,000,000
With Donor Restrictions	$	853,000,000
Total Net Assets	**$**	**2,603,000,000**
Total Liabilities & Net Assets	***$***	***4,615,000,000***

continued

Here is the statement of activities for the free clinic:

Free Medical Clinic
Statement of Activities

For the year ending December 31, 20XX

	Without Donor Restrictions	With Donor Restrictions	Total
Revenues			
Contributions	$ 1,500,000	$ 50,000	$ 1,550,000
Grant Revenue	$ 100,000	$ 1,500,000	$ 1,600,000
Special Events	$ 500,000	$ -	$ 500,000
Investment Income	$ 100,000	$ -	$ 100,000
Donated Services, Materials & Facilities	$ 5,750,000	$ -	$ 5,750,000
Released from Restrictions	$ 1,000,000	$ (1,000,000)	$ -
Total Revenue	**$ 8,950,000**	**$ 550,000**	**$ 9,500,000**
Expenses			
Program	$ 4,000,000	$ -	$ 4,000,000
Support	$ -	$ -	$ -
Management & General	$ 250,000	$ -	$ 250,000
Fundraising	$ 200,000	$ -	$ 200,000
Total Expenses	**$ 4,450,000**	**$ -**	**$ 4,450,000**
Increase in Net Assets	$ 4,500,000	$ 550,000	$ 5,050,000
Net Assets at Beginning of Year	$ 1,250,000	$ 415,000	$ 1,665,000
Net Assets at End of Year	$ 5,750,000	$ 965,000	$ 6,715,000

This is the statement of activities for the hospital:

Hospital
Statement of Activities

For the year ending December 31, 20XX

	Without Donor Restrictions	With Donor Restrictions	Total
Revenues			
Net Patient Revenue	$ 2,750,000,000	$ -	$ 2,750,000,000
Grants & Contracts	$ 200,000,000	$ 150,000,000	$ 350,000,000
Contributions	$ 50,000,000	$ 600,000,000	$ 650,000,000
Other Revenue	$ 20,000,000	$ -	$ 20,000,000
Released from Restrictions	$ 125,000,000	$ (125,000,000)	$ -
Total Revenues and Support	**$ 3,145,000,000**	**$ 625,000,000**	**$ 3,770,000,000**
Expenses			
Salaries, Wages, Benefits	$ 1,500,000,000	$ -	$ 1,500,000,000
Medical Supplies	$ 1,000,000	$ -	$ 1,000,000
Interest	$ 50,000,000	$ -	$ 50,000,000
Depreciation	$ 150,000,000	$ -	$ 150,000,000
Other Operating Expenses	$ 700,000,000	$ -	$ 700,000,000
Total Expenses	**$ 2,401,000,000**	**$ -**	**$ 2,401,000,000**
Operating Income	**$ 744,000,000**	**$ 625,000,000**	**$ 1,369,000,000**
Non-operating Income			
Investment Income	$ 10,000,000	$ 700,000	$ 10,700,000
Other	$ 2,000,000	$ 200,000	$ 2,200,000
Total non-operating income	$ 12,000,000	$ 900,000	$ 12,900,000
Increase in Net Assets	**$ 732,000,000**	**$ 624,100,000**	**$ 1,356,100,000**
Net Assets at Beginning of Year	$ 1,018,000,000	$ 228,900,000	$ 1,246,900,000
Net Assets at End of Year	$ 1,750,000,000	$ 853,000,000	$ 2,603,000,000

The following is the statement of functional expenses for the clinic:

Free Medical Clinic
Statement of Functional Expenses

For the year ending December 31, 20XX

	Program	Management & General	Fundraising	Total
Wages	$ 1,000,000	$ 75,000	$ 30,000	$ 1,105,000
Payroll Related Expenses	$ 150,000	$ 15,000	$ 6,000	$ 171,000
Accounting	$ 10,000	$ 20,000	$ 8,000	$ 38,000
Advertising	$ -	$ -	$ 34,750	$ 34,750
Consulting	$ -	$ 1,500	$ 5,000	$ 6,500
Dues & Licenses	$ 25,000	$ 1,000	$ 500	$ 26,500
Legal Fees	$ 5,000	$ 1,000	$ 750	$ 6,750
Postage, Printing, Telephone	$ 4,000	$ 7,500	$ 10,000	$ 21,500
Clinic supplies & Pharmaceuticals	$ 700,000	$ -	$ -	$ 700,000
Medical & professional Services	$ 2,000,000	$ -	$ -	$ 2,000,000
Office Expenses	$ 35,000	$ 80,000	$ 55,000	$ 170,000
Depreciation	$ 30,000	$ 20,000	$ 25,000	$ 75,000
Rent Expense (donated)	$ 41,000	$ 29,000	$ 25,000	$ 95,000
Total	**$ 4,000,000**	**$ 250,000**	**$ 200,000**	**$ 4,450,000**

Finally, this is the statement of functional expenses for the hospital:

Hospital
Statement of Functional Expenses

For the year ending December 31, 20XX

	Program	Management & General	Fundraising	Total
Wages	$ 1,000,000,000	$ 200,000,000	$ 50,000,000	$ 1,250,000,000
Payroll Related Expenses	$ 200,000,000	$ 40,000,000	$ 10,000,000	$ 250,000,000
Accounting	$ 5,000,000	$ 15,000,000	$ 10,000,000	$ 30,000,000
Advertising	$ 2,000,000	$ -	$ 5,000,000	$ 7,000,000
Consulting	$ 1,000,000	$ 17,500,000	$ -	$ 18,500,000
Dues & Licenses	$ 2,500,000	$ 100,000	$ -	$ 2,600,000
Legal Fees	$ 1,000,000	$ 5,000,000	$ 2,700,000	$ 8,700,000
Postage, Printing, Telephone	$ 500,000	$ -	$ -	$ 500,000
Medical supplies	$ 1,000,000	$ -	$ -	$ 1,000,000
Office Expenses	$ 1,000,000	$ 8,000,000	$ 2,700,000	$ 11,700,000
Depreciation	$ 120,000,000	$ 20,000,000	$ 10,000,000	$ 150,000,000
Rent Expense	$ 400,000,000	$ 200,000,000	$ 21,000,000	$ 621,000,000
Interest Expense	$ 40,000,000	$ 10,000,000	$ -	$ 50,000,000
Total	**$ 1,774,000,000**	**$ 515,600,000**	**$ 111,400,000**	**$ 2,401,000,000**

RATIO ANALYSIS

While there are many ratios used to evaluate publicly traded companies, not all of them make sense for nonprofits. Nonprofits are mission driven, and unlike for-profit entities, they are not created to generate profits and returns for investors. Selecting ratios specifically for the nonprofit sector is very important. While we'll look at a variety of ratios, the right mix will depend on the individual nonprofit and its subindustry.

A ratio analysis for a hospital will look very different from that of a soup kitchen. So it's best to compare nonprofits to others of a similar size and mission. Nonprofits that have significant exchange revenues will have different ratios than those that rely heavily on donations. We provide some best practices here, but there are no hard-and-fast rules for evaluating ratios.

There are different types of ratios, including liquidity, operating, and spending.

Liquidity Ratios

One of the most important types, *liquidity ratios* help to determine whether the nonprofit has sufficient funds to support its payments.

DAYS CASH ON HAND

The first ratio is the days cash on hand. This ratio helps a nonprofit understand how long they would be able to pay their bills if no additional revenues came in. When COVID hit in 2020, many nonprofits were forced to close their doors due to curfews and stay-at-home orders. Likely, very little cash was coming in. Those who survived were able to continue to pay their bills despite the drop in revenues. It's important for nonprofits to have sufficient reserves.

To calculate days cash on hand, divide the operating expenses (noncash items like depreciation can be removed from operating expenses, as they do not require cash) by 365, and then divide the cash on hand by the result.

$$\text{Days Cash on Hand} = \frac{\text{Cash on Hand}}{\left(\text{Operating Expenses} - \text{Noncash Expenses}\right) \div 365}$$

When evaluating operating expenses, include all items that are expected to reoccur each month (e.g., utilities, rent, salaries). Most nonprofits should try to have at least three to six months of operating expenses on hand in case of an emergency.

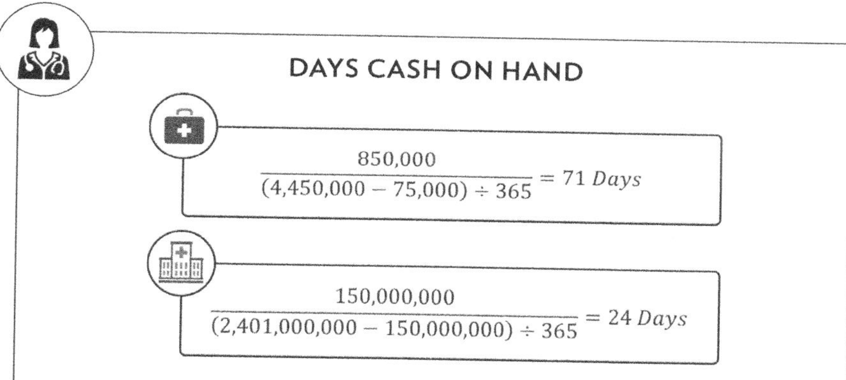

Zara first reviews the information provided by Luna for the clinic. Based on the calculation, days cash on hand is now seventy-one days. The goal of the clinic is to have ninety days on hand. Luna explains that the liquidity policy to hold more cash on hand and only commit to investments when certain cash levels are hit is the primary cause of the improvement. The fact that the organization has significant gifts in kind reduces the need to use its cash and allows it to be more strategic with its funding.

On the other hand, Levi continues to be concerned with the cash on hand for the hospital. He has calculated that the organization only has twenty-four days on hand. There has been a slowdown in collection of receivables for patient services with a mix of late payments from third-party payers. Levi has already communicated with the collections department to see if they can increase their calls to improve the cash standing. Zara notes to discuss this with operations before the board meeting.

CURRENT RATIO

Another useful liquidity ratio, the *current ratio*, evaluates whether the nonprofit has sufficient funds to pay its current obligations.

The ratio is calculated as current assets (cash, inventory, accounts receivable) divided by current liabilities (accounts payable, salaries payable, etc.).

$$Current\ Ratio = \frac{Current\ Assets}{Current\ Liabilities}$$

The goal is to have at least two to three times the amount of current assets as current liabilities. If an entity has more current liabilities than current assets, they are unable to pay their bills as they become due.

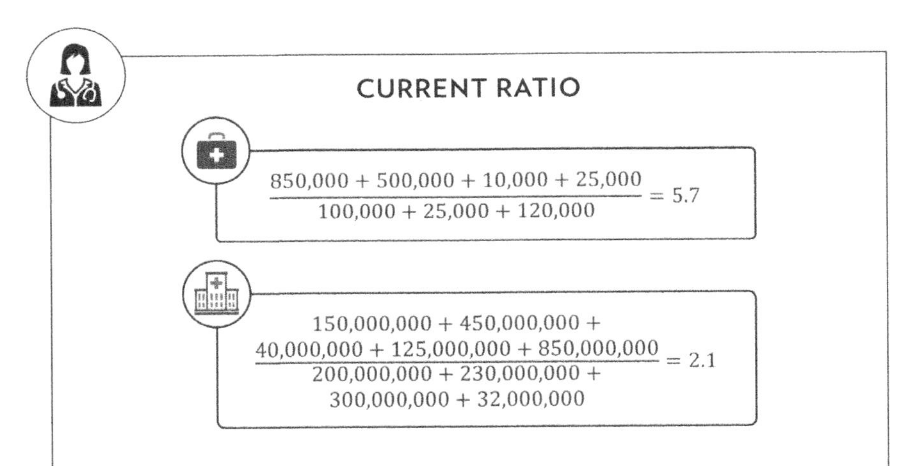

Luna is happy to report another strong ratio for the clinic. Because all of the assets of the organization are short term, with the exception of investments and PP&E, the clinic can very easily cover the liabilities. All liabilities of the clinic are short term, as the clinic has no debt. They occasionally have to draw on their line of credit, but due to the cash on hand, the team had already paid off the line at the beginning of the current year.

> Levi is also pleased with the current ratio for the hospital. While not as high as the clinic, the hospital is reporting a 2.1 current ratio, which indicates that the current assets are double the current liabilities. So long as the current assets convert into cash, there should be no issues with the liquidity of the hospital, despite the low cash count.
>
> Zara is very happy to see improvement in the current ratio for both entities. She knows the board tracks liquidity very carefully.

DEBT COVERAGE RATIO

Another important liquidity ratio, the *debt coverage ratio*, focuses on the ability of the nonprofit to pay its debt.

The debt coverage ratio takes change in net assets and adds back interest and noncash items like depreciation. The adjusted change in net assets is then divided by required debt payments (principal and interest).

$$\text{Debt Coverage Ratio} = \frac{\text{Change in Net Assets} + \text{Noncash Expenses} + \text{Interest on Debt}}{\text{Required Debt Payments}}$$

The goal is to have a higher ratio here to show that there is sufficient coverage of the payments. Sometimes banks will include a minimum ratio in the debt covenants to protect themselves from a situation in which the nonprofit is not able to make payments.

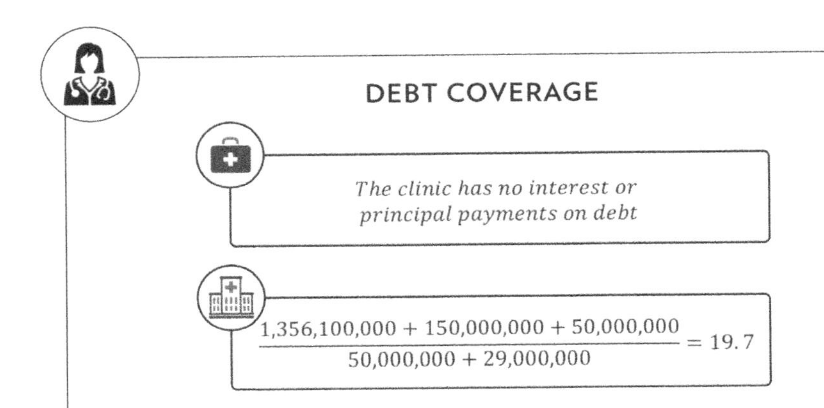

Levi leads the discussion here, as the clinic has no debt. The debt for the clinic includes several bonds payable over multiple maturities. However, the required debt payments are still rather small compared to the overall income of the organization. The debt service for the year includes both principal and interest. Principal payments for the year totaled $29 million. As a result, the organization is showing a debt coverage ratio of nearly twenty times the debt payment. The hospital's policy is to ensure that debt coverage ratio is at least two times. The current ratio is ten times that—a clear sign that the debt of the organization is reasonable.

Operating Ratios

Operating ratios look at how entities generate their funds.

CONTRIBUTION RATIO

The *contribution ratio* considers contributions and grants as a percentage of revenue. This helps the nonprofit understand how much they rely on external support as opposed to program revenues.

This simple calculation takes contribution and grant revenues and divides by total revenue.

$$\text{Contribution Ratio} = \frac{\text{Contribution Revenue} + \text{Grant Revenue}}{\text{Total Revenue}}$$

This can be a very interesting ratio. For many churches, for example, contribution ratio can be very high, as they typically have fewer programs generating revenue. On the other hand, universities might have a significantly lower contribution ratio, as they often have significant fees for service (e.g., tuition revenue). Hospitals also have significant patient revenues that will impact the contribution ratio.

The importance of this ratio is to understand how the organization would be affected if there were ever a drop in external support. Some entities prepare a contribution ratio separate from a grant/federal funds ratio if that helps them better evaluate the organization.

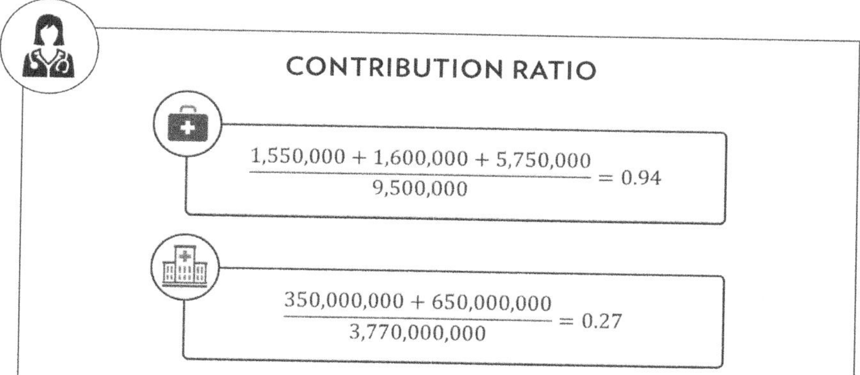

CONTRIBUTION RATIO

$$\frac{1{,}550{,}000 + 1{,}600{,}000 + 5{,}750{,}000}{9{,}500{,}000} = 0.94$$

$$\frac{350{,}000{,}000 + 650{,}000{,}000}{3{,}770{,}000{,}000} = 0.27$$

The clinic is funded almost entirely by contributions, so it's no surprise to see a contribution ratio of 94 percent. The clinic is run with the donated services of the doctors and nurses, and most of the pharmaceuticals are also donated. If doctors were to stop donating their time or pharmaceutical companies were to stop donating the pharmaceuticals, the organization would be in financial distress. However, the clinic has a good reputation in the community, and the doctors appear to enjoy their time helping the less fortunate. Zara notes that a recent requirement to provide detailed disclosures regarding contributed nonfinancial assets will continue to show donors and grantors the importance of these funds. That new disclosure will be a focus of the upcoming board meeting.

Levi, on the other hand, notes that the organization receives only 27 percent of its funding from government grants that are treated as contributions

continued

and general contributions. The organization is primarily financed by patient revenue received from individuals and third-party payers. Levi notes that grants covering the cost of uninsured or underinsured individuals are treated as exchange transactions and reported with patient revenues.

Zara notes that a significant portion of the nonexchange revenue has donor restrictions. That will be a topic at the next board meeting as well.

EXCHANGE RATIO

Organizations can also evaluate the percentage of their revenues that come from exchange revenues.

$$Exchange\ Ratio = \frac{Exchange\ Revenue}{Total\ Revenue}$$

This is important to look at from a subindustry perspective and is often most helpful when evaluated for trends—not looking at a particular year.

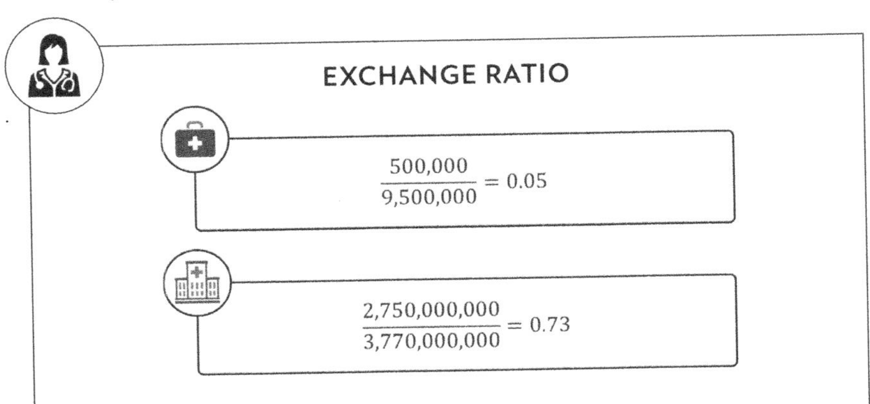

Luna notes that the only exchange revenue stems from special events put on as fundraisers to generate cash for the organization. The special events have been growing in size, and she notes that the amount increased from the prior year. When she first started, there were no special events, but the two put on in the prior year brought in 5 percent of total revenue. There is even discussion of potentially adding another event. The staff will be discussing this at their next development meeting. They want to be careful to not overcommit the volunteers, as these events are very labor intensive.

Levi notes that exchange revenue continues to make up nearly 75 percent of all revenue sources. It is actually lower than some hospitals, which are closer to being 90 percent funded with exchange revenues. The ability to generate contributions and grants has been a key focus of management. Zara makes a note to include a bullet on the slide deck with a comparison to the three competitor hospitals that they use for ratio analysis purposes. Both the positive trend and competitor information should be pleasing to the board.

FUNDRAISING EFFICIENCY RATIO

While entities often look at fundraising as a percentage of expenses, another useful tool for evaluating a nonprofit's development department is the *fundraising efficiency ratio*. This ratio evaluates the amount of contributions raised for each dollar of fundraising.

The goal is for each dollar spent on fundraising to bring in more revenue. The higher the fundraising efficiency ratio, the more efficient the fundraising is. If a nonprofit spends a dollar in fundraising and brings in less than a dollar in contributions, that indicates that the fundraising attempt was not effective. While fundraising expenses may be small in comparison to total expenses, the ratios still need to work for a fundraising campaign to be considered effective.

To calculate this ratio, the nonprofit takes total contributions (excluding government grants) and divides by fundraising expenses.

$$\begin{matrix} Fundraising \\ Efficiency \end{matrix} = \frac{Total\ Contributions\ (less\ government\ grants)}{Fundraising\ Expenses}$$

FUNDRAISING EFFICIENCY

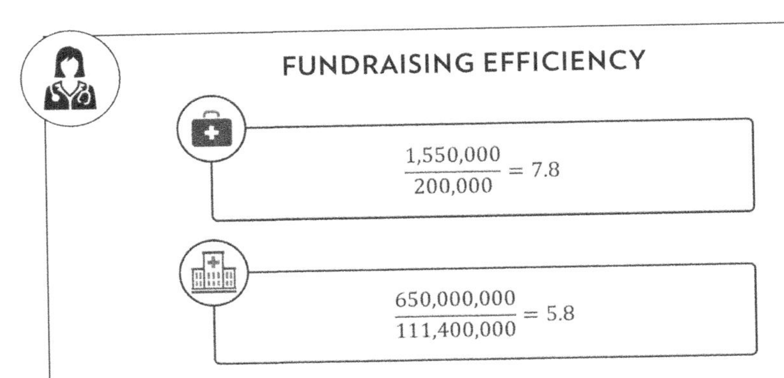

Luna indicates that as contributions were up over the prior year, the fundraising efficiency ratio shows a nice increase. While there has been little change in the amount of fundraising expenses recognized, the improvement in contributions has led to a ratio of nearly 8. For every dollar spent in fundraising, the nonprofit brings in $7.80 in contributions. The clinic chooses not to include donated gifts in kind in the calculation, since the majority of these funds are contributed services and contributed medical supplies that are not a result of the fundraising effort of the development department.

Levi also notes a positive trend in the efficiency ratio for the hospital. The group has continued to grow contributions, despite holding costs for fundraising relatively flat. Most donors increased their donations over the prior year due to a matching campaign that was set up by a large benefactor. The agreement matched each individual's increase over the prior year. Therefore, if someone had donated $200 in the prior year and donated $250 in the current year, not only did the hospital get an additional $50 from the donor, but the matching campaign also generated an extra $50. Many donors chose to increase their donation to max out the match. The fundraising ratio has hovered at under 5 for some time and is now approaching 6.

While the clinic is able to treat most patients that have non-life-threatening emergencies, it is not able to provide surgical care and other emergency care. As a result, the hospital provides charity care based on household income to federal poverty guidelines. In addition, the hospital provides services under the Medicare program, for which payments received were less than the full cost of providing the services. The hospital's donors allow the hospital to provide excellent care to those in need through their support. The hospital uses funds restricted to aiding low-income individuals to supplement the costs of these services.

Zara notes that the development department has already indicated they intend to discuss the campaign results at the next meeting because it was such a huge success.

FUNDRAISING RATIO

The opposite of the fundraising efficiency ratio is the *fundraising ratio*, which measures the percentage of fundraising costs to contribution revenues (effectively flipping the numerator and denominator). This looks at the cost of fundraising to generate one dollar of a donation.

$$\text{Fundraising Ratio} = \frac{\text{Fundraising Expenses}}{\text{Total Contributions (less government grants)}}$$

The goal for most nonprofits is to have a lower ratio. A rule of thumb is to shoot for a ratio under 33 percent.

Fundraising expenses spent today may not elicit a donation for several years. Maintaining a longer-term view of fundraising is important.

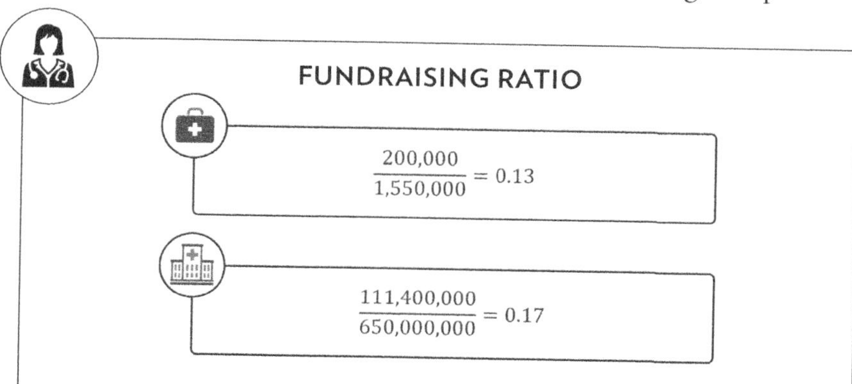

Zara notes that the fundraising ratios also reflect the good work of the organization to elicit more contributions. As a result, the ratio continues to improve. While both the clinic and the hospital have development staff, both departments are lean and have worked hard to develop relationships with donors. Their efforts are clearly paying off!

OPERATING RELIANCE RATIO

The *operating reliance ratio*, or *self-sufficiency ratio*, takes unrestricted program revenues and divides by total expenses.

$$\text{Operating Reliance Ratio} = \frac{\text{Unrestricted Program Revenues}}{\text{Total Expenses}}$$

The goal is to have a higher ratio, as this provides favorable feedback on the ability of the nonprofit to pay its expenses through program revenues.

This ratio can be problematic for entities such as churches, which are heavily reliant on donations. As with all ratios, boards need to decide whether the ratio is relevant to their organization.

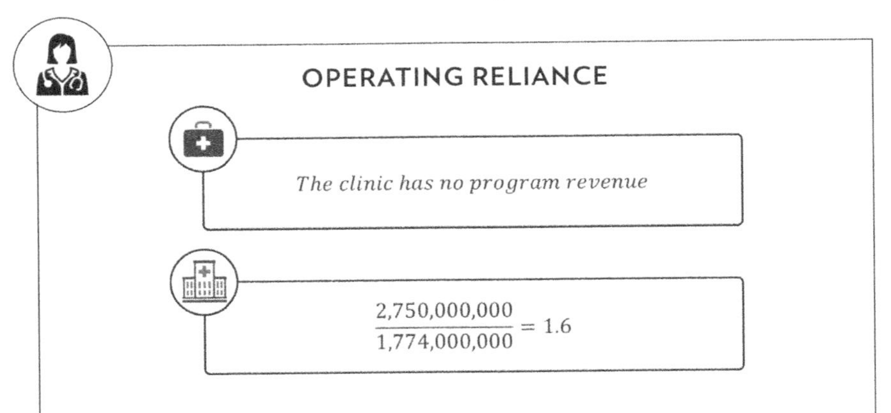

The hospital calculates its operating reliance, focusing on its patient revenue and related program expenses. The clinic does not calculate an operating reliance, as it does not charge for the services provided. A reliance of 1.6 indicates that the revenues sufficiently cover the related expenses while still retaining margin. The hospital understands that revenue is often negotiated with third-party payers and that there are confines for what can be charged. As a result, while they would like to see a higher number, they understand that they are competitive compared to other hospitals who operate under similar conditions. In addition, many patients are provided services that are covered by Medicare or Medicaid, which have very low negotiated rates.

The hospital focuses on providing care efficiently while maintaining the highest levels of patient experience. For the past three years, the ratio has come in at 1.2, 1.4, and 1.5, so the trend is favorable. The board will be happy to see another increase. While not as big an increase as the prior year, the trend is positive.

Spending Ratios

The final type of ratios we'll discuss, *spending ratios*, focus on the various types of functional expenses as compared to overall expenses.

PROGRAM SERVICE EXPENSE RATIO

The first ratio is the *program service expense ratio*, which is sometimes referred to as the *program efficiency ratio*. This ratio looks at the expenses incurred for mission or purpose as a percentage of total expenses.

$$\text{Program Service Expense Ratio} = \frac{\text{Program Expenses}}{\text{Total Expenses}}$$

Most donors want the vast majority of their donations to go to the programs of the nonprofit. So, the higher the ratio, the better—but only to a point. A nonprofit *must* have overhead (management and general expenses) in order to grow, plan, and sustain. This is often referred to as the *overhead myth*. Entities want to reduce overhead to appease donors. However, we need to remember that nonprofit organizations need appropriate support to have a long-lasting impact.

When evaluating programs, people often focus on how much cash is spent on them. Another key focus is on the impact the program has on its mission. Nonprofits should also evaluate how effectively the program is achieving its mission. Spending a very high percentage of a nonprofit's expenses on a program that doesn't produce results is problematic.

Entities that are well staffed and have sufficient resources that make a lasting impact may have lower ratios here but actually have a better impact on society. And, as already noted, one ratio on its own is insufficient to evaluate an organization.

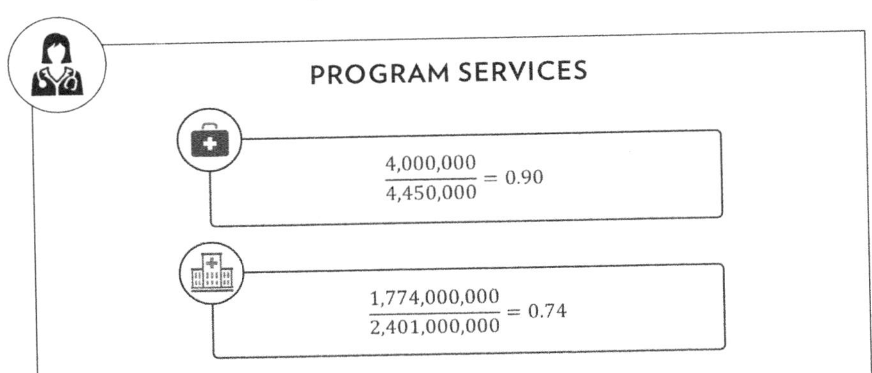

Luna kicks off the conversation around program services. Program expenses have been over 85 percent for the past few years but just crossed the 90 percent mark. This is predominantly due to increases in the fair value of contributed services and contributed nonfinancial assets. As these expenses increase, the revenue increases the same amount. However, as other expenses have been constant, it shows as an increase in program expenses as a percentage of total expenses. Donors and grantors view this ratio favorably.

The hospital's financials also show a favorable program services ratio. The hospital recognizes there is overhead that must be paid to operate. Unlike other nonprofits, a hospital operates much more closely to a for-profit entity with significant regulatory, legal, and other requirements. As a result, the management and general ratio is much higher than the clinic but still competitive for the hospital industry. Department heads spend more time addressing management and general and less time in the program than the clinic. However, the size of the organization warrants significant oversight. The ratio has hovered around 75 percent for years. The steady nature of that ratio and the fact that it is competitive with others in the industry results in it generating very little discussion at board meetings. The board is committed to having sufficient staffing to support overhead functions, such as accounting, human resources, and IT. So long as there isn't a material change, it is unlikely to be a topic of discussion.

MANAGEMENT EXPENSE RATIO

The *management expense ratio*, sometimes referred to as the *administrative ratio*, takes management and general expenses and divides by total expenses to determine management and general costs as a percentage of total expenses.

$$\text{Management Expense Ratio} = \frac{\text{Management \& General Expenses}}{\text{Total Expenses}}$$

Donors generally want this ratio to be lower, but the nonprofit doesn't want it to be so low that it may jeopardize the effectiveness of the organization. A low management expense ratio may also be an indicator that the nonprofit is too lean, leading to consistent turnover, low morale among the staff, and general ineffectiveness.

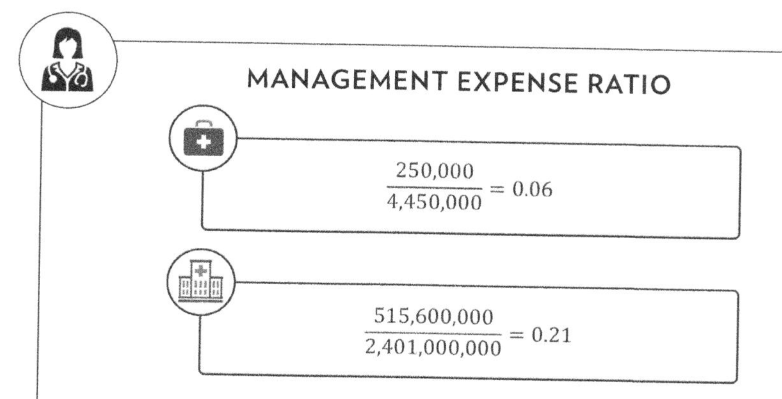

Zara notes that management expense is consistent with the explanations provided for program services. As management ratio plus program ratio plus fundraising ratio always equals one, any adjustments to one will impact the others. Her team has provided additional analysis should a question pop up at the meeting, but Zara feels like these ratios will likely not receive much attention.

FUNDRAISING EXPENSE RATIO

The final spending ratio looks at the last functional expense type—fundraising—as a percentage of total expense. The *fundraising expense ratio* takes total fundraising divided by total expenses.

$$\text{Fundraising Expense Ratio} = \frac{\text{Fundraising Expenses}}{\text{Total Expenses}}$$

We would not want a nonprofit to spend 90 percent of its revenue on fundraising, but we have to consider this ratio in concert with the quality of the funds generated—another example of how a single ratio is not sufficient to evaluate a nonprofit.

Other Ratios

There are a variety of other ratios that can be used by nonprofits to suit their individual needs.

DAYS SALES OUTSTANDING RATIO

If nonprofits have significant accounts receivable, calculating days sales outstanding (the DSO ratio) of accounts receivable may be helpful to evaluate how long it takes to collect cash for its services. These receivables may be from customers, government agencies, or third-party payers. The number of days varies, but tracking the trend can be very helpful.

The ratio is calculated by taking total accounts receivable and dividing by annual revenue, then multiplying the result by 365. Cash sales can be excluded from the denominator because here we are only tracking outstanding accounts receivable.

$$\text{Days Sales Outstanding} = \frac{\text{Accounts Receivable}}{\text{Annual Revenue}} \times 365$$

This tells you how many days it takes from billing to collection. If this number starts trending upward, that may be an indicator that customers are struggling to pay.

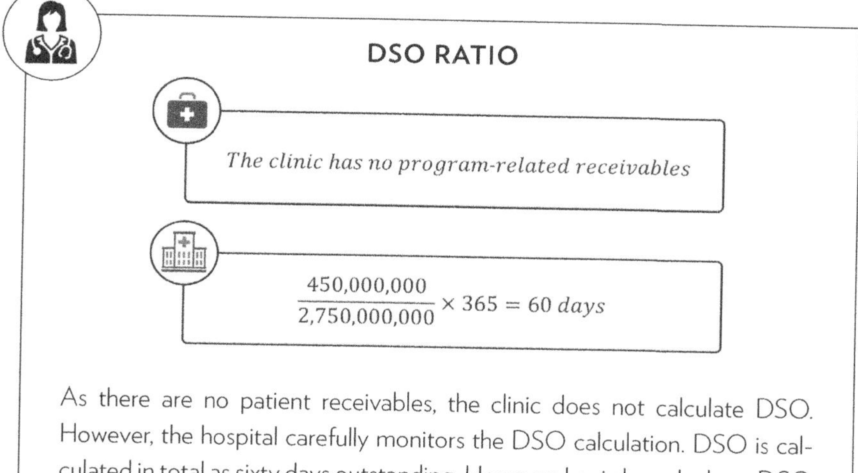

As there are no patient receivables, the clinic does not calculate DSO. However, the hospital carefully monitors the DSO calculation. DSO is calculated in total as sixty days outstanding. However, Levi also calculates DSO for commercial payers, Medicare, Medicaid, self-pay, and other third-party payers. The government continues to have terms that allow them longer than average to pay. However, most self-pay terms are thirty days, and most commercial payers have agreed to forty-five days. As a result, each category is reviewed to ensure there are no significant changes.

OPERATING MARGIN

Most nonprofits do not use profitability ratios because their goal is not to generate a profit. However, calculations like operating margin can be helpful in determining whether exchange transactions are properly priced, or the extent of deficit created by programs that would need to be funded by other sources.

Operating margin at the program level is calculated by taking the revenue a program receives and subtracting its related operating expenses to calculate margin.

$$\begin{matrix}Program \\ Revenues\end{matrix} - \begin{matrix}Operating \\ Expenses\end{matrix} = \begin{matrix}Operating \\ Margin\end{matrix}$$

The nonprofit can also look more holistically at the operating margin by taking all operating revenues and subtracting all operating expenses. Negative margins indicate that programs are being funded by other revenue sources (e.g., fundraising or grants).

PRIMARY RESERVE RATIO (OPERATING RESERVE RATIO)

Another ratio used by nonprofits compares expendable net assets to total expenses. This allows the nonprofit to understand how long it could function using just its expendable reserves (i.e., without relying on any additional net assets from operations). Expendable net assets are the net assets without donor restrictions minus physical assets (like buildings and equipment, as they can't be expended). The denominator is the total expenses of the organization (i.e., salaries, utilities, supplies, etc.) but excludes noncash items like depreciation. Some organizations use operating expenses in lieu of total expenses.

$$Primary\ Reserve\ Ratio = \frac{\begin{matrix}Net\ Assets\ Without \\ Donor\ Restrictions\end{matrix} - PP\&E}{Total\ Expenses\ - Noncash\ Expenses}$$

This provides an estimation of how long the nonprofit could continue its operations without generating any new revenue. Typically, the minimum ratio would be 0.4, or 40 percent of the year (just about 5 months). This ratio helps the nonprofit evaluate whether its resources are sufficient and flexible enough to support its mission.

LEVERAGE RATIOS

Leverage ratios are another useful set of ratios for nonprofits. The two most common leverage ratios are debt to assets and debt to net assets.

The debt-to-asset ratio helps the nonprofit understand what percentage of the assets are financed by debt. This is calculated by taking total liabilities from the statement of financial position and dividing it by total assets.

$$\textit{Debt to Asset Ratio} = \frac{\textit{Total Liabilities}}{\textit{Total Assets}}$$

This helps the organization understand how much of their assets comes from debt. If this percentage gets too high, the entity may have difficulty paying its debt or be unable to take out additional debt.

Debt to net assets works similarly, by dividing the total liabilities of the organization by its net assets.

$$\textit{Debt to Net Asset Ratio} = \frac{\textit{Total Liabilities}}{\textit{Total Net Assets}}$$

The higher the ratio, the more the organization is reliant on debt. Debt is not a bad thing, but too much debt can become an issue.

BENCHMARKING

Ratios are only a piece of the puzzle. On their own, they lack context. Comparing ratios within subindustries can help evaluate the nonprofit more effectively.

Nonprofits can consider other nonprofits in their subindustry that have a similar size and check to see if they issue their financial statements publicly on their website. If they don't, the 990 has many of the details that are used to calculate these ratios, and it is always publicly available. Entities often pick three to five organizations they consider peers and compare their results with those of the peers to identify where they perform well comparatively, as well as where they may want to focus attention.

BENCHMARKING

As many nonprofit hospitals receive federal funding, it is easy for the hospital to identify similarly sized hospitals with similar geographic and demographic constituents. Zara uses the Federal Audit Clearinghouse to obtain the financial statements of the organizations and then reviews the three comparison hospitals each year to see if they are still relatively similar or if there were any major changes that would make them different. Luna and Levi calculate most ratios for those organizations to serve as a benchmark. Broader industry averages, if available, are also appropriate benchmarks.

TRENDS

Often a single calculation of a ratio doesn't provide enough context. Looking at a ratio year over year or on a monthly or quarterly basis will provide insight into how the ratios are trending. Are they improving? Are they getting worse? Generally, the longer the period of time that a ratio is tracked, the more informative it is. For example, if you have only two years of information, it may be hard to know if one of those years was an anomaly. It typically takes three to five years of data to see the strength of a trend. It also helps to identify anomalies that need to be examined further. A large, unexpected gift in one year can throw off ratios and would be difficult to evaluate in other years.

Trend analysis helps entities identify these types of issues and evaluate whether their strategy is working when they see changes in the ratio over time. Not everything can be a quick fix, but identifying movement in the right direction can be very helpful.

TRENDS

After each ratio is calculated, Zara adds it to the scorecard. The scorecard keeps a running list of the past five years. This allows the board to not only evaluate the current-year ratio but also notice trends. The board often asks for the reasons for trends upward or downward. As a result, Luna and Levi both evaluate the causes as part of their analysis.

ANALYSIS

While ratios are helpful for evaluating a nonprofit, there are other analyses that can be used as well.

For example, the liquidity disclosures required for nonprofits can be evaluated over time. These disclosures tell a lot about the nonprofit's solvency. Boards can evaluate the trends to determine if there are steps needed to improve the liquidity of the organization. For example, a nonprofit may choose to implement a gift acceptance policy when a large volume of small restricted contributions is making it difficult for them to pay for general expenses. Creating a policy that prevents donors from restricting small-dollar donations reduces inefficiency. These small restricted donations can sometimes cost more for the nonprofit to track than the amount provided. However, unless the nonprofit has the information to make that determination, it doesn't have a basis for making the change.

Looking at the financial statements year over year to evaluate significant changes can be helpful. Comparative financial statements can be useful for the board to identify where major shifts are occurring. A board can ask management to prepare an analysis of fluctuations between the current year and the prior year and provide an explanation to help them understand the drivers of the changes and whether they indicate any issues.

Analyzing common-size financials can help provide context. A common-size financial statement shows each line item as a percentage of a base instead of actual cash. For example, on the statement of activities, a nonprofit can show all line items as a percentage of revenue. On the statement of financial position, the line items can be presented as a percentage of total assets. This is helpful for tracking percentages over time. It can also be used for comparison to other organizations that are of a different size, to reduce the impact of size on the evaluation.

COMMON-SIZE FINANCIALS

Zara prepares the common-size financials for the board. These help the board look at very dissimilar entities by showing them based on percentage of revenue. It also helps when comparing with benchmarks of organizations larger or smaller than the hospital.

Free Medical Clinic
Common Size Statement of Activities

	For the year ending December 31, 20XX		
	Without Donor Restrictions	**With Donor Restrictions**	**Total**
Revenues			
Contributions	15%	1%	16%
Grant Revenue	1%	16%	17%
Special Events	5%	0%	5%
Investment Income	1%	0%	1%
Donated Services, Materials & Facilities	61%	0%	61%
Released from Restrictions	11%	-11%	0%
Total Revenue	**94%**	**6%**	**100%**
Expenses			
Program	42%	0%	42%
Support			
Management & General	3%	0%	3%
Fundraising	2%	0%	2%
Total Expenses	**47%**	**0%**	**47%**
Increase in Net Assets	47%	6%	53%

The common-size financials for the clinic use total revenues as the denominator for both revenues and expenses. This can help users understand the types of revenues and how that revenue is spent on expenses.

Hospital
Common Size Statement of Activities

	For the year ending December 31, 20XX		
	Without Donor Restrictions	With Donor Restrictions	Total
Revenues			
Net Patient Revenue	73%	0%	73%
Grants & Contracts	5%	4%	9%
Contributions	1%	16%	17%
Other Revenue	1%	0%	1%
Released from Restrictions	3%	-3%	0%
Total Revenues and Support	**83%**	**17%**	**100%**
Expenses			
Salaries, Wages, Benefits	40%	0%	40%
Medical Supplies	0%	0%	0%
Interest	1%	0%	1%
Depreciation	4%	0%	4%
Other Operating Expenses	19%	0%	19%
Total Expenses	**64%**	**0%**	**64%**
Operating Income	**19%**	**17%**	**36%**
Non-operating Income			
Investment Income	0%	0%	0%
Other	0%	0%	0%
Total non-operating income	0%	0%	0%
Increase in Net Assets	**19%**	**17%**	**36%**

The common-size financials for the hospital also uses total revenue as its base. It is now easy to compare the types of revenue between the two organizations even though the hospital is considerably larger than the clinic.

Reviewing balance sheet reconciliations performed by management can help the board analyze reconciling items and accounting issues identified. For smaller entities that do not have sufficient segregation of duties, the board can act as the reviewer and approver to provide the oversight needed. For larger organizations, periodic review can provide insight into the types of reconciling items. It also helps reduce fraud risk.

The board should be proactive in seeking out ways to stay informed about the health of the nonprofit.

NONFINANCIAL ANALYSIS

Along with ratios and trends, nonprofits often need to evaluate measures of program efficiency and effectiveness. Nonprofit board members should be evaluating the organization and considering potential risks to the organization.

KPIs

Key performance indicators (KPIs) are used to measure the implementation of programs. They allow nonprofits to evaluate the number of people served or number of hours volunteered. Membership tracking—looking at the percentage of members who renewed or the number of new members brought on—helps to evaluate the health of the organization. Trends can also be reviewed to determine causes of declines in membership, and perhaps offer an opportunity to interview members who didn't renew to find out why and see what improvements can be made.

Another way to evaluate a program is through a cost-benefit analysis, an evaluation of how efficiently the nonprofit is providing services. If the cost to provide the program exceeds the impact provided, perhaps the program should be run differently, or needs to be replaced with a more effective program.

Tracking program activities and impact can help the nonprofit stay on course and identify programs that may need to be revisited when not effective. However, it is important that a nonprofit not track too many items. An organization could keep finance busy all day just tracking various metrics, leaving them no time to devote to their real work. Selecting the right mix of metrics, including leading and lagging indicators with trend analysis, is vital. Each year the metrics can be reviewed and evaluated to decide whether some can be discontinued because they are clearly meeting targets and others can be added for renewed focus. Nonprofits that get too involved in the minutiae may lose sight of the bigger picture.

Process-based evaluations help nonprofits understand how a program works. They look at the activities of the program and the inputs that go into them (e.g., materials used, activities implemented). They can help identify efficiencies in the program or perhaps friction in processes that need to be addressed to be more successful.

Equally important, however, is the impact an organization makes. Outcome-based evaluations look at the mission and how the nonprofit has contributed to that mission. If the mission is to improve test scores for low-income individuals, tracking test scores can help determine whether the organization is hitting its outcome goals.

KPIs can be created out of any strategic plan. Wherever the board wants to focus, a metric can be identified to measure it and then track it to see if it's trending in the correct direction. Determining the value provided by a program is another important factor in building KPIs. Do we want to see a decline in dropout rates? We have to track it, along with the leading and lagging indicators, to help move the needle in the right direction. If we want to see higher test scores from students in an after-school program, we have to track contact hours to see what impact it makes on the actual score.

KPIs

Zara reviews the KPIs provided by both Levi and Luna. Different KPIs are used for each division. Levi tracks the average hospital stay, bed turnover, and average patient wait times. As the services provided in the clinic are usually treated same day, Luna does not track the average hospital stay. However, the number of patients served continues to be the key focus of the clinic.

Levi also tracks insurance processing time, claims denial rates, and patient satisfaction. Luna is more focused on the patient follow-up rate and number of educational programs. The clinic offers programs about immunizations, CPR, and other public healthcare items to help serve the population. Learning about prevention and proper health practices is often the best medicine, especially for the underserved.

The board evaluates annually whether there should be any metrics removed or new ones added. This keeps the information relevant for decision-making.

Board Self-Evaluation

How are we tracking compared to our strategic plan KPIs and priorities?

Each board meeting is an opportunity to look at the long term and evaluate how the organization is performing compared to plan.

In what ways did the organization move forward in terms of mission, resources, public attention, and other identified objectives? What were our achievements this year? What things did we struggle with? What lessons did we learn?

Asking these questions can help the organization identify gaps and set the stage for better KPIs and tracking in the future.

CHAPTER 8

COMPILATIONS, REVIEWS, AND AUDITS

In order to build public trust in their financial information, nonprofits hire independent public accountants to provide various levels of assurance about the accuracy of the numbers.

Sometimes an independent accountant is hired because of a bank requirement in a debt covenant that requires the nonprofit to provide the bank with audited financial statements on an annual basis. Sometimes a grantor requires assurance as part of the grant agreement to ensure the funds are being spent in alignment with the purpose of the funding. If an organization receives federal funding, an audit may also be required.

Sometimes the board unilaterally decides to have the books reviewed and to get feedback from an objective third party. Having financial statements reviewed by an independent accountant is a best practice. It helps ensure any material errors are caught and the nonprofit is correctly applying the rules of accounting. Some boards will voluntarily engage an accountant to protect the organization from fraud. This is not always an annual engagement and does not always start with an audit. CPAs offer a variety of engagement types.

Board Best Practices

The board should carefully review debt agreements, grant agreements, and other contracts that contain audit or review requirements. They should ensure that if an audit requirement is triggered, the audit firm is hired and the work is performed. When reviewing the grants and contracts, if a Yellow Book or Single Audit requirement is triggered, the board must ensure the work is performed. The audit standards require that the auditor communicate with "those charged with governance," starting with signing the engagement letter, through planning and risk assessment, all the way to the closeout of the engagement and issuance of the report. There are special communication letters for the board that provide the qualitative aspects of the audit. These communications are critical, and the board should actively participate in the discussions and ensure they understand the information the independent accountant is providing.

ATTEST VS. ASSURANCE

When an accountant provides an attest service, they are issuing a report. Audits, reviews, and compilations require the CPA to provide their report in writing to management and those charged with governance. Other services are non-attest and do not require the issuance of a report. An example of a non-attest service is preparation of financial statements.

CPAs can provide varying levels of assurance. Some engagements provide no assurance. For example, in a compilation, the CPA does not verify the accuracy of the financial statements. In a review, the CPA provides limited assurance based on a handful of procedures performed. In an audit, the CPA provides reasonable assurance, which is the highest level of assurance. No matter the level of service, a CPA cannot provide absolute assurance.

COMPILATIONS

Compilations are the most basic level of service an accountant can provide. Compilation engagements are performed under the Statements on Standards for Accounting and Review Services (SSARS), written by the AICPA's Accounting and Review Services Committee.

Compilations provide no assurance. The accountant merely takes the information provided by management and assists them in preparing complete financial statements. SSARS AR-C Section 80 states that the objective "is to apply accounting and financial reporting expertise to assist management in the presentation of financial statements . . . without undertaking to obtain or provide any assurance." So while the CPA helps the nonprofit create a complete set of financial statements, the CPA is not verifying the accuracy of the underlying records.

Some compilation engagements are nondisclosure compilations, which means the accountant prepares only the basic financial statements without any disclosures. Entities often hire accountants to perform this level of service when they do not have the capabilities in house to prepare a complete set of financial statements.

Unlike other attestation engagements, a compilation does not require the accountant to be independent. Therefore, the accountant is not required to assess management's skill, knowledge, or experience. If the accountant is not independent, the accountant has to disclose the lack of independence in the compilation report.

While a compilation does not provide any assurance, the accountant is still required to obtain an engagement letter from the nonprofit agreeing to the terms and conditions. The CPA must understand the financial reporting framework used by management (e.g., GAAP or cash basis), as well as the accounting policies of the entities. The accountant is then required to read the financial statements to consider whether they appear to be in the appropriate form and free from obvious material misstatements.

In a compilation engagement, the accountant neither verifies the accuracy of the information nor evaluates internal controls or source documents.

While a compilation provides no assurance, it is still an attest engagement because the CPA provides a report. The report must be on the CPA firm's letterhead. The most basic version of the report would look much like the following example:

ACCOUNTANT'S COMPILATION REPORT

Management is responsible for the accompanying financial statements of Wonderful NFP, which comprise the statement of financial position as of December 31, 20X2 and 20X1, and the related statements of activities, functional expenses, and cash flows for the years then ended, and the related notes to the financial statements in accordance with accounting principles generally accepted in the United States of America. We have performed compilation engagements in accordance with Statements on Standards for Accounting and Review Services promulgated by the Accounting and Review Services Committee of the AICPA. We did not audit or review the financial statements, nor were we required to perform any procedures to verify the accuracy or completeness of the information provided by management. We do not express an opinion, a conclusion, nor provide any assurance on these financial statements.

[Signature of accounting firm or accountant]
[Accountant's city and state]
[Date of the accountant's report]

The report is modified if the accountant was not independent or if the basis of accounting was not GAAP (i.e., cash basis). While the accountant is not required to perform procedures to verify the information, sometimes information might come to their attention during the preparation process. If there is a known error (referred to as a departure from the framework), the accountant notes that in the report.

Compilations are a lower level of service, so they are less expensive and therefore budget friendly. However, because they do not provide any level of assurance, this is often used only as a substitute for an entity having a qualified CPA on staff that can prepare the financial statements.

REVIEW ENGAGEMENTS

A review engagement is a lower level of engagement than an audit but higher than a compilation. Financial statement review engagements are also performed under the Statements on Standards for Accounting and Review Services written by the AICPA's Accounting and Review Services Committee.

A review engagement provides limited assurance. The accountant issues a conclusion as to whether any material modifications are needed to make the financial statements conform with the financial reporting framework. AR-C Section 90 states the objective of the accountant is to "obtain limited assurance, primarily by performing analytical procedures and inquiries, as a basis for reporting whether the accountant is aware of any material modifications that should be made to the financial statements for them to be in accordance with the applicable financial reporting framework." Limited assurance is less than what you would receive with an audit (reasonable assurance) but substantial enough for the accountant to issue a conclusion. The accountant performs some procedures (primarily analytical procedures and inquiry) and evaluates any material errors that come to their attention during these procedures.

As the accountant concludes whether a material modification needs to be made to the financial statements, the accountant is required to calculate materiality. An error is material if it would influence the user's judgments on the financial statements. AR-C Section 90 states that "misstatements, including omissions, are considered to be material if there is a substantial likelihood that, individually or in the aggregate, they would influence the judgment made by a reasonable user based on the financial statements." Thus, the accountant is not looking to find every minor error but only ones large enough that they would influence a user's judgment.

Misstatements occur when an amount (or classification or disclosure) is different from what is required by the financial reporting framework. For example, if revenue is not calculated correctly or if a required disclosure is missing, those are misstatements. Misstatements can be caused by fraud (intentional) or error (unintentional).

In order to perform a review engagement, the accountant must be knowledgeable about the entity, the industry, and the financial reporting framework used by the nonprofit. The primary procedures in a review engagement are inquiry (asking questions of management and others as necessary) and analytical procedures. Analytical procedures include trend analysis, comparing information in the financial statements with expectations of the accountant, comparing ratios, and making comparisons with the prior year. If an inconsistency is identified between the accountant's expectations and the information provided by management, the accountant will discuss the difference with management and perform other procedures as necessary to get comfortable with the numbers.

The accountant will also read the financial statements to ensure they are presented appropriately and provide the correct disclosures according to the financial reporting framework. The accountant also reconciles the financial statements back to the trial balance provided by management. As part of the procedures of the review engagement, the accountant will ask management to provide a management representation letter, which requires management to put various statements in writing, including that management takes responsibility for the financial statements and that all transactions have been included and properly accounted for. In addition, management must agree to include the accountant's review report in any financial documents that contain the financial statements.

The accountant is required to be independent of the entity when performing reviews. If the accountant is not independent, they are required to withdraw from the engagement.

In a review engagement, management is still responsible for preparation and fair presentation of the financial statements. Management and the accountant agree to the terms and conditions of the engagement in an engagement letter that must be in writing. Both the accountant and management (or those charged with governance) are required to sign the agreement.

The accountant's review report is longer than a compilation report but shorter than an audit report.

Here is an example report:

INDEPENDENT ACCOUNTANT'S REVIEW REPORT

[Appropriate Addressee]

We have reviewed the accompanying financial statements of ABC Nonprofit, which comprise the statements of financial position as of December 31, 20X2 and 20X1, and the related statements of activities and cash flows for the years then ended, and the related notes to the financial statements. A review includes primarily applying analytical procedures to management's financial data and making inquiries of company management. A review is substantially less in scope than an audit, the objective of which is the expression of an opinion regarding the financial statements as a whole. Accordingly, we do not express such an opinion.

Management's Responsibility for the Financial Statements

Management is responsible for the preparation and fair presentation of these financial statements in accordance with accounting principles generally accepted in the United States of America; this includes the design, implementation, and maintenance of internal control relevant to the preparation and fair presentation of financial statements that are free from material misstatement whether due to fraud or error.

continued

Accountant's Responsibility

Our responsibility is to conduct the review engagements in accordance with Statements on Standards for Accounting and Review Services promulgated by the Accounting and Review Services Committee of the AICPA. Those standards require us to perform procedures to obtain limited assurance as a basis for reporting whether we are aware of any material modifications that should be made to the financial statements for them to be in accordance with accounting principles generally accepted in the United States of America. We believe that the results of our procedures provide a reasonable basis for our conclusion.

We are required to be independent of ABC Nonprofit and to meet our other ethical responsibilities, in accordance with the relevant ethical requirements related to our reviews.

Accountant's Conclusion

Based on our reviews, we are not aware of any material modifications that should be made to the accompanying financial statements in order for them to be in accordance with accounting principles generally accepted in the United States of America.

[Signature of accounting firm or accountant, as appropriate]
[Accountant's city and state]
[Date of the accountant's review report]

The report can be modified for any known departures, as well as for items the accountant wishes to emphasize (which are referred to as *emphasis* and *other matter* paragraphs). The report can also address things like supplementary information and required supplementary information, as well as the use of a special-purpose framework like cash basis.

Reviews incorporate only inquiries and analytical procedures and therefore are less expensive than audits but provide only limited assurance. Some entities start with review engagements and work their way up to audits as they become larger and have enough funding to support an audit.

AUDIT ENGAGEMENTS

An audit is the highest level of service accountants provide on financial statements. Financial statement audits are performed under the Statement of Auditing Standards issued by the Auditing Standards Board of the AICPA. They provide reasonable assurance as to whether the financial statements are fairly stated. Reasonable assurance is the highest level of assurance offered by CPAs, though it is not absolute. There may still be material errors in the financial statements that were not found by the auditor even if the audit was properly performed. It is not possible for the auditor to give absolute assurance, as the auditor does not look at every transaction. In addition, fraud often involves concealment, making it harder to identify the misstatement. AU-C Section 200 states that the objective of the auditor is to "obtain reasonable assurance about whether the financial statements as a whole are free from material misstatement, whether due to fraud or error."

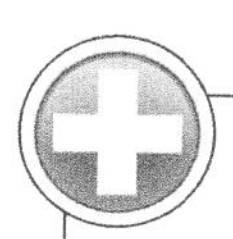

MEET LILLIAN

Lillian is the CFO of a disaster recovery organization. The nonprofit provides medicine, emergency supplies, and other disaster relief to those in need around the world. The organization is funded through a combination of contributions and government grants. They also receive significant contributions of medical inventory and disaster supplies. The three largest contributors accounted for almost 40 percent of the gifts in kind during the year. They receive several grants from the U.S. Agency for International Development. As a result of the grants received, the organization is required to have an annual financial statement audit as well as a Yellow Book and Single Audit.

For an audit, the auditor is required to obtain an engagement letter signed by both the firm and the client that covers the terms and conditions of the engagement and clarifies the respective responsibilities of management and the auditor.

An audit requires significant planning and risk assessment. No two audits are exactly the same. The auditor is required to identify and assess the risks of material misstatement and then to identify audit procedures responsive to those risks. This is referred to as a *risk-based approach.* While nonprofits are all in the same industry, each entity has its own risks, and therefore audits are tailored to the procedures needed to mitigate those specific risks.

The auditor is required to understand the entity and its environment, including internal controls. The auditor must understand the design of the internal controls and determine whether they have been implemented but is not required to test internal controls to determine whether the controls are truly effective, unless they plan to reduce the work performed as a result of relying on those controls. As part of the risk assessment, the auditor considers fraud and brainstorms how management might commit fraud, in order to design procedures to mitigate fraud risk. The auditor also considers laws and regulations affecting the entity that could have a material impact on the financial statements.

Similar to a review, the auditor calculates materiality thresholds. These thresholds help the auditor ensure that they perform procedures to mitigate the risk that the financial statements are materially misstated and that the auditor does not identify the misstatement.

Based on the risks identified, the auditor designs audit procedures responsive to those risks. This includes confirming balances with external parties like banks and customers, performing substantive analytical procedures, and sampling items for the auditor to vouch from the books and records to support (or trace from support back to the books and records). The auditor may elect to observe an inventory count or reperform an inventory count to verify its accuracy. The procedures in an audit are much more in-depth than in a review, such that the auditor can issue an opinion on whether the financial statements are fairly presented.

An opinion is the highest level of assurance provided by CPAs. If an error is found, the CPA is required to extrapolate the error and propose adjusting journal entries to management in order for them to correct the financials. CPAs verify the accuracy of estimates, related party transactions, subsequent events, and whether the entity is financially sound enough to be considered a *going concern* (i.e., financially secure enough to make it another year).

The requirements for audit evidence and documentation are substantial. The auditor has to be able to show that they had sufficient and appropriate evidence to support their opinion. Sometimes the auditor has to bring in an individual with expertise in an area outside of accounting or auditing, like a valuation expert or actuary. These specialists assist the auditor in obtaining evidence.

Once the auditor has obtained all the evidence, they must evaluate whether it is sufficient and appropriate. This includes evaluating the quality and quantity of evidence, as well as a review of identified and extrapolated errors to reduce the possibility of a material misstatement to an acceptable level.

The auditor is required to communicate with the board (which is referred to as "those charged with governance") throughout the audit, starting with planning all the way through issuing the report. At the end of the engagement, they issue a governance letter that includes a discussion of the auditor's views about qualitative aspects of the entity's significant accounting practices, including accounting policies, accounting estimates, and financial statement disclosures.

The auditor also communicates about significant unusual transactions, significant difficulties encountered during the audit, any disagreements with management that took place during the audit, and matters that were difficult or contentious, for which the auditor consulted outside the engagement team. This assists board members with upholding their fiduciary responsibilities. The auditor communicates any uncorrected misstatements and their effects related to prior periods and provides the board with a list of material, corrected misstatements that were brought to the attention of management as a result of audit procedures. These communications should help facilitate a dialogue between the auditor and the board, and the board and management.

The audit report is significantly longer than a review or compilation report. It provides explicit information about the role of management and the auditor. It also provides an overview of the procedures performed by the auditor to obtain sufficient appropriate evidence.

Here is an example audit report.

INDEPENDENT AUDITOR'S REPORT

[Appropriate Addressee]

Report on the Audit of the Financial Statements

Opinion

We have audited the financial statements of XYZ Not-for-Profit Organization, which comprise the statement of financial position as of September 30, 20X1, and the related statements of activities and cash flows for the year then ended, and the related notes to the financial statements.

In our opinion, the accompanying financial statements present fairly, in all material respects, the financial position of XYZ Not-for-Profit Organization as of September 30, 20X1, and the changes in its net assets and its cash flows for the year then ended in accordance with accounting principles generally accepted in the United States of America.

Basis for Opinion

We conducted our audit in accordance with auditing standards generally accepted in the United States of America (GAAS). Our responsibilities under those standards are further described in the Auditor's Responsibilities for the Audit of the Financial Statements section of our report. We are required to be independent of XYZ Not-for-Profit Organization and to meet our other ethical responsibilities, in accordance with the relevant ethical requirements relating to our audit. We believe that the audit evidence we have obtained is sufficient and appropriate to provide a basis for our audit opinion.

Responsibilities of Management for the Financial Statements

Management is responsible for the preparation and fair presentation of the financial statements in accordance with accounting principles generally accepted in the United States of America, and for the design, implementation, and maintenance of internal control relevant to the preparation and fair presentation of financial statements that are free from material misstatement, whether due to fraud or error.

In preparing the financial statements, management is required to evaluate whether there are conditions or events, considered in the aggregate, that raise substantial doubt about XYZ Not-for-Profit Organization's ability to continue as a going concern for within one year after the date that the financial statements are available to be issued.

Auditor's Responsibilities for the Audit of the Financial Statements

Our objectives are to obtain reasonable assurance about whether the financial statements as a whole are free from material misstatement, whether due to fraud or error, and to issue an auditor's report that includes our opinion. Reasonable assurance is a high level of assurance but is not absolute assurance and therefore is not a guarantee that an audit conducted in accordance with GAAS will always detect a material misstatement when it exists. The risk of not detecting a material misstatement resulting from fraud is higher than for one resulting from error, as fraud may involve collusion, forgery, intentional omissions, misrepresentations, or the override of internal control. Misstatements are considered material if there is a substantial likelihood that, individually or in the aggregate, they would influence the judgment made by a reasonable user based on the financial statements.

In performing an audit in accordance with GAAS, we:

- Exercise professional judgment and maintain professional skepticism throughout the audit.

continued

- Identify and assess the risks of material misstatement of the financial statements, whether due to fraud or error, and design and perform audit procedures responsive to those risks. Such procedures include examining, on a test basis, evidence regarding the amounts and disclosures in the financial statements.
- Obtain an understanding of internal control relevant to the audit in order to design audit procedures that are appropriate in the circumstances, but not for the purpose of expressing an opinion on the effectiveness of XYZ Not-for-Profit Organization's internal control. Accordingly, no such opinion is expressed.
- Evaluate the appropriateness of accounting policies used and the reasonableness of significant accounting estimates made by management, as well as evaluate the overall presentation of the financial statements.
- Conclude whether, in our judgment, there are conditions or events, considered in the aggregate, that raise substantial doubt about XYZ Not-for-Profit Organization's ability to continue as a going concern for a reasonable period of time.

We are required to communicate with those charged with governance regarding, among other matters, the planned scope and timing of the audit, significant audit findings, and certain internal control-related matters that we identified during the audit.

[Signature of the auditor's firm]
[City and state where the auditor's report is issued]
[Date of the auditor's report]

An audit is more expensive than other engagements offered by CPA firms, but it provides the most detailed review of the financials and includes the highest level of assurance. Having an annual audit is a best practice for nonprofits. It is an opportunity to get feedback on the quality of the financial statements, internal controls, and processes used by management.

ANNUAL AUDIT

Lillian has just had her closing meeting with the auditors. The same firm has performed the audit for the past five years. She really enjoys the insights that the partner provides, and she uses the feedback on her staff to provide spot bonuses. The audit typically takes four weeks, and during that time it consumes most of her staff's time. From providing copies of invoices and payments to providing detailed explanations for various questions, the audit is very time consuming. The auditors have completed their work and will be attending next week's board meeting to present the financial statements. Lillian is proud that there were only a handful of adjusting journal entries proposed by the auditor this year. Her staff worked hard to implement the new standards, including investing in new software for their leases. In preparation for the audit, her staff completed their analytical reviews of the statement of activities and prepared balance sheet reconciliations for Lillian's review. Several errors were spotted by this analysis, which made the audit go much more smoothly. Lillian met with the partner to discuss comments on the management letter and those charged with governance. She feels it accurately portrays the overall audit experience. Her staff has started the process of collecting all the audit samples from the auditors, and next week she plans to surprise them with a nice lunch and early release to thank them for their hard work.

ROLE OF MANAGEMENT

The role of management includes the "preparation and fair presentation" of the financial statements. This means that management should have the competence to prepare the financial statements and comply with the rules of accounting. Management is also responsible for designing, implementing, and maintaining internal controls. Internal controls help to mitigate the risk that the financial statements could be materially misstated.

Internal controls can be *detective* and identify misstatements after the fact. An example would be performing reconciliation of the statement of financial position accounts to support the numbers in the financials, or reconciling the cash account back to a bank statement. Internal controls can also be *preventative* controls. For example, a nonprofit might have the staff auditor prepare a journal entry and then have it reviewed and approved by a supervisor, who then posts the entry and corrects any errors prior to posting.

When management is unable to take responsibility for preparation and fair presentation because they lack the expertise, the CPA is not independent. Often, a nonprofit hires another CPA or CPA firm to prepare the financials, so that the audit firm does not impair their independence.

Sometimes, in addition to an audit or review, management may hire the CPA to perform services unrelated to the audit, which are referred to as *non-attest services*. These non-attest services can sometimes lead to independence issues. Management is required to have the skill, knowledge, or experience to oversee the accountant performing these other services and to accept responsibilities for these services in order to preserve independence. Examples of non-attest services include preparing the financial statements or preparing the 990 return (IRS information tax return).

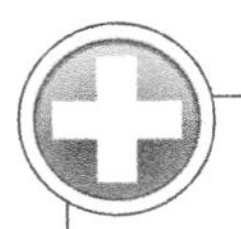

MANAGEMENT'S RESPONSIBILITIES

Lillian knows that her team is small but mighty. Segregation of duties is important to her. Prior to working at the disaster recovery organization, Lillian worked in public accounting for a CPA firm about the same size as her current auditor. She often found that the nonprofits with the strongest internal controls were the ones that had the least number of issues.

Over the last few years, she's added a few new internal controls to improve the effectiveness of the system. She introduced park and post, whereby her accountant can enter a journal entry into the system. However, it has to be reviewed by either Lillian or her boss before it can be posted into the system. This identifies errors on the front end and reduces the number of balance sheet reconciliation adjustments needed.

She also implemented park and post for accounts receivable and accounts payable. While it requires more of her time, the preparation of the annual financial statements has become much easier, as the numbers have already been reviewed once!

Lillian's team has a lot on its hands. While Lillian prepared many financial statements as an auditor, she has engaged her auditor to prepare the notes to the financial statements. Lillian uses the disclosure checklist provided by her auditor to look for missing disclosures and ensure the verbiage is accurate. Lillian maintains her CPA license and attends several nonprofit conferences to stay on top of changes in financial reporting. She also attends the webinars put on by the CPA firm, which she finds very helpful. The CPA firm also provides timely newsletters about changes in financial reporting so that she can follow up as the deadlines come closer.

Lillian reviews the financial statements one last time. She then reviews the representation letter provided by the CPA firm. Her boss will sign the letter indicating that management accepts responsibility for preparation and fair presentation of the financial statements, as well as for design, implementation, and maintenance of internal control. It also indicates that Lillian and her team provided all the information requested and have not lied to the auditors in any of their discussions. Lillian feels good about the representation letter and takes it to her boss for review in preparation for the board meeting. The auditors won't date the report until the letter is signed.

When a CPA performs non-attest services, management must perform all management responsibilities. If the CPA assumes a management responsibility, the management participation threat is so significant that no safeguards can reduce the threat to an acceptable level, and independence is impaired. Examples of management responsibilities that would impair the CPA's independence from the AICPA Code of Professional Conduct include setting policy or strategic direction for the attest client; directing or accepting responsibility for actions of the attest client's employees; authorizing, executing, or consummating transactions; preparing source documents; deciding which recommendations of the member or other third parties to implement or prioritize; and accepting responsibility for the management of an attest client's project.

Accepting responsibility for the preparation and fair presentation of the attest client's financial statements in accordance with the applicable financial reporting framework automatically impairs the auditor's independence, as does accepting responsibility for designing, implementing, or maintaining internal control. Therefore, even when the CPA firm prepares the financial statements for the nonprofit, management must still accept responsibility for preparation and fair presentation. In addition, management must provide a staff person with the skills, knowledge, or experience to oversee the preparation service. If a CPA's independence is impaired, they cannot perform the attest service (review or audit).

ROLE OF AUDITOR/ACCOUNTANT

In order for users and the public to trust their work, CPAs are required to follow a very strict code of professional conduct that focuses on integrity and objectivity, including independence rules to ensure the CPA's report is unbiased and objective. The AICPA Code of Professional Conduct (hereafter referred to as the Code) uses a threats and safeguards approach incorporated into a principles-based approach to ethics. If a certain action is expressly prohibited, then it clearly cannot be done. But if there is no specific guidance as to the impact of a certain conduct on independence or ethics, the accountant is required to identify the potential threats and evaluate their significance. If they are significant, the accountant must apply safeguards to reduce the threat to an acceptable level. There are seven broad categories of threats—*adverse interest, advocacy, familiarity, management participation, self-interest, self-review,* and *undue influence.*

EXAMPLES OF THREATS TO INDEPENDENCE

- *Adverse interest threats* occur when the CPA's interests are in opposition to the client's. For example, if the client is suing the CPA firm for an error or negligence, the CPA firm cannot be objective.
- *Advocacy threats* are related to promoting the client's interest to the point that independence is compromised.
- *Familiarity threats* stem from long or close relationships with the client. For example, if the CFO and the partner of the CPA are best friends and go on vacation together, a third party might find that the CPA can no longer be objective.
- *Management participation threats* stem from the CPA taking on a role of management. For example, if the CPA designed the internal controls of the organization, they are unable to objectively evaluate the controls.
- *Self-interest threats* stem from the CPA having a financial or other interest in the client. For example, holding stock in the client's publicly traded company impairs the independence of the CPA.
- *Self-review threat* is a common threat for nonprofits. If the CPA prepares the financial statements as part of the audit, they are reviewing their own work. Safeguards have to be applied to reduce the threat to an acceptable level.
- *Undue influence* occurs when an external actor attempts to exercise excessive influence to get their way. For example, if management threatens to fire the CPA to get them to approve their accounting practices, that is undue influence.

The Code includes rules around gifts and entertainment, financial interests, fees, family relationships with attest clients, and current or former employment with a client. Board members should have discussions with the accountant about threats identified and safeguards applied. (See Appendix.)

In addition to performing reviews, compilations, and audits, CPA firms offer a host of other advisory and supporting services to nonprofits.

These are referred to as non-attest services. Self-review, management participation, or advocacy threats may exist when a CPA performs non-attest services.

If a CPA is asked to perform a non-attest service for an attest client, *all* the following safeguards must be met to ensure threats are at an acceptable level and independence is not impaired:

- The CPA must determine that the attest client and its management agree to assume all management responsibilities.
- Management must oversee the service by designating an individual with skill, knowledge, or experience.
- Management must evaluate the adequacy and results of the services performed and accept responsibility for the results of the services.

The CPA cannot assume management responsibilities. The nonprofit must make an informed judgment on the results of the member's non-attest services and accept responsibility for making the significant judgments and decisions that are the responsibility of management. If management is unable or unwilling to assume these responsibilities, the CPA's independence would be impaired if they perform the non-attest service.

The engagement letter is also required to have specific language regarding the objectives of the engagement, the services to be performed, the attest client's acceptance of its responsibilities, the CPA's responsibilities, and any limitations of the engagement.

Examples of non-attest services for which there are special rules include consulting/advisory services, appraisal and valuation services, bookkeeping and payroll services, recruiting, IT services, and tax services.

YELLOW BOOK (GAGAS) ENGAGEMENTS

Sometimes a nonprofit may receive a grant or contract that requires the audit or review to be performed in accordance with Generally Accepted Government Auditing Standards (GAGAS). GAGAS, also referred to as Yellow Book, requires the auditor to perform additional performance and reporting above and beyond a GAAS audit.

Yellow Book audits are often required in grant agreements but also in state law. For example, North Carolina state law requires nonprofits receiving $500,000 in state funds to obtain a Yellow Book audit. When receiving federal funding, if a nonprofit receives more than $750,000 in federal funding, a Single Audit is required. When a Single Audit is required, the audit must be performed in accordance with GAAS, GAGAS, and the Uniform Guidance.

GAGAS is written by the Government Accountability Office and has its own set of regulations. GAGAS includes its own ethics and independence rules that are different and often more stringent than the AICPA Code of Professional Conduct. The ethical principles in a GAGAS engagement are the public interest, integrity, objectivity, proper use of government information, resources, positions, and professional behavior.[1] As these engagements are often funded with federal or state funds (i.e., tax dollars), the public interest is first and foremost in these engagements.

When performing any Yellow Book engagement, the auditor is required to be independent. Yellow Book includes a conceptual framework approach similar to the AICPA, where the auditor is required to identify and assess threats. If a threat is significant, the auditor must identify safeguards that eliminate the threat or reduce it to an acceptable level. Similar to the Code, GAGAS includes guidance around non-audit services.[2] One key difference between the AICPA Code and GAGAS is that GAGAS states that when the CPA prepares financial statements in their entirety from a client-provided trial balance, it is a significant threat to independence. As such, safeguards must be applied to reduce the threat. The AICPA Code permits the auditor to assess the threat and potentially determine it is not a significant threat. GAGAS also states that when evaluating management's skills, knowledge, or experience (SKE), an indicator that management has acceptable SKE is that they can recognize a material error, omission, or misstatement in the results of the non-audit services provided.

GAGAS also has a more stringent definition of a safeguard. Safeguards under GAGAS are "actions or other measures, individually or in combination, that auditors and the audit organization take that effectively eliminate threats to independence or reduce them to an acceptable level." As such, safeguards must be performed by the CPA. Management's SKE is not a safeguard, as it is not an action taken by the audit organization. Figures 1 and 2 at the end of Chapter 3 of GAGAS provide an excellent flowchart for evaluating threats to independence.

In addition to additional ethics requirements, GAGAS also includes additional continuing professional education (CPE) requirements for CPAs performing these types of engagements. CPE are required classes a CPA takes to stay up to date with changes in rules and regulations. Typically, CPE requirements are set by the state, and each state's requirements are unique. Membership in quality centers of the AICPA may also impact the CPE requirements for a CPA. When performing GAGAS engagements, auditors are required to obtain twenty-four hours of CPE in "subject matter directly related to the government environment, government auditing, or the specific or unique environment in which the audited entity operates." In this case, the term *government* includes nonprofits, as they are the subject of Yellow Book engagements. As a result, nonprofit-related topics fall in the twenty-four-hour category. In addition, auditors are required, with certain exceptions, to obtain an additional fifty-six hours of CPE in a "subject matter that directly enhance auditors' professional expertise to conduct engagements." Therefore, most tax classes, financial planning courses, and so on may qualify for CPE for state law but would not meet the requirements for GAGAS.

In addition to the GAAS performance requirements set out by the AICPA, the auditor must follow Chapter 6 for additional Yellow Book–specific requirements that layer on to GAAS when performing an audit. These requirements require the auditor to follow up on results of previous engagements. In a GAAS audit, the auditor has no requirement to see if the client took corrective action. In a GAGAS audit, the auditor would need to evaluate whether corrective action was taken. AU-C 250 of GAAS requires the auditor to consider laws and regulations that have a material effect on the financial statements. GAGAS layers on noncompliance with provisions of contracts and grant agreements.

When internal control deficiencies or noncompliance is identified, the auditor is required to develop the criteria, condition, cause, and effect of the findings to be compliant with GAGAS.

GAGAS also includes the concepts of waste and abuse. *Waste* is "the act of using or expending resources carelessly, extravagantly, or to no purpose." *Abuse* is "behavior that is deficient or improper when compared with behavior that a prudent person would consider reasonable and necessary business practice given the facts and circumstances, but excludes fraud and noncompliance with provisions of laws, regulations, contracts, and grant agreements. Abuse also includes misuse of authority or position for personal financial interests or those of an immediate or close family member or business associate." While Yellow Book does not require the auditor to consider waste or abuse required findings, it does indicate that waste or abuse may be indicative of noncompliance or an internal control deficiency.

On top of the additional performance requirements in a GAGAS audit, the auditor also has supplementary reporting requirements. In a GAAS audit, the auditor only reports on internal controls if there is a significant deficiency or material weakness in internal controls.

- A *significant deficiency* is "a deficiency, or a combination of deficiencies, in internal control over financial reporting that is less severe than a material weakness yet important enough to merit attention by those charged with governance."[3]
- A *material weakness* is "a deficiency, or a combination of deficiencies, in internal control over financial reporting, such that there is a reasonable possibility that a material misstatement of the entity's financial statements will not be prevented, or detected and corrected, on a timely basis."[4]

In a GAGAS engagement, an auditor always provides a report on internal controls over financial reporting, even if no significant deficiencies or material weaknesses were identified. The auditor also reports explicitly on noncompliance even if no noncompliance is identified. The auditor is also required to request the views of responsible officials for any findings identified.

Here is an example of a Yellow Book report:

INDEPENDENT AUDITOR'S REPORT

[Appropriate Addressee]

We have audited, in accordance with the auditing standards generally accepted in the United States of America and the standards applicable to financial audits contained in Government Auditing Standards issued by the Comptroller General of the United States, the consolidated financial statements of Helpful Nonprofit, which comprise Helpful Nonprofit's consolidated statement of financial position as of June 30, 20X1, and the related consolidated statements of activities, and cash flows for the year then ended, and the related notes to the financial statements, and have issued our report thereon dated August 15, 20X1.

Report on Internal Control Over Financial Reporting

In planning and performing our audit of the financial statements, we considered Helpful Nonprofit's internal control over financial reporting (internal control) as a basis for designing audit procedures that are appropriate in the circumstances for the purpose of expressing our opinions on the financial statements, but not for the purpose of expressing an opinion on the effectiveness of Helpful Nonprofit's internal control. Accordingly, we do not express an opinion on the effectiveness of Helpful Nonprofit's internal control.

A deficiency in internal control exists when the design or operation of a control does not allow management or employees, in the normal course of performing their assigned functions, to prevent, or detect and correct, misstatements on a timely basis. A material weakness is a deficiency, or a combination of deficiencies, in internal control, such that there is a reasonable possibility that a material misstatement of the entity's financial statements will not be prevented, or detected and corrected, on a timely basis. A significant deficiency is a deficiency, or a combination of deficiencies, in internal control that is less severe than a material weakness, yet important enough to merit attention by those charged with governance.

Our consideration of internal control was for the limited purpose described in the first paragraph of this section and was not designed to identify all deficiencies in internal control that might be material weaknesses or significant deficiencies. Given these limitations, during our audit we did not identify any deficiencies in internal control that we consider to be material weaknesses. However, material weaknesses or significant deficiencies may exist that were not identified.

Report on Compliance and Other Matters

As part of obtaining reasonable assurance about whether Helpful Nonprofit's financial statements are free from material misstatement, we performed tests of its compliance with certain provisions of laws, regulations, contracts, and grant agreements, noncompliance with which could have a direct and

continued

material effect on the financial statements. However, providing an opinion on compliance with those provisions was not an objective of our audit, and accordingly, we do not express such an opinion. The results of our tests disclosed no instances of noncompliance or other matters that are required to be reported under Government Auditing Standards.

Purpose of This Report

The purpose of this report is solely to describe the scope of our testing of internal control and compliance and the results of that testing, and not to provide an opinion on the effectiveness of the entity's internal control or on compliance. This report is an integral part of an audit performed in accordance with Government Auditing Standards in considering the entity's internal control and compliance. Accordingly, this communication is not suitable for any other purpose.

[Signature of the auditor's firm]
[City and state where the auditor's report is issued]
[Date of the auditor's report]

This report indicates that the auditor found no internal control deficiencies that were material weaknesses nor noncompliance material to the financial statements.

UNIFORM GUIDANCE AUDITS (AKA SINGLE AUDITS)

Many nonprofits who apply for federal grants to help support their mission are unaware of the terms and conditions that come along with many of these grants. When a nonprofit expends $750,000 or more of federal awards in a fiscal year, they will be subject to a Single Audit performed under the Uniform Guidance. Unlike a financial statement audit that is primarily concerned with identifying material misstatements, a Single Audit is focused on identifying material noncompliance. Federal financial assistance includes grants, cooperative agreements, noncash contributions, or donations of property, food commodities, and other financial assistance.

A Single Audit is conducted in accordance with the Uniform Guidance in addition to the GAAS financial statement audit performed under the Statement of Auditing Standards. When a Single Audit is required, the financial statements must also be subject to Yellow Book requirements.

The Uniform Guidance requires nonfederal agencies to establish and maintain effective internal control over the federal award. The internal control must provide reasonable assurance the entity is in compliance with federal statutes, regulations, and the terms and conditions of the award. These are referred to as *internal controls over compliance.* The internal control should be designed to prevent or detect and correct noncompliance with the terms and the conditions of the award.

The Uniform Guidance provides requirements on cost sharing, the use of program income, detailed rules on the use of property, procurement standards, and performance and financial monitoring and reporting. The government also has very explicit rules for what can and cannot be purchased with federal funds. These are referred to as the *cost principles,* which are found in Subpart E of the Uniform Guidance.

When performing a Single Audit, the auditor is required to identify, using a risk-based approach, the major programs that are subject to audit. A nonprofit may receive funding from a variety of programs. The federal government requires the auditor to audit only a portion of the programs received each year based on a risk assessment. Some nonprofits receive money from hundreds of programs. The auditor evaluates each program, and then—based on factors such as the size of the program, date of the last audit, and whether there were issues in the past—the auditor selects a subset of the programs to be audited. So, instead of providing an opinion on compliance overall, the auditor provides an opinion on the major programs selected for that year.

For a Single Audit, the nonprofit is required to prepare a special financial statement called the *Schedule of Expenditures of Federal Awards* (SEFA). This details the amount expended by the federal program. Federal programs are identified by assistance listing numbers (ALN). The first two digits of the ALN tell us what federal agency provided the funding (e.g., 10 is the Department of Agriculture and 84 is the Department of Education). Then, there is a period followed by another three digits that identify the program. For example, 93.498 is the Provider Relief Fund, which is funded by the Department of Health and Human Services, and 14.856 is the Lower Income Housing Assistance Program—Section 8 Moderate Rehabilitation program, which is funded by the Department of Housing and Urban Development.

Auditors use the annually updated Compliance Supplement to determine how to audit programs. The Compliance Supplement identifies the compliance requirements subject to audit for each program. The compliance requirements in the 2022 Compliance Supplement were Activities Allowed or Unallowed, Allowable Costs/ Cost Principles, Cash Management, Eligibility, Equipment and Real Property Management, Matching, Level of Effort, Earmarking, Period of Performance, Procurement and Suspension and Debarment, Program Income, Reporting, Subrecipient Monitoring, and Special Tests and Provisions. Of the potential twelve compliance requirements, the federal government picks six that the auditor should test for each federal program. The compliance requirements subject to audit are found in Part 2 of the Compliance Supplement, which is referred to as the Matrix.

GOVERNMENT GRANTS

During the year, the organization received funds from the Department of Health and Human Services for disaster relief, as well as from the Department of Homeland Security for disaster grants for public assistance in presidentially declared disasters. These funds are used to help communities recover from major disasters. The auditors selected 97.036, Disaster Grants—Public Assistance, as a major program in the current year. There were several hurricanes where states had received funding from the federal government and had passed the funding through to the organization. No funding was received directly from the federal government.

Once the auditor identifies the compliance requirements subject to audit, they determine which ones are direct and material to the entity, then they perform a risk assessment at the compliance requirement level to identify what could go wrong. For example, for allowable costs, the risk is that the nonprofit purchases and charges something that is unallowable (e.g., alcohol) to the federal award. For eligibility, the risk is that an individual who did not meet the eligibility requirements (i.e., had too much income) received federal funding. Once the risks have been identified, the auditor and will document the internal controls implemented by the nonprofit to mitigate these risks.

Unlike in a financial statement audit, for which the auditor is required only to determine the design and implementation of internal controls, a Single Audit requires the auditor to plan the audit to support a low control risk. Therefore, the auditor is required to test the operating effectiveness of the internal controls. The auditor reports any significant deficiencies or material weaknesses in internal controls over compliance identified in the audit. The auditor is *not* required to opine on the quality of internal controls.

The auditor then performs actual tests of compliance by selecting samples of invoices, eligibility files, and so on to determine whether the entity complied with the laws, regulations, and terms and conditions of the contract. This testing doesn't focus on material misstatement but instead noncompliance with the compliance requirements identified by the federal government. Once tests of compliance are completed, the auditor is required to opine on whether the nonprofit complied in all material respects with the laws, regulations, and terms and conditions of federal awards that could have a direct and material effect on the federal program. Similar to a financial statement audit, this is an opinion based on reasonable assurance. Therefore, the auditor must obtain sufficient appropriate evidence to support the opinion.

INTERNAL CONTROL AND COMPLIANCE TESTING

The grants received were used to support hurricane relief. As a result, the auditors reviewed invoices to determine if they met the requirements of the Federal Emergency Management Agency (FEMA) for allowable cost/cost principles. Thankfully, Lillian is proud of her team's documentation. They were easily able to demonstrate that the costs were directly tied to the disaster relief and were adequately documented. As labor is reimbursed based on actual hourly rates and actual fringe benefits, all expenses funded with federal funding are appropriately tagged in the financial reporting system. Time is tracked by project to ensure proper accounting for actual time and cost. FEMA also reimburses mileage for use of vehicles, as well as equipment such as generators. Lillian's team was able to provide detailed records to demonstrate the funds were used for allowable activities. The use of parking and posting was also very helpful to ensure that the invoices and payroll were properly reviewed and approved. All federal funds are subjected to an extra step of documenting which paragraph in the award indicates the funding is permitted, so that a reviewer can ensure all the funds were allowable. This is reviewed during the park-and-post process.

While the grants sometimes have matching requirements, all the hurricane funds this year waived these requirements, and the federal government covered 100 percent of the costs. As a result, Lillian did not have to provide evidence about a split between federal and state funding.

The auditors did review reporting requirements this year, including the SF-425 Federal Financial Report. That report requires Lillian to provide detailed information about the organization and the grant. The report provides details of the organization, including its employer identification number, address, and contact person. It also provides information about the accounting for the program, including the basis of accounting and the period of the grant. Lillian's team then provides detailed schedules to document the cash received and disbursed, total federal funds authorized, and any program income that was generated. Once prepared and reviewed, the report is signed by the CFO, who provides their contact information. The auditor verifies the report was reviewed and approved by someone other than the preparer and reviews the supporting documentation for each number.

The report on compliance includes information on both the auditor and management's responsibility, an opinion on each major program, and a report on internal controls over compliance. Here is an example of a Single Audit report:

INDEPENDENT AUDITOR'S REPORT

[Appropriate Addressee]

Report on Compliance for Each Major Federal Program
Opinion on Each Major Federal Program

We have audited Example Entity's compliance with the types of compliance requirements identified as subject to audit in the Office of Management and Budget's Compliance Supplement that could have a direct and material effect on each of Example Entity's major federal programs for the year ended June 30, 20X1. Example Entity's major federal programs are identified in the summary of auditor's results section of the accompanying schedule of findings and questioned costs.

In our opinion, Example Entity complied, in all material respects, with the compliance requirements referred to above that could have a direct and material effect on each of its major federal programs for the year ended June 30, 20X1.

Basis for Opinion on Each Major Federal Program

We conducted our audit of compliance in accordance with auditing standards generally accepted in the United States of America (GAAS); the standards applicable to financial audits contained in *Government Auditing*

continued

Standards issued by the comptroller general of the United States; and the audit requirements of Title 2 U.S. Code of Federal Regulations Part 200, Uniform Administrative Requirements, Cost Principles, and Audit Requirements for Federal Awards (Uniform Guidance). Our responsibilities under those standards and the Uniform Guidance are further described in the Auditor's Responsibilities for the Audit of Compliance section of our report.

We are required to be independent of Example Entity and to meet our other ethical responsibilities, in accordance with relevant ethical requirements relating to our audit. We believe that the audit evidence we have obtained is sufficient and appropriate to provide a basis for our opinion on compliance for each major federal program. Our audit does not provide a legal determination of Example Entity's compliance with the compliance requirements referred to above.

Responsibilities of Management for Compliance

Management is responsible for compliance with the requirements referred to above and for the design, implementation, and maintenance of effective internal control over compliance with the requirements of laws, statutes, regulations, rules, and provisions of contracts or grant agreements applicable to Example Entity's federal programs.

Auditor's Responsibilities for the Audit of Compliance

Our objectives are to obtain reasonable assurance about whether material noncompliance with the compliance requirements referred to above occurred, whether due to fraud or error, and express an opinion on Example Entity's compliance based on our audit. Reasonable assurance is a high level of assurance but is not absolute assurance and therefore is not a guarantee that an audit conducted in accordance with GAAS, *Government Auditing Standards*, and the Uniform Guidance will always detect material noncompliance when it exists. The risk of not detecting material noncompliance resulting from fraud is higher than for that resulting from error, as fraud may involve collusion, forgery, intentional omissions, misrepresentations, or the override of internal control. Noncompliance with the compliance requirements referred to above is considered material if there is a substantial likelihood that, individually or in the aggregate, it would influence the judgment made by a reasonable user of the report on compliance about Example Entity's compliance with the requirements of each major federal program as a whole.

In performing an audit in accordance with GAAS, *Government Auditing Standards*, and the Uniform Guidance, we

- exercise professional judgment and maintain professional skepticism throughout the audit.
- identify and assess the risks of material noncompliance, whether due to fraud or error, and design and perform audit procedures responsive to those risks. Such procedures include examining, on a test basis, evidence regarding Example Entity's compliance with the compliance requirements referred to above and performing such other procedures as we considered necessary in the circumstances.
- obtain an understanding of Example Entity's internal control over compliance relevant to the audit in order to design audit procedures that are appropriate in the circumstances and to test and report on internal control over compliance in accordance with the Uniform Guidance, but not for the purpose of expressing an opinion on the effectiveness of Example Entity's internal control over compliance. Accordingly, no such opinion is expressed.

We are required to communicate with those charged with governance regarding, among other matters, the planned scope and timing of the audit and any significant deficiencies and material weaknesses in internal control over compliance that we identified during the audit.

Report on Internal Control Over Compliance

A *deficiency in internal control over compliance* exists when the design or operation of a control over compliance does not allow management or employees, in the normal course of performing their assigned functions, to prevent, or detect and correct, noncompliance with a type of compliance requirement of a federal program on a timely basis. A *material weakness in internal control over compliance* is a deficiency, or a combination of deficiencies, in internal control over compliance, such that there is a reasonable possibility that material noncompliance with a type of compliance requirement of a federal program will not be prevented, or detected

continued

and corrected, on a timely basis. A *significant deficiency in internal control over compliance* is a deficiency, or a combination of deficiencies, in internal control over compliance with a type of compliance requirement of a federal program that is less severe than a material weakness in internal control over compliance, yet important enough to merit attention by those charged with governance.

Our consideration of internal control over compliance was for the limited purpose described in the Auditor's Responsibilities for the Audit of Compliance section above and was not designed to identify all deficiencies in internal control over compliance that might be material weaknesses or significant deficiencies in internal control over compliance. Given these limitations, during our audit we did not identify any deficiencies in internal control over compliance that we consider to be material weaknesses, as defined above. However, material weaknesses or significant deficiencies in internal control over compliance may exist that were not identified.

Our audit was not designed for the purpose of expressing an opinion on the effectiveness of internal control over compliance. Accordingly, no such opinion is expressed.

The purpose of this report on internal control over compliance is solely to describe the scope of our testing of internal control over compliance and the results of that testing based on the requirements of the Uniform Guidance. Accordingly, this report is not suitable for any other purpose.

Report on Schedule of Expenditures of Federal Awards Required by the Uniform Guidance

We have audited the financial statements of Example Entity as of and for the year ended June 30, 20X1, and have issued our report thereon dated August 15, 20X1, which contained an unmodified opinion on those financial statements. Our audit was performed for the purpose of forming an opinion on the financial statements as a whole. The accompanying schedule of expenditures of federal awards is presented for purposes of additional analysis as required by the Uniform Guidance and is not a required part of the financial statements. Such information is the responsibility of management and was derived from and relates directly to the underlying accounting and other records used to prepare the financial statements. The information has been subjected to the auditing procedures applied in the audit of the financial statements and certain additional procedures, including comparing and reconciling such information directly to the underlying accounting and other records used to prepare the financial statements or to the financial statements themselves, and other additional procedures in accordance with auditing standards generally accepted in the United States of America. In our opinion, the schedule of expenditures of federal awards is fairly stated in all material respects in relation to the financial statements as a whole.

[Signature of the auditor's firm]
[City and state where auditor's report is issued]
[Date of the auditor's report]

As part of the reporting phase of a Single Audit, the auditor must include in the reporting package the financial statements of the nonprofit, the SEFA, and the auditor's report on the financial statements. The reporting package also includes the auditor's report on the SEFA, the GAGAS report, and the auditor's report on compliance. In addition to the audit reports, the auditor must complete a schedule of findings and questioned costs. If there are any findings from the Yellow Book or Single Audit, the nonprofit completes a Corrective Action Plan, which details who is responsible for taking corrective action, what corrective action will be done, and when it will be completed. They are also responsible for preparing a Summary Schedule of Prior Audit Findings that provides a status update on all previous audit findings. All of these items are then loaded in the Federal Audit Clearinghouse (FAC), which is public information. Anyone can see the reporting package.

PUBLIC INFORMATION

As federal funds come from taxpayer dollars, all nonprofits and governments that expend federal funds are required to provide their information in the FAC. Individuals who are interested in how a nonprofit uses federal

continued

funding can search the FAC website—https://facweb.census.gov/uploadpdf.aspx—to review the financial statements and the SEFA of the entity. They can also review if the auditor identified any internal control deficiencies or noncompliance. It is important that nonprofits put sufficient attention to these requirements, as anyone can see the information with a simple search.

As you can imagine, Single Audits require significant effort and can be quite expensive. Selecting an auditor who is an expert in Single Audit and has experience with the types of federal awards received by the entity is very important.

Board Self-Evaluation

Did the auditor identify any internal control deficiencies? Were there material entries? Did they express any concern over the competence of management or the quality of financial reporting?

The auditor is an objective provider of information. Using the audit report solely as a compliance mechanism limits the value received. To get the full benefit of the audit, see it as a way to benchmark, get feedback, and improve processes. Take what is provided and utilize it to move the organization forward. If your auditor doesn't provide management comments or suggestions for improvements, consider putting the audit out for a request for proposal to find an auditor who provides feedback and helps the organization move forward.

CONCLUSION

We've covered a lot of material here, including what it means to be a board member, the basics of financial statements, and the elements and disclosures needed to prepare them. We've covered some basic evaluation techniques to help you identify what's working well and where the board needs to devote time. We've analyzed the role of the independent CPA and how you can interact with them to move the nonprofit forward.

There were many new terms, situational examples, and suggested resources. I hope that this has given you a glimpse into the importance of the role of the board in protecting the organization and its beneficiaries from a whole host of potential issues. Now that you are armed with the information you need to start the conversation, I encourage you to take the time to engage with management and with the auditor—ask the probing questions, and help push your organization into the top tier of nonprofit governance.

You can be an amazing asset to your nonprofit board when you apply what you've learned. You've invested the time to learn the terminology and how to read the financials. Now go out there and make a difference!

APPENDIX

QUESTIONS FOR THE INDEPENDENT ACCOUNTANT

HIRING/SELECTING A CPA?

What experience do you have with our type of nonprofit? How many nonprofits do you serve?

- It is important that the nonprofit evaluate whether the firm has experienced, qualified staff. Not only is the firm's overall experience important, but it is also important to determine that they have experience relevant to your organization. Auditing a hospital is very different from auditing a soup kitchen. Even a firm with a concentration in nonprofits may not have experience with a subindustry (e.g., healthcare or education) within the sector.

How many Yellow Book or Single Audits do you perform (if applicable)?

- Many auditors may have a large nonprofit practice, but that does not necessarily mean they have significant experience with Single Audits or Yellow Book. If an audit firm is not familiar with their requirements, they may perform subpar audits.

Will the team presented in your proposal be the team that serves the audit long term?

- Audit firms can have high rates of turnover, especially at the staff level. If the nonprofit has to re-explain its organization, mission, and processes each year, it can be taxing on staff and create unnecessary work. No one can guarantee that a particular employee will be on a particular engagement, but it is helpful to find out whether anyone on the proposal team is scheduled to be on the engagement.

Do you bill extra for phone calls during the year?

- It is important to understand the true fees for the audit or review engagement. Some firms charge by the hour, and others charge a fixed fee. Make sure, when evaluating and comparing alternatives, that the nonprofit has all of the relevant information. Someone with an inexpensive fee that nickels-and-dimes every interaction may end up being more expensive in the long run or make staff hesitant to reach out when they have questions.

What educational offerings do you provide to clients that can help keep management and the board informed?

- Many firms offer webinars, newsletters, seminars, and other methods of keeping clients up to date with what's going on in financial reporting, as well as other industry impacts. Some firms offer these additional educational offerings for free; others will charge a fee. It's a good idea to find out if the firm provides these offerings outside of the audit.

Do we need to budget additional dollars for additional billings related to the implementation of new accounting or audit standards?

- Accounting standards change frequently. Some standards require more effort on behalf of the auditor to obtain sufficient appropriate evidence. *Sufficient* is the quantity of evidence and *appropriate* is the quality of evidence such that the evidence is persuasive. Audit standards can also change, requiring the auditor to do more work. Being up-front about upcoming changes is important. Surprises are not acceptable. Frequent communication between the auditor and the nonprofit is crucial.

Do you bill extra for when management does not meet deadlines or creates inefficiencies in the audit?

- Many engagement letters include language around additional billing. Staff are assigned for a particular engagement for a particular period. If the client is not prepared, the staff may sit idle and then be unavailable when the client is ready. As a result, many firms will bill for unexpected inefficiencies to offset this avoidable issue. Scheduling the audit when management is ready to provide documentation is a critical consideration.

What types of advisory services or non-attest services do you offer? What services would you recommend for our nonprofit?

- Many firms offer non-attest services to their clients, ranging from bookkeeping and tax preparation to technology consulting and process improvement, but, of course, firms must be careful to ensure they do not take on work that may impair their independence. Assessing a firm's commitment to independence is important.

What were the results of the firm's most recent peer review?

- CPA firms receive feedback from a peer firm at least every three years about the quality of their work and how well they follow the required standards. Firms can receive a rating of pass, pass with deficiencies, or fail. Firms who have poor audit quality should be avoided. If a firm doesn't provide the results of its latest peer review with its proposal, ask for it. If there were issues, understand what the issues were and what the firm is doing to fix them. A poorly performed audit will not provide the appropriate level of assurance. While a CPA firm should provide their last peer review report when requested, the AICPA does maintain a repository of reports on a website: https://peerreview.aicpa.org/public_file_search.html.

Is your firm a member of the AICPA's Governmental Audit Quality Center (GAQC)? (Only ask if your nonprofit needs a Yellow Book or Single Audit.)

- Another indicator of a firm's commitment to quality can be shown by a firm's membership in AICPA resource centers. The GAQC includes resources relating to financial statement audits of both governments and nonprofits and Single Audits. This can show that the firm invests in its people and wants to follow the standards.

How many of your staff are a member of the AICPA's Not-For-Profit Section? How many have obtained the nonprofit certificates from the AICPA? Will they be on our engagement?

- Having a firm show a commitment to quality and education—and especially a commitment to the nonprofit industry—is important. Questions like this can help you focus in on firms that pride themselves on working with nonprofits.

Do you have any references of current clients similar to our organization?

- Taking the opportunity to talk to current clients about their experiences with the firm can be helpful. Do they get the attention they need? Does the firm provide benchmarking and offer suggestions for improvements? Are management comment letters useful to help the nonprofit improve?

Has the firm been the subject of any AICPA or state CPA society ethics referrals?

- Ethics violations are a big deal. If the firm is performing poor-quality engagements or is not compliant with ethics rules, steer clear at all costs! Each state has a board of accountancy that is responsible for oversight. Actions taken against CPAs are public information and are published on their website. The AICPA's enforcement actions can be found on their website: https://us.aicpa.org/forthepublic/disciplinaryactions.

What training did the partner on the engagement and other staff receive in the prior year relevant to our engagement?

- CPAs are required to obtain around forty hours of CPE a year, depending on their state. Yellow Book requires eighty hours of CPE over a two-year period. Many states provide a lot of flexibility to individuals to decide where to get their continuing education. Look to see if firms were taking update classes in nonprofit subjects. Were they mostly taking classes that were not helpful to your organization? This can help you assess the quality of the organization's commitment to competence in your subindustry.

If you currently have an auditor and are considering making a change, or if you are looking to hire an auditor for the first time, you can ask their references questions like the following:

- Did they discuss the audit plan and areas of risk such that you understood it and it added value to the organization?

- Does the audit team understand your organization, economic trends, and environments? Do they ask the same questions each year without really understanding your processes or model?

- What percentage of their audit work is with nonprofits? Does the firm have people they can go to when they have questions, and can they get responses in a timely fashion?

- Did the firm demonstrate its independence? Do you feel that the firm cares about the independence rules? Do they discuss the implications of non-audit/non-attest services?

- Did the team follow the audit plan based on preliminary discussions? Did they issue the report on time? Were there a lot of last-minute issues that popped up without prior notice?
- Did the audit provide details on the quality of your reporting? Did they give you insights into how you were performing, and provide benchmarks?
- Did the auditor compare your accounting policies with industry best practices and provide feedback?
- Did the auditor inform you of upcoming changes to accounting or auditing standards? Was it in a timely fashion?
- Did the partner communicate regularly with management and the board? Were the communications complete? Did you understand? Did they encourage you to ask questions?
- Was the engagement appropriately staffed?
- Did the auditor ask for feedback?
- Were there changes in your audit team from the prior year? Is turnover a problem with the staff?
- Did they listen to you and answer your questions?
- Did they help you understand areas for improvement?
- Did they provide you valuable feedback in the management letter about areas for improvement?

INDEPENDENCE

How do you determine whether you are independent?

- Independence is the cornerstone of the CPA profession when it comes to attest services. Firms are required to identify whether there are any threats to independence. Some non-attest services (e.g., bookkeeping, consulting) are threats to independence. The CPA must evaluate the threat and determine appropriate safeguards. Familiarity (having a long relationship with a client or a close friendship) is also a threat to independence. Has the firm identified these threats? What safeguards did they apply?

If a firm provides non-attest services: What safeguards did you apply with respect to non-attest services provided? How did you evaluate our management's skill, knowledge, or experience?

- Safeguards are used to minimize threats to an acceptable level. Firms can use independent reviews by a non-engagement team member, separation of staff providing the non-attest service from the engagement staff, and a whole host of other safeguards. The firm should be able to clearly explain the threats and safeguards so you feel confident in their independence. If a non-attest service was provided, the auditor is required to evaluate management's SKE. Knowing how they evaluate this SKE can help you with your overall evaluation. Evaluate their response. Did it seem reasonable or like they added a lot of fluff? You can also determine if your auditor is simply checking the box or making an accurate assessment of management.

How did the cumulative fees for consulting (and other non-attest services) impact the assessment of independence?

- The auditor must assess threats to independence individually and in the aggregate. Providing multiple non-attest services can increase the threats to independence. A firm should be able to provide an explanation of their assessment, and you should evaluate whether there is an overreliance on the firm and if you need to bring in another consultant if you are concerned with a self-review threat.

BENCHMARKING

What are the biggest risks you see to our organization over the next year, five years, and ten years?

- A CPA from James Moore, a firm located in Florida that does extensive work with nonprofits, indicated in a survey that they wished more nonprofits and the nonprofit's board in particular would ask them about their risks. Firms perform a detailed risk assessment in an audit to understand what could go wrong in financial reporting. They are also experts in the industry and can be great advisers to firms. Leverage the firm's experience and knowledge of your organization to discuss risks and to learn about areas of focus that the board can use in their risk assessment.

Is our accounting/finance department adequately and appropriately staffed?

- Nonprofits are known for being lean in operations, but a properly staffed finance department is a must. Whether the department is staffed by employees or outsourced advisers, it is imperative the nonprofit has the right people to handle the accounting and financial reporting. The CPA firm works closely with these individuals and can often identify gaps in knowledge or skillset.

Tell us about trends you are seeing in our industry/subindustry. What is the state of the nonprofit industry?

- Again, if the firm isn't providing this during their normal conversations with management and the board, ask! Good CPA firms want to share this information and provide context.

How do our costs of providing services compare with those of similar nonprofit organizations?

- If your CPA firm specializes in nonprofits, they will have lots of details about costs of services for similar organizations to help you benchmark.

How do our functional expense percentages benchmark against other organizations for program vs. management/general?

- While functional expense ratios vary by type of nonprofit, if your CPA has other clients similar to your organization, you can learn a lot about how you stack up against other nonprofits.

Do you have any concerns about management? Is our team effective?

- This gives the CPAs an opportunity to provide feedback on staffing and the quality of the staff.

GOVERNANCE

How does our executive compensation compare to other similar organizations?

- IRS regulations include the "Rebuttable Presumption of Reasonableness." Your CPA should be able to provide benchmarks as to the reasonableness of compensation and raise red flags regarding excessive executive compensation.

How can we (the board) be supporting the organization better and fulfilling our board responsibilities?

- This is a great way to get feedback from your auditor on the effectiveness of the board. Your CPA likely works with a variety of boards and can help you assess where to focus attention.

INTERNAL CONTROLS

How adequate are our internal controls? Where can we improve them? What types of internal controls can a small organization effectively apply?

- If you search "nonprofit fraud" online, you'll likely find that nonprofits that are victims of fraud make the news. Funds diverted from the mission and abuse of power are commonplace. Internal controls are one way to combat fraud. Review and approval of executive travel and expenses, reviews of invoices by multiple layers, and check signers on the board are all excellent controls that can limit risk. The CPA should be able to provide you with an overview of the existing controls and where they see room for improvement. They may also have suggestions regarding new controls to consider. CPAs cannot design or implement these for the nonprofit as they would impair their independence. But CPAs can assist with gap analysis. They may recommend implementing a whistleblower policy or a cybersecurity policy that the board had not previously considered.

Board Best Practices

CPAs are required to provide a management letter and a communication of significant deficiencies and material weaknesses in internal controls. Is the CPA providing useful information in these communications? Are they truly providing advice and actionable methods for improvement?

If your CPA has little information in the management letter, that can be a sign of a lazy auditor or perhaps one that is afraid to tell you the truth. No organization is perfect, and there is always room for improvement. The suggestions for improvements in a management letter can be of the utmost importance to the success of a nonprofit. If your CPA isn't giving you quality information, ask for it or find a firm that will.

How can our organization that is lean in staff improve segregation of duties?

- Frequently the board can assist with segregation-of-duty issues by signing checks, reviewing invoices for approval, and reviewing executive expenses. The CPA can also provide other suggestions to help reduce risk.

How adequate is our timekeeping system? Does it allow for proper allocation of payroll costs? Is there a better way to track salaries and functional expenses?

- Because of the heightened scrutiny of the functional expense allocations, the CPA can provide feedback on the quality of records and suggestions for areas for improvement to ensure quality financial reporting.

AUDITING

Did you identify any transactions with related parties not previously documented by management? Did you identify any transactions not properly approved?

- Related party transactions are typically not an arm's-length transaction. These require disclosure in the financial statements. Auditors perform tests to determine the completeness of related parties and related party transactions.

Are there any major changes to accounting or auditing standards that could affect the organization?

- CPAs should be proactive in sharing information about changes in accounting and auditing standards. Because many standards require time to implement, CPAs should provide this information during planning and closing meetings.

Did management give you everything you requested in a timely manner? Did management cooperate and make themselves available?

- Audits run smoothly when management is cooperative. If management is slow to provide information or makes the process difficult, it can cause overruns in the audit schedule. In addition, if management is difficult to work with, this is often a sign of other issues. The CPA firm should be honest with you in its assessment of management.

Were there any disagreements between you and management?

- This is a required communication but is often better presented through conversation than a letter. It's important to understand the disagreements and how they were resolved.

What was the cause of adjusting entries that were proposed by the CPA firm?

- It is important to understand the root cause of errors in the financial statements. Were they due to a lack of training or misinterpretation of the rules, or were they just standard adjustments? This can assist the board in determining what needs to change to reduce adjusting entries going forward. If the auditor doesn't give root causes and instead gives high-level reasons that are unhelpful, consider finding a new firm.

Are our policies in line with best practice?

- Accounting policies often allow for accounting policy election. Some industries have certain expectations for accounting policy. CPAs can give insight into whether the nonprofit is taking extreme positions or pushing the envelope on what is appropriate.

Were there any significant unusual transactions that caused concern for the CPA firm?

- This is another required communication. Discussing the transactions, the purpose, and the approval process can be beneficial to the auditor and the board.

What is your risk-assessment process, and what significant risks have you identified?

- An AICPA Peer Review Program study found that more than one in ten firms are not properly assessing risk or linking their assessments to their audit procedures. The accounting standards require the auditor to communicate significant risks with the board. However, the quality of these communications varies. If they don't help the board with their risk assessment or don't help the board with their responsibility for mitigating risk, look for another auditor.

Is there anything else you would like to discuss with us?

- This is a great way to give the auditor an opportunity to freely communicate anything you may have missed. Strong two-way communication is the best practice!

NOTES

CHAPTER 1

1. BoardSource, "Key Questions to Ask Before Joining a Nonprofit Board," February 17, 2017, https://boardsource.org/resources/key-questions-ask-joining-nonprofit-board/.
2. Model Nonprofit Corporation Act, 3rd Ed. 8165 (2008) § 8.01. Cf. Model Business Corporation Act (2016 8166 Revision), § 8.01.
3. BoardSource, "What Does Board Service Entail?" 2016, https://boardsource.org/wp-content/uploads/2017/01/Board-Service-Graphic.pdf.
4. Independent Sector, "Principles for Good Governance and Ethical Practice," accessed December 2021, https://independentsector.org/programs/principles-for-good-governance-and-ethical-practice/.
5. Financial Accounting Standards Board (FASB). *Accounting Standards Codification*, Master Glossary (hereafter cited as FASB, *ASC*, Master Glossary), accessed March 2022, https://asc.fasb.org/.
6. GlobeNewswire, "90% of S&P 500 Index Companies Publish Sustainability Reports in 2019, G&A Announces in Its Latest Annual 2020 Flash Report," July 16, 2020, https://www.globenewswire.com/news-release/2020/07/16/2063434/0/en/90-of-S-P-500-Index-Companies-Publish-Sustainability-Reports-in-2019-G-A-Announces-in-its-Latest-Annual-2020-Flash-Report.html.
7. H. Ott, R. Wang, and D. Bortree, "Communicating Sustainability Online: An Examination of Corporate, Nonprofit, and University Websites," *Mass Communication and Society* 19(5): 671–87, July 22, 2016, https://doi.org/10.1080/15205436.2016.1204554.

8. Independent Sector, "Principles for Good Governance and Ethical Practice," accessed December 2021, https://independentsector.org/programs/principles-for-good-governance-and-ethical-practice/.
9. March of Dimes, "Who We Are," accessed December 2021, https://www.marchofdimes.org/mission/who-we-are.aspx.
10. *Oxford English Dictionary* defines *key performance indicator* as "a quantifiable measure used to evaluate the success of an organization, employee, etc. in meeting objectives for performance." OED Online, Oxford University Press, March 2022, https://www.oed.com/view/Entry/103130?redirectedFrom=Key+Performance+Indicator#eid1289559030.
11. COSO, *COSO Enterprise Risk Management—Integrating with Strategy and Performance: Compendium of Examples*, accessed December 2021, https://future.aicpa.org/cpe-learning/publication/coso-enterprise-risk-management-integrating-with-strategy-and-performance-compendium-of-examples.
12. Wounded Warrior Project, "Who We Are," accessed December 2021, https://www.woundedwarriorproject.org/mission.
13. For Purpose Law Group, "Wounded Warrior Project: 'So Many Lessons . . . ,'" August 25, 2016, https://forpurposelaw.com/wounded-warrior-project-governance/.
14. Military.com, "After Public Crisis and Fall from Grace, Wounded Warrior Project Quietly Regains Ground," August 9, 2019, https://www.military.com/daily-news/2019/08/09/after-public-crisis-and-fall-grace-wounded-warrior-project-quietly-regains-ground.html.
15. Committee of Sponsoring Organizations of the Treadway Commission, "Enterprise Risk Management—Integrated Framework: Executive Summary," September 2004, https://www.coso.org/Documents/COSO-ERM-Executive-Summary.pdf.
16. Committee of Sponsoring Organizations of the Treadway Commission, "About Us," accessed December 2021, https://www.coso.org/Pages/aboutus.aspx.
17. Committee of Sponsoring Organizations of the Treadway Commission, "Internal Control—Integrated Framework: Executive Summary," May 2013, https://www.coso.org/documents/990025p-executive-summary-final-may20.pdf.

18. Donorbox, "20 KPIs for Nonprofits to Track—Key Performance Indicators," August 4, 2021, https://donorbox.org/nonprofit-blog/kpis-for-your-nonprofit/.
19. A great article on developing KPIs can be found in the *CPA Journal*: "How to Create Key Performance Indicators," April 2019, https://www.cpajournal.com/2019/04/22/how-to-create-key-performance-indicators/.
20. Jaqcueline Trescott and James V. Grimaldi, "Smithsonian Chief Quits in Wake of Inquiry," *NBC News*, March 26, 2007, https://www.nbcnews.com/id/wbna17804796.

CHAPTER 2

1. Financial Accounting Standards Board, "About the FASB," September 2021, https://www.fasb.org/facts/.
2. Some entities that appear to be nonprofit may be governmental. For example, private universities and private hospitals use GAAP written by the FASB. However, a public hospital or public university is deemed to be a governmental organization and therefore follows GAAP written by the Governmental Accounting Standards Board. Governmental GAAP has different requirements than GAAP for nonprofits and commercial entities.
3. American Institute of Certified Public Accountants (AICPA). *Statement on Auditing Standards*, AU-C Glossary: Glossary of Terms, accessed March 2022 (hereafter cited as AICPA SAS Glossary of Terms).
4. Financial Accounting Standards Board (FASB). *Accounting Standards Update* (hereafter cited as FASB *ASU*) No. 2020-07, "Not-for-Profit Entities (Topic 958): Presentation and Disclosures by Not-for-Profit Entities for Contributed Nonfinancial Assets," September 2020.
5. FASB, *ASU* No. 2019-03, "Not-for-Profit Entities (Topic 958): Updating the Definition of Collections," March 2019.
6. FASB, *ASU* No. 2019-06, "Intangibles—Goodwill and Other (Topic 350), Business Combinations (Topic 805), and Not-for-Profit Entities (Topic 958): Extending the Private Company Accounting Alternatives on Goodwill and Certain Identifiable Intangible Assets to Not-for-Profit Entities," May 2019.

7. Net income is calculated by for-profit entities to determine the amount left over after all expenses are deducted from total revenue. It is an important measure of profitability.
8. FASB, *ASC*, Master Glossary.

CHAPTER 3

1. A performance obligation is "a promise in a contract with a customer to transfer to the customer either a good or service (or a bundle of goods or services) that is distinct or a series of distinct goods or services that are substantially the same and that have the same pattern of transfer to the customer." FASB, *ASC*, Master Glossary.
2. FASB, *ASC*, Master Glossary.
3. FASB, ASC, Master Glossary.
4. Office of Management and Budget Guidance for Grants and Agreements, *Code of Federal Regulations* [Title 2 Grants and Agreements, Part 200 Uniform Administrative Requirements, Cost Principles, and Audit Requirements for Federal Awards, Subpart E Cost Principles], accessed March 2022, https://www.ecfr.gov/current/title-2/subtitle-A/chapter-II/part-200/subpart-E?toc=1.
5. Nonprofits can no longer imply time restrictions from donors for long-lived assets as a result of ASU 2016-14.
6. FASB, *ASC*, Master Glossary.
7. Independent Sector, "Independent Sector Releases New Value of Volunteer Time of $28.54 Per Hour," April 20, 2021, https://independentsector.org/news-post/independent-sector-releases-new-value-of-volunteer-time-of-28-54-per-hour/.
8. To learn more, see https://www.goodwill.org/wp-content/uploads/2021/05/2020-Goodwill-Industries-International-Audited-Financial-Statements.pdf.
9. To learn more, see https://www.habitat.org/sites/default/files/documents/2021%20Habitat%20for%20Humanity%20FS%20SF.pdf.
10. To learn more, see https://www.capital.edu/WorkArea/DownloadAsset.aspx?id=12884903502

11. To learn more, see https://corporate.dukehealth.org/sites/default/files/2021-09/FY21%20DUHS%20Issued%20Consolidated%20Financial%20Statements.pdf.
12. To learn more, see https://www.lls.org/sites/default/files/2022-01/FY21%20-%20LLS%20USA%20Financials[2].pdf.
13. To learn more, see https://www.lls.org/sites/default/files/2022-01/FY21%20-%20LLS%20USA%20Financials[2].pdf.

CHAPTER 4

1. A FICO score is a credit score created by the Fair Isaac Corporation (FICO). Lenders use a borrowers' FICO score, along with other details on borrowers' credit reports, to assess credit risk and determine whether to extend credit. A score over 800 is an exceptional credit score. A score less than 580 is a poor credit score.
2. Prior to the adoption of ASC 842, most of these leases were "off balance sheet," meaning that monthly or annual expense was recognized in the statement of activities as incurred, but no asset or liability was recognized. The change to adopt ASC 842, which included putting the right-of-use asset (and related liability) on the books, was issued in 2016 but had a delayed implementation date, so these changes are relatively new to nonprofits. Board members should understand that these new assets and liabilities don't necessarily mean new leases, just the adoption of the standard. Note disclosures should explain the impact of implementation. Topic 842 was effective for nonprofits with conduit debt for periods ending after December 15, 2020, and for nonprofits without conduit debt for periods ending after December 15, 2022.
3. The incremental borrowing rate is the rate the bank would charge if the nonprofit were to go to the bank to borrow money for the same amount of time and same amount of money.
4. FASB, *ASC*, Master Glossary.
5. To learn more, see https://www.si.edu/osp/Reports/Smithsonian%20Annual%20Financials/FY20%20Single%20Audit%20Report.pdf.
6. FASB, *ASC*, Master Glossary.

7. FASB, *Concepts Statements*, accessed December 2021, https://fasb.org/page/PageContent?pageId=/standards/concepts-statements.html.
8. Prior to ASC 842, entities were able to keep operating leases off the statement of financial position.
9. To learn more, see https://d2x0djib3vzbzj.cloudfront.net/FAF_2020AR_StandardsThatWork_FromMainStreetToWallStreet.pdf.
10. To learn more, see https://www.elon.edu/u/fa/accounting/wp-content/uploads/sites/707/2021/10/2021-Elon-University-Final-9.22.2021.pdf.

CHAPTER 5

1. FASB, *ASC*, Master Glossary.
2. Ann Goggins Gregory and Don Howard, "The Nonprofit Starvation Cycle," *Stanford Social Innovation Review*, Fall 2009, https://ssir.org/articles/entry/the_nonprofit_starvation_cycle.
3. FASB, *ASC*, Master Glossary.
4. FASB, ASC, Master Glossary.
5. To learn more, see https://www.birminghamzoo.com/wp-content/uploads/2021/05/Birmingham-Zoo-Inc.-2020-Audited-Financial-Statements-FINAL.pdf.
6. To learn more, see https://www.rmhc.org/-/media/Feature/RMHC-Production-Images/About-Us/Files/Media-Resources-and-Financials/2020-Signed-Final-Report-and-Financial-Statements.pdf.
7. To learn more, see https://docs.gatesfoundation.org/documents/F_151002C-1B_Bill&MelindaGatesFoundation_FS.pdf.
8. There are specific tests that must be performed—outlined in ASC 958-720-45—to determine compliance. For example, the compensation or fees tests, a separate and similar activities test, or other evidence test. These require significant accounting experience.
9. To learn more, see https://www.aicpa.org/resources/download/illustrative-financial-statements-save-our-charities.

CHAPTER 6

1. To learn more, see https://www.fftc.org/sites/default/files/2021-09/2020.12.31_Audited_Financial_Statements.pdf.
2. To learn more, see https://docs.gatesfoundation.org/documents/F_151002C-1B_Bill&MelindaGatesFoundation_FS.pdf.

CHAPTER 8

1. To learn more, see Paragraph 3.06: https://www.gao.gov/assets/gao-21-368g.pdf.
2. The AICPA uses the term non-attest services. GAGAS uses the term non-audit.
3. AICPA SAS Glossary of Terms.
4. AICPA SAS Glossary of Terms.

ACKNOWLEDGMENTS

First and foremost, I would like to thank my team at Galasso Learning Solutions for their tireless work in getting this book ready. Their hard work and dedication made all the processes that go into writing a book (more than I could have ever imagined) were made so much easier. I am so thankful for my amazing team. Frank, Kristina, and Teresa—you guys are the best!

I would also like to thank my clients who encouraged me to write this book. Many of them were prereaders of the book and some even went above and beyond to provide endorsements. GLS clients are passionate about serving the nonprofit community and their work is so important as many nonprofits rely on their auditors and audit report for financing and grants. Thank you all for your support and for the amazing work you do. I'm honored to partner with you!

I would like to especially thank Jeff Mechanick and Kathryn Fletcher for their technical reviews. Writing a book on an accounting topic while trying to make the text approachable takes a lot of creativity. Thank you to Jeff and Kathryn for making sure I didn't get too far from the standards!

A big thanks goes out to all the nonprofits who generously gave me permission to use their financial statements as examples in this book. Allowing readers to experience the diversity of presentation was really important to me. These nonprofits believed in the purpose of the book and graciously gave permission for their usage. The book is better because of your generosity!

I want to thank everyone on the Greenleaf team and especially my lead editor, Lee Zarnikau. I had no idea what I was getting into when I started this project and the project management, the conversations, and the guidance made it doable. I'm especially grateful to Lee who was committed to keeping me sane throughout the process, and for that I am forever grateful!

Last, but certainly not least, I would like to thank my family for their support in writing the book. We're a busy family to begin with and there are always lots of moving parts to our schedules. I appreciate you helping me find the time to write this book and for encouraging me throughout the process. Being a female CEO is much easier when the family is there to support and champion success!

ABOUT THE AUTHOR

Photo by Ebony Stubbs

MELISA F. GALASSO is the founder and CEO of Galasso Learning Solutions LLC. A CPA with nearly twenty years of experience in the accounting profession, Melisa designs and facilitates courses in advanced technical accounting and auditing topics, including not-for-profit and governmental accounting. Melisa is a Certified Public Accountant (CPA), a Certified Speaking Professional (CSP), and a Certified Professional in Talent Development (CPTD) and has earned the Association for Talent Development Master Trainer™ designation.

Melisa is passionate about the accounting profession and has been involved at the local, state, and national level. She currently serves on the FASB's Not-for-Profit Advisory Committee (NAC) and AICPA Council. She previously served on the AICPA's Technical Issues Committee (TIC) and the Virginia Society of CPA's Board of Directors and is a past chair of the North Carolina Association of CPA's Accounting & Attestation committee. She is a 2014 graduate of the AICPA Leadership Academy.

Melisa was honored as a "40 under 40" leader in the accounting field by CPA Practice Advisor in 2017, 2018, and 2019 and was named one of the Top 50 Women in Accounting for 2021 by Ignition. She also received the Don Farmer award for achievement in technical content instruction, and earned several other awards for public speaking and technical training. Melisa has also been recognized as a leading entrepreneur, having been named the 2019 Rising Star by the Charlotte chapter of the National Association of Woman Business Owners and honored in the 2020 Enterprising Women of the Year Awards by *Enterprising Women*.

Before establishing Galasso Learning Solutions, Melisa worked in public accounting, industry, internal audit, and academia. She received a bachelor of science in business administration with a concentration in accounting and international business from Georgetown University. On a personal level, Melisa enjoys traveling, watching her daughter ride her horse, and spending quality time with family. She finds balance through yoga, is an avid reader, and frequents local performing arts shows. Melisa actively supports several causes that empower women.